THE ART OF HOLIDAY PHOTOGRAPHY

How to preserve those precious memories

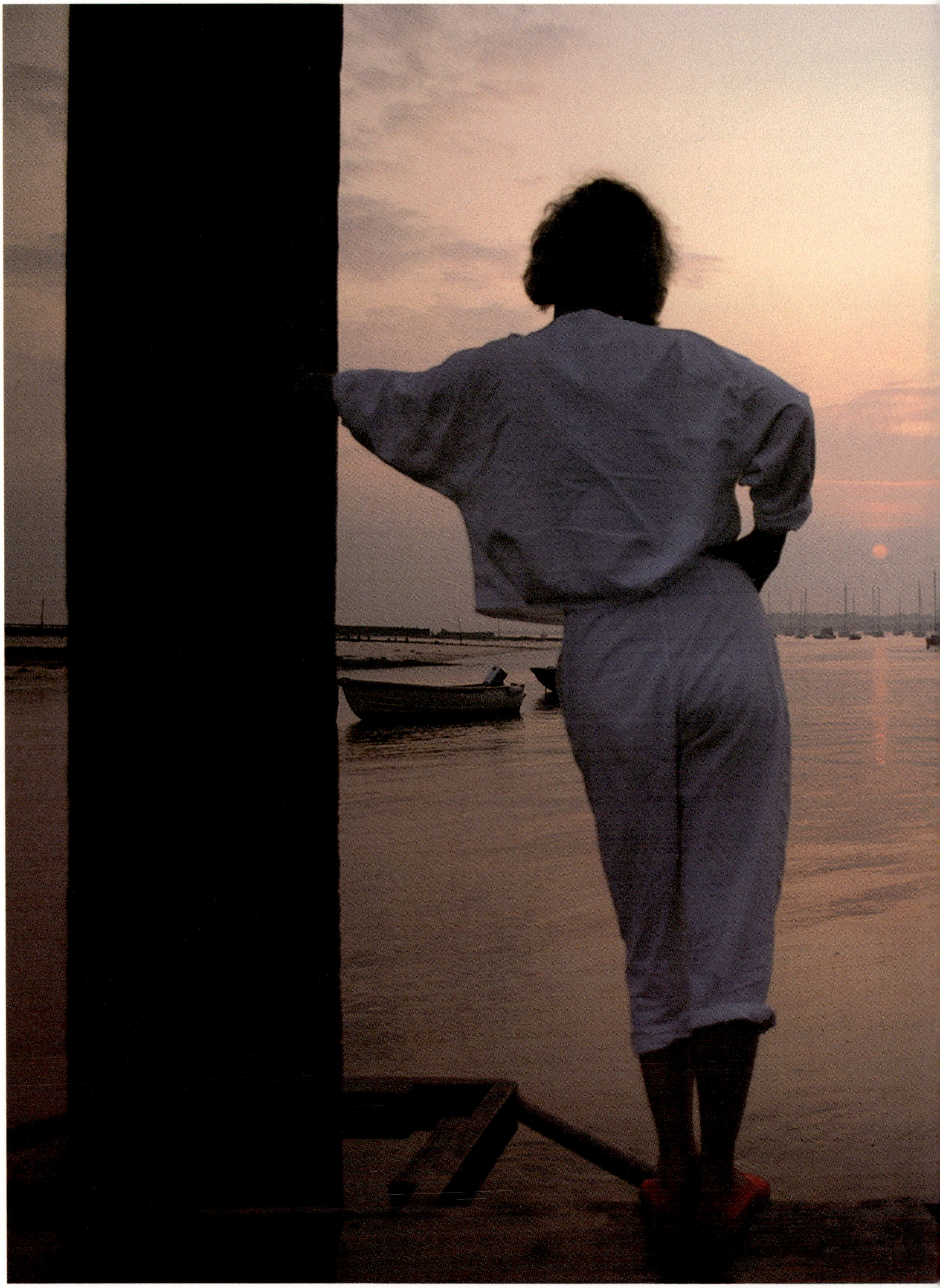

THE ART OF HOLIDAY PHOTOGRAPHY

How to preserve those precious memories

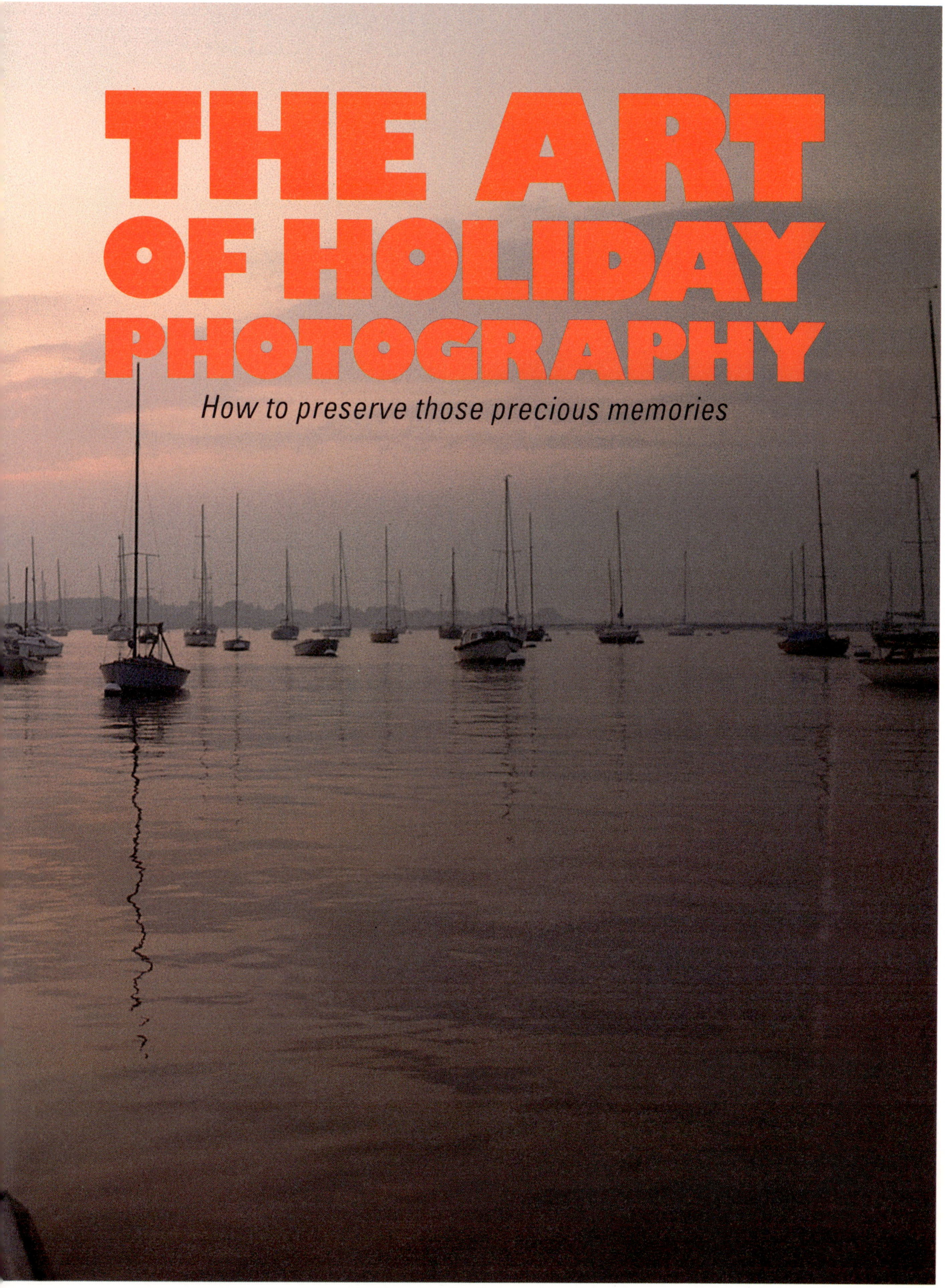

FBB

A Fotobank book published in association
with the English Tourist Board.

Great care has been taken to ensure that all factual information contained in this book is accurate. Any errors which appear are the responsibility of the Publisher and not that of the English Tourist Board. Any opinions or subjective views are those of the Author and do not necessarily reflect the opinion or policy of the Publisher or the English Tourist Board

English Tourist Board

First published 1987 copyright © Fotobank Books
32/33 Kingly Court, London W1R 5LE
Telephone: 01-734 2915/4764. Telex: 25367. Fax 4375220

ISBN 1-869911-01-6

Art Director: Andrew Fenton
Production Directors: Ray Daffurn, Brian Goodall
Editor: Roger Hicks
Editorial Contributors: John Easterby, Susanne Haines
Design/Art Work: Chameleon Graphic Design
Picture Research: Fotobank International Colour Library Ltd.

Contributors

Fotobank International Colour Library Ltd.
England Scene Colour Library
Britain on View Photographic Library
Royal Photographic Society
Michael Busselle
Ray Daffurn
Barry Hicks
Colin Molyneux
Patrick Thurston
Glyn Williams
Oliver Ben
Anthony Blake
Marcus Brown
Robert Eames
John Farnham
Julia Fryer
Andy Gordon
Roger Hicks
Neil Holmes
Ian Howes
Rayment Kirby
Peter Kowal
Robert Lawrence
Richard Littlewood
Steve Moss
Tony Page
Roger Scruton
Roger Tidman
Andy Williams
Patrick Wise
Adam Woolfitt
John Wyand

Contents

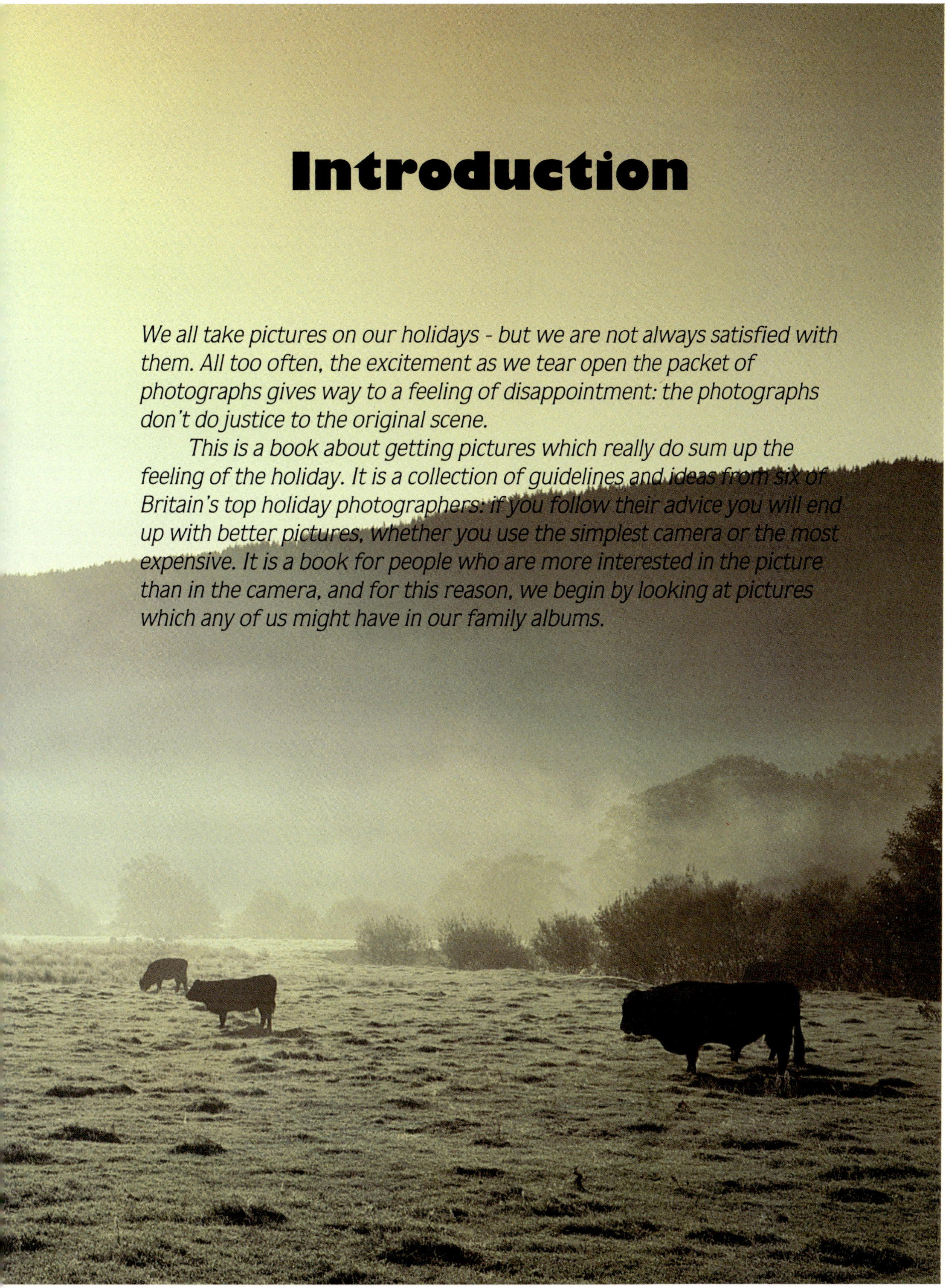

Introduction

We all take pictures on our holidays - but we are not always satisfied with them. All too often, the excitement as we tear open the packet of photographs gives way to a feeling of disappointment: the photographs don't do justice to the original scene.

This is a book about getting pictures which really do sum up the feeling of the holiday. It is a collection of guidelines and ideas from six of Britain's top holiday photographers: if you follow their advice you will end up with better pictures, whether you use the simplest camera or the most expensive. It is a book for people who are more interested in the picture than in the camera, and for this reason, we begin by looking at pictures which any of us might have in our family albums.

Glyn Williams

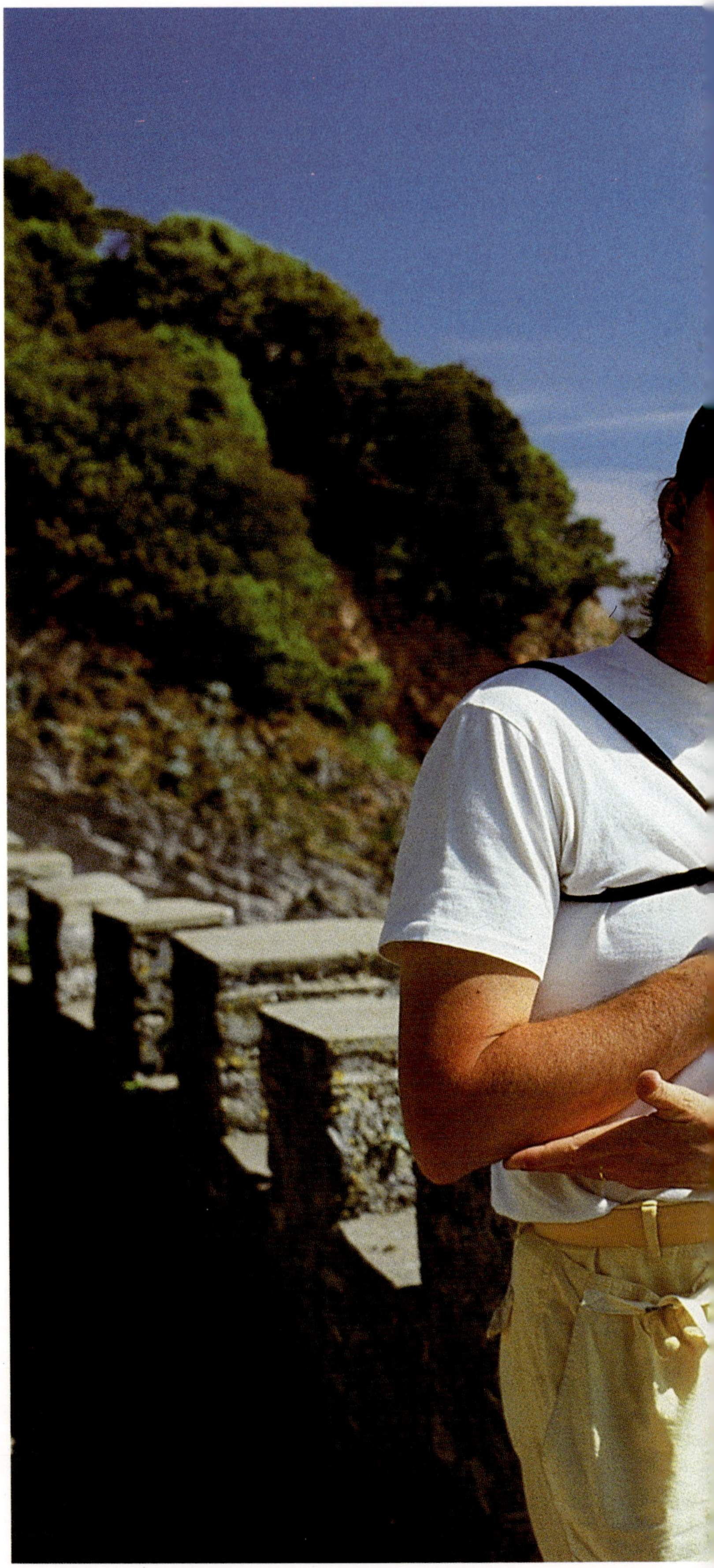

In my view, a holiday photograph can be one of two things: a picture-postcard view, or a personal record.

The ones I call 'picture postcards' are much easier: you can learn how to take them. You find your subject; you get in close; you change your viewpoint until you find the best one; and you go for bright colours, blue skies, and basically simple images - images that everyone can identify with. For example, if I see a multicoloured umbrella on a beach, or outside a pub, I am drawn to it like a bee to honey because I know that it will be the kind of colourful, attractive picture that will look good in a brochure. Don't get me wrong: I'm not knocking this kind of picture, because it's the kind of picture that means something to everyone and makes them feel good.

Personal pictures are another matter. Many of them are completely spontaneous; they may mean something only to you, or they may convey a particular mood which was very personal and perhaps very fleeting - a feeling of hope, or yearning, or mystery, or awe, or maybe even humour. They may make you feel good; they may make you feel all kinds of other things. Learning to take this sort of picture is much more difficult. You have to work quickly, so that you can capture the mood while it is still there - though I suppose that is true of any sort of photography. You also have to decide what is important to *you:* I like simple graphic shapes, and I often use black and white for my personal photography.

Because we live in a very visual age, with posters and magazines and television everywhere, I think that our photography constantly improves whether we work at it or not; but we can improve it faster if we really look at our pictures. Put them on the table and ask yourself which ones worked best. Why did they work, or fail? Would they have been better if we had been a few feet to the left or right, or if we had crouched down low or stood on a wall? What do they say to you? You can learn a lot from this kind of exercise.

I love photography. I do it for a living; I do it for fun. I look back on my days as a schoolteacher, and I think just how hard I had to work. Now, it sometimes seems almost fraudulent to take money for doing something I like doing so much. But my photography does serve a purpose: people hire me because I can communicate the ideas that they want communicated, and I think this is the key to it. You have to think about what you're doing.

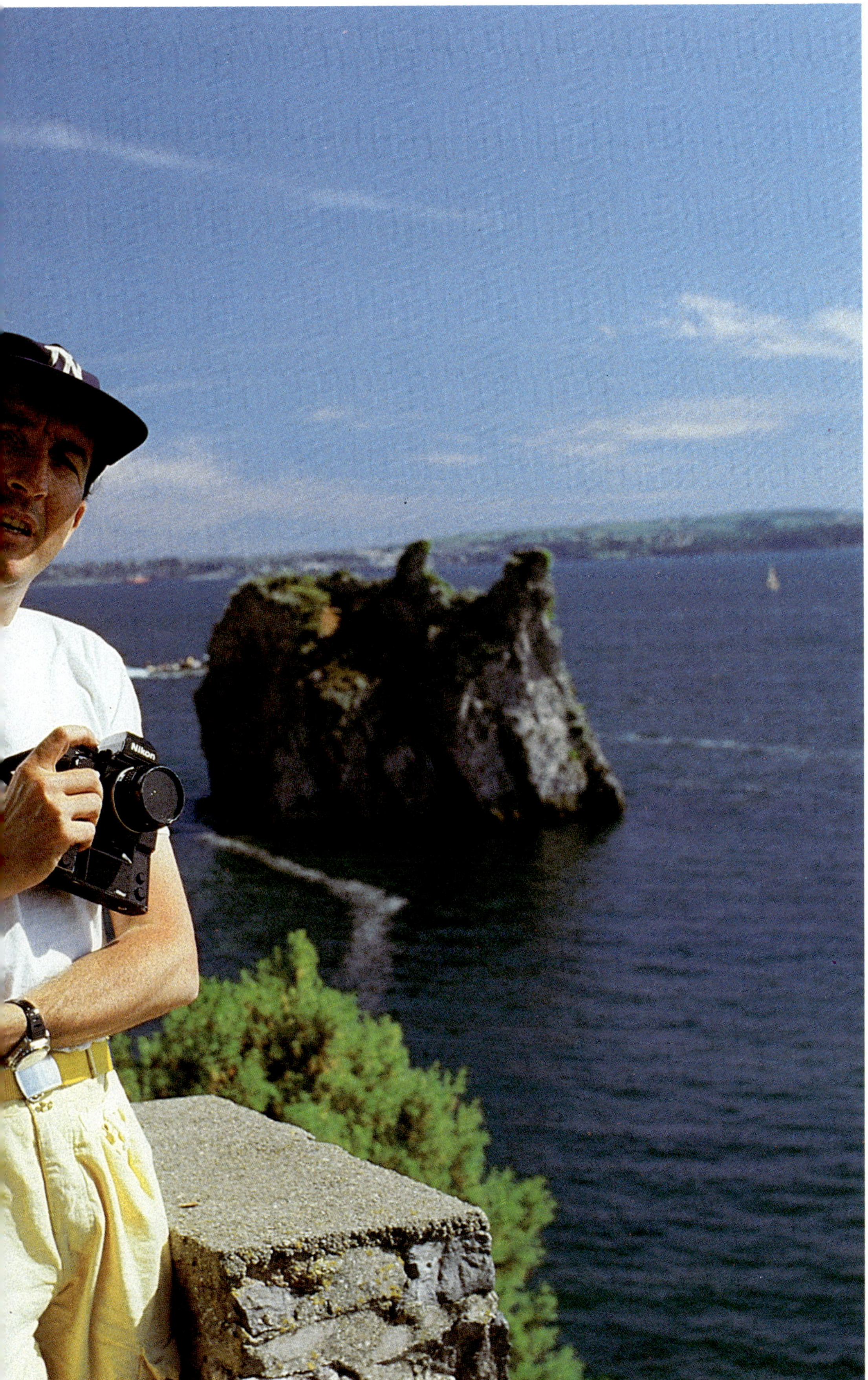

Glyn has, in Mae West's words, 'been things and seen places'. He started out as a schoolteacher in England, and then when he was teaching in the West Indies he became interested in photography: the availability of cheap cameras at the Free Port encouraged him. After a couple of summer schools in Colorado, he came back to the UK and took a BA degree in photography at the Polytechnic of Central London. Straightforward enough so far...

His final year thesis, though, involved a trip to Japan. In order to earn the money to get there, he took a job at the Hard Rock Café in London. When he graduated, instead of going straight into photography he went back to the Hard Rock Café for a while, and then he went to Sweden (his wife is Swedish) to run a similar place there. All the while, though, he was getting more and more photographic work, mainly holiday/travel and annual reports, though including all kinds of other things. Eventually, he became a full-time photographer and moved back to London. He says he has a love-hate relationship with the city, but that he couldn't really imagine being based anywhere else.

Patrick Thurston

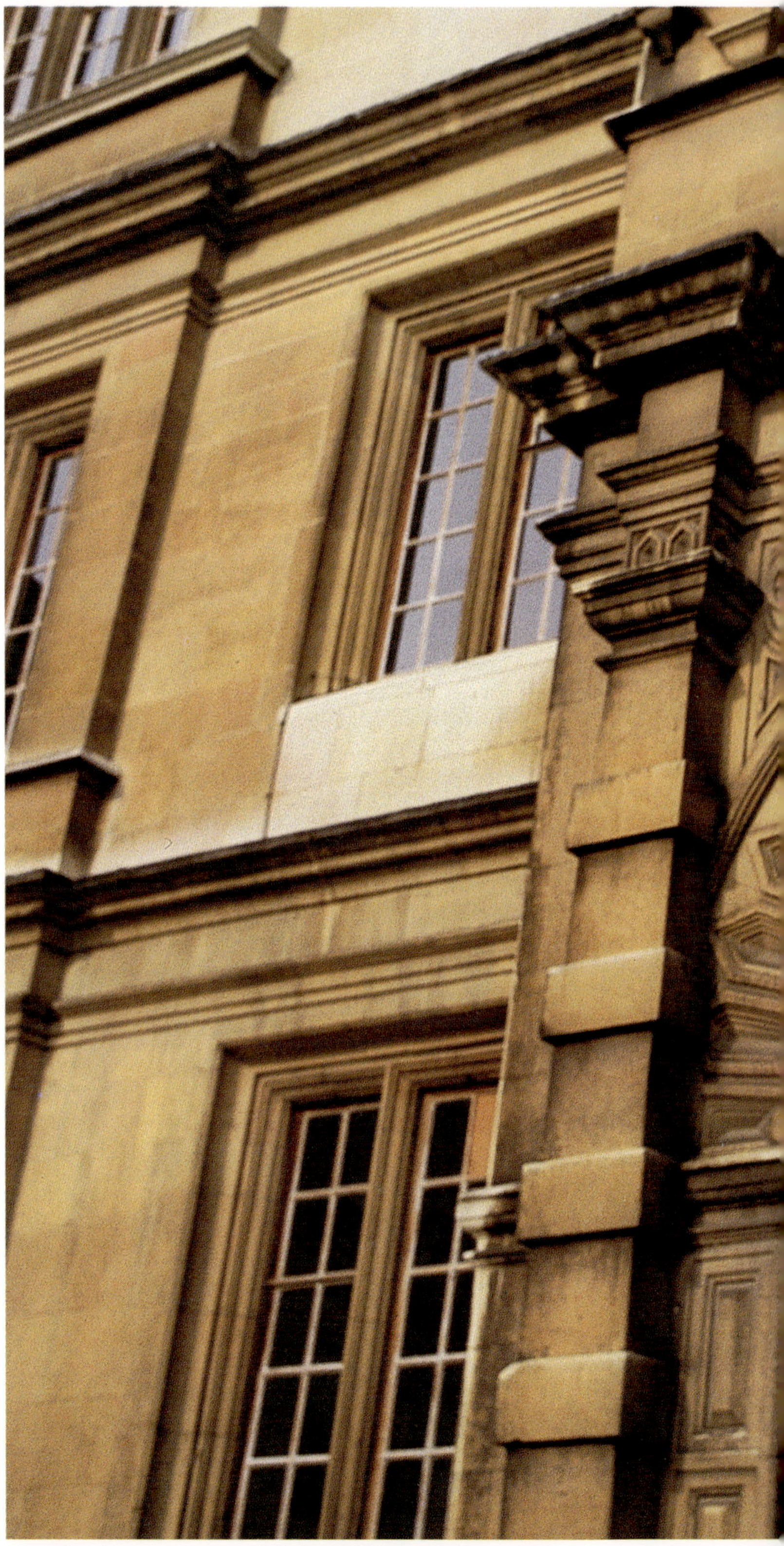

The best advice for anyone who wants to take pictures is to go out and do it: there's no faster way to learn. Certainly, books are useful, but 'read' the pictures as well as the words; ask yourself how the photographer achieved a certain effect, and whether that effect worked or not.

Equipment isn't all that important, though it's obviously useful to have the best you can afford. I like to travel light, so I normally only use three lenses, all Nikon: an 80-200mm zoom, a 25-50mm zoom, and a 20mm. The zooms are on the two camera bodies around my neck, and the 20mm goes in a pocket. I find that wide-angles are indispensable for landscapes, particularly; I would buy a 13mm if I could justify the expense, but even professionals have to worry about these things! You do have to be very careful about foregrounds when you are using a wide-angle, though: unless you have some real foreground interest, such as flowers, or a gate, or a tree, or something like that, the picture usually looks flat and boring. I think it is important to have a focal point or main centre of interest in a picture; it doesn't have to be the main subject of the picture, but it does have to be something for the eye to start with before it explores the picture any further. Even something like a shovel which a workman left sticking in the earth when he went off for his lunch can provide this sort of centre of interest. Once you've got it, you can have as much space behind it as you like, but a wide-angle shot without it is often impossible to make attractive.

Generally, I prefer to work without a tripod, because I find that I can grab the shot instantly, for example to capture a deer running across moorland, or rapidly changing light conditions. On the other hand, if I'm running out of light, which is always a risk with zooms because of their comparatively small maximum apertures, I'd rather use a tripod than a faster film; I much prefer the kind of image quality that the slower films give.

To finish, I'd like to repeat what I said at the beginning: get out there and take pictures. That's how I learned, and I now make my living by it!

Like so many professional photographers, Patrick is self-taught. He began with a box camera, and then moved on to an old Kodak Autographic, with a trap-door in the back, because it was a more versatile camera!

During his National Service, in Singapore, he met another photographer whose work had been published in *Picture Post*, then the leading British picture magazine; he was, he says, 'knocked out' by the pictures, and decided that maybe this

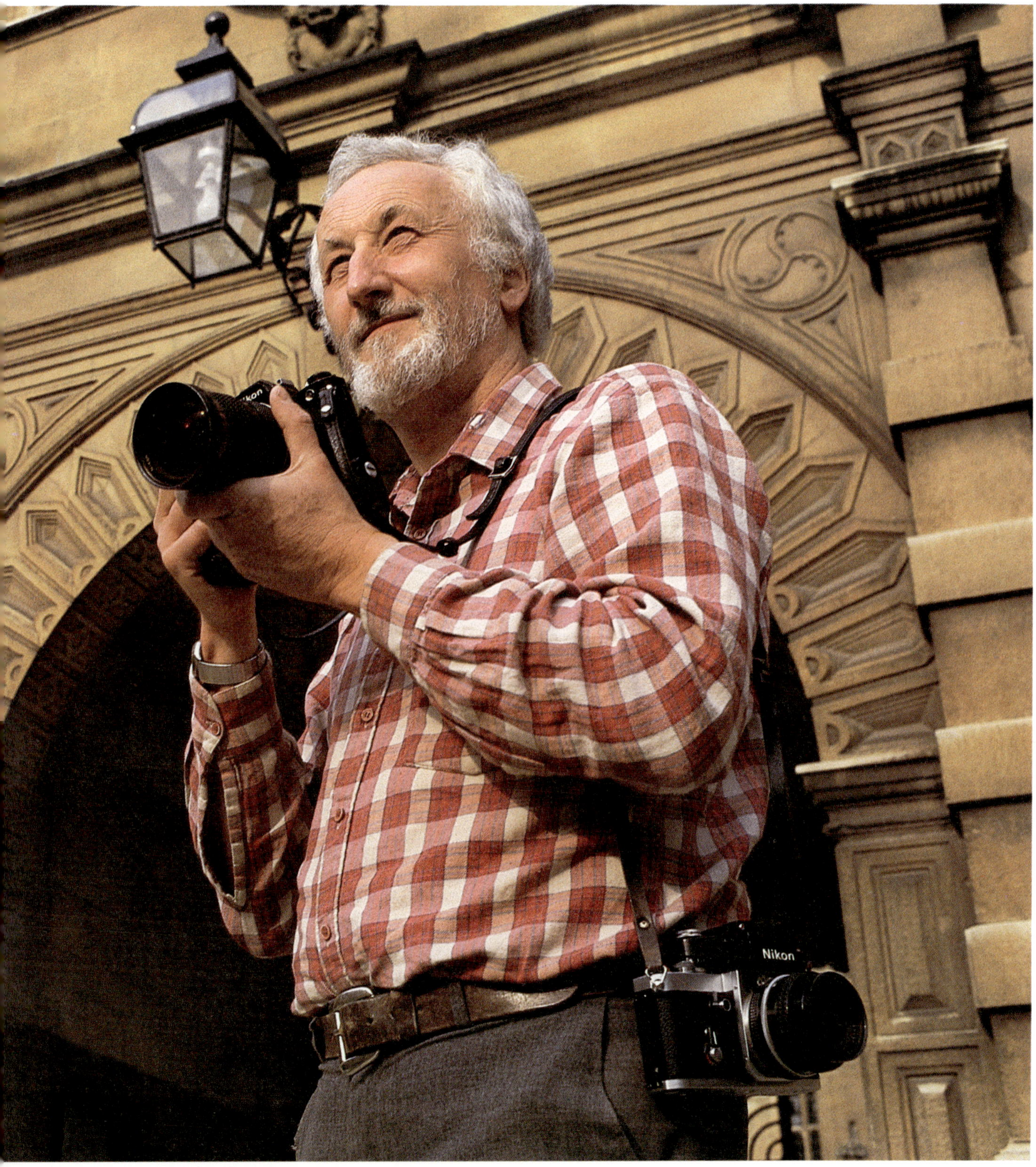

was what he wanted to do with the rest of his life. Of course, cameras were much cheaper and more easily available at that time in Singapore than in Britain, so he bought himself an expensive German Contaflex, one of the first modern-style single-lens reflex cameras (see page 118).

When he came back from Singapore, he spent a term at the Regent Street Polytechnic, where he learned 'an enormous amount about portraiture' but decided he could do better in the rough-and-tumble commercial world. Since then, he has earned his living with his cameras for more years than he cares to admit.

Colin Molyneux

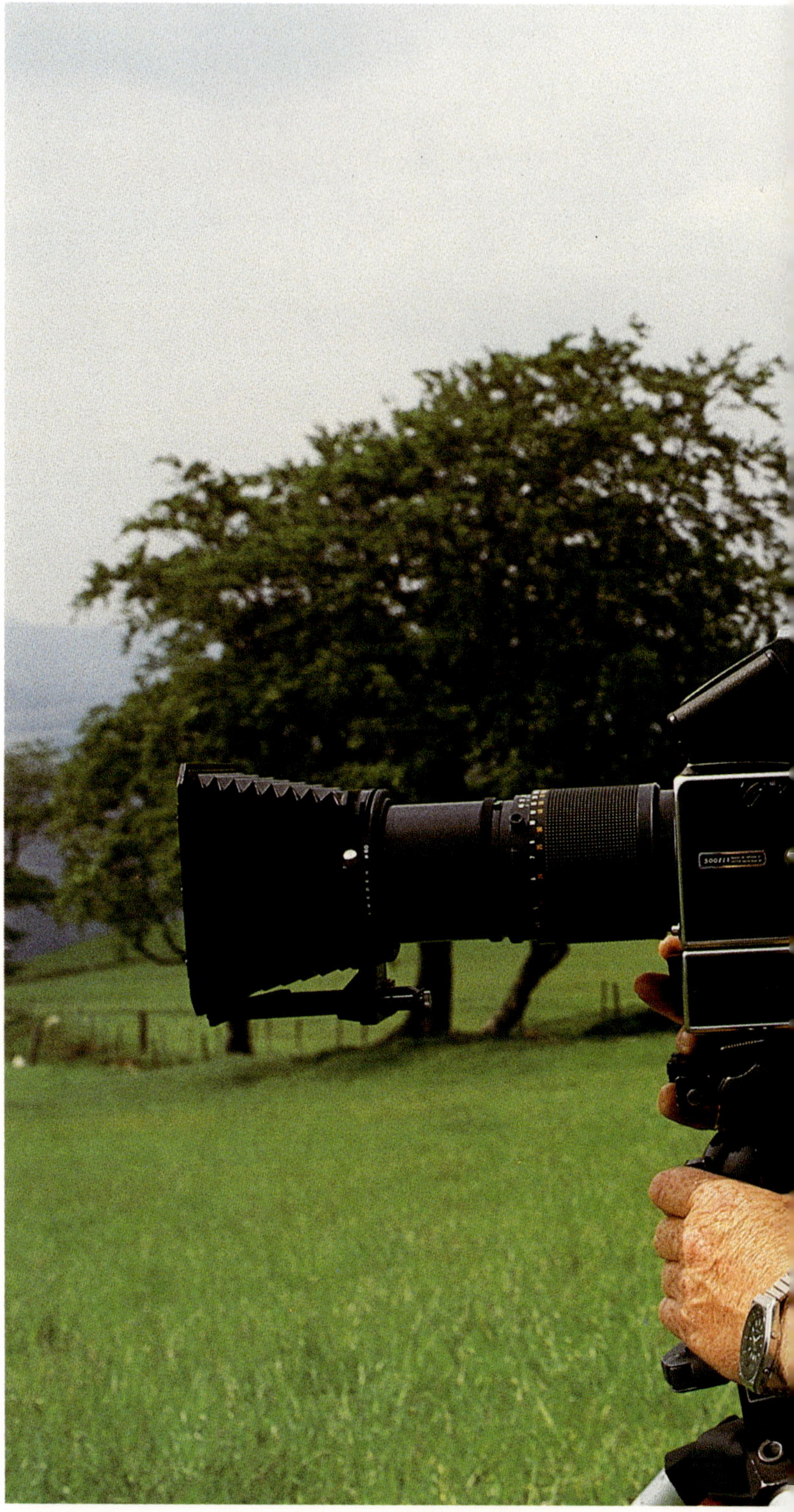

Photography is fifty per cent luck and fifty per cent patience. You can spend three quarters of an hour waiting for the picture to be just right, and as soon as the one element that you are waiting for falls into place, another one disappears. For example, I was photographing a farmhouse once, with a sheep perched on a rock that formed the real centre of interest of the picture. I waited for ages for the light to be just right, and just as the sun broke through, the sheep jumped off the rock. I've got a beautiful picture of the sheep's hindquarters!

I know that not everyone likes tripods, but I am a great believer in them. They are a great help in getting sharp pictures, and they also allow you to just *look* through the viewfinder, waiting for the shapes to come together. This thing about shapes is very important: it's hard to explain, but you can *see* when it happens, because everything suddenly looks just right.

Of course, you can carry this counsel of perfection too far. I remember shooting sheep-dog trials once, and I got far fewer pictures than I should have done, because while I was waiting for the dog to get to the right place, the shepherd and the sheep would move, and so on. On the other hand, I find that I tend to take fewer and fewer pictures on each shoot as time goes on anyway; instead of shooting anything and everything, and then throwing half the pictures away when I get home, I now throw them away in the viewfinder before I take them! This sounds a bit odd, but it's a good description of the way I work: I imagine that I am looking at the final picture, not at the image in the viewfinder, and if I don't like the picture, I don't take it.

I find that using a single-lens reflex camera (page 118) makes this process very much easier. With other sorts of camera, the ones with a separate viewfinder, it's much harder to isolate the picture and to look at it as if you had already taken it. The reflex also gives you a much better idea of what is going to be sharp and what isn't: masses of out-of-focus flowers in the foreground, for example, can be used to cover up parked cars, gasometers, and all kinds of ugly things.

The foreground is a very important part of the picture, I think, for two reasons. First, it provides some extra interest in what could otherwise be very empty areas of the picture, and second, it is invaluable for creating a sense of depth in distance shots, which otherwise just look hazy, flat and blue. You can use anything - a stone wall, the overhanging bough of a tree, a gateway - but you do need something.

All in all, I think I've been very lucky to be able to earn a living doing what I like doing, and I reckon that thinking about how you take the picture is a part of the clue to success.

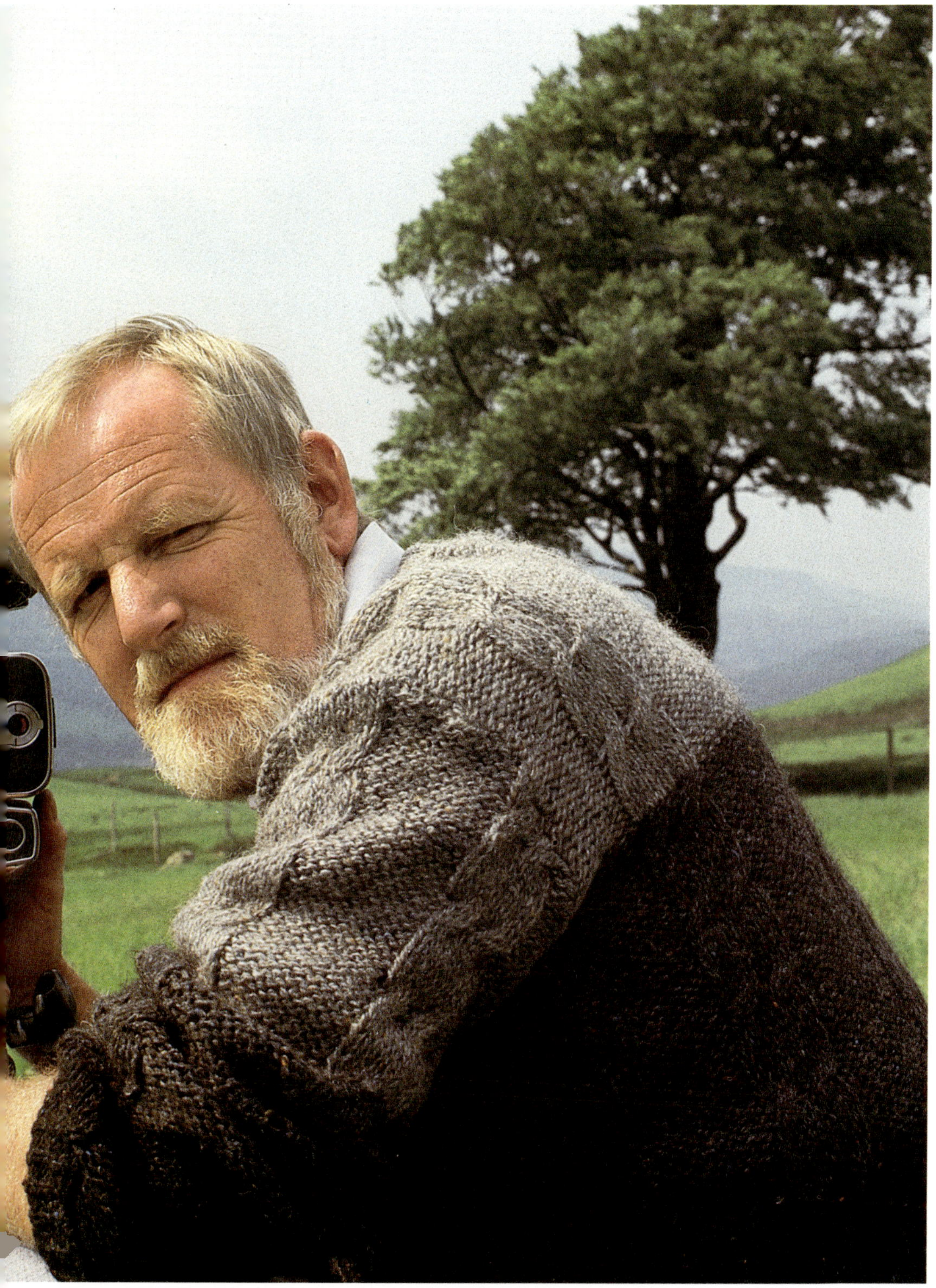

Colin began his career as a graphic designer; he had studied photography at art school, but only as a part of the graphic arts course. What he did, though, was to persuade each of his employers in turn to set up a photography department, which he also ran; by degrees, he became more and more a photographer, and less and less a graphic designer. It was an offer of two years' guaranteed work from the Wales Tourist Board which finally made him decide to go into photography full-time, and since the early 1970s he has been involved in holiday and travel photography, in annual report photography, and in other fields. Based in Wales, he works all over the British Isles and indeed all over the world.

Barry Hicks

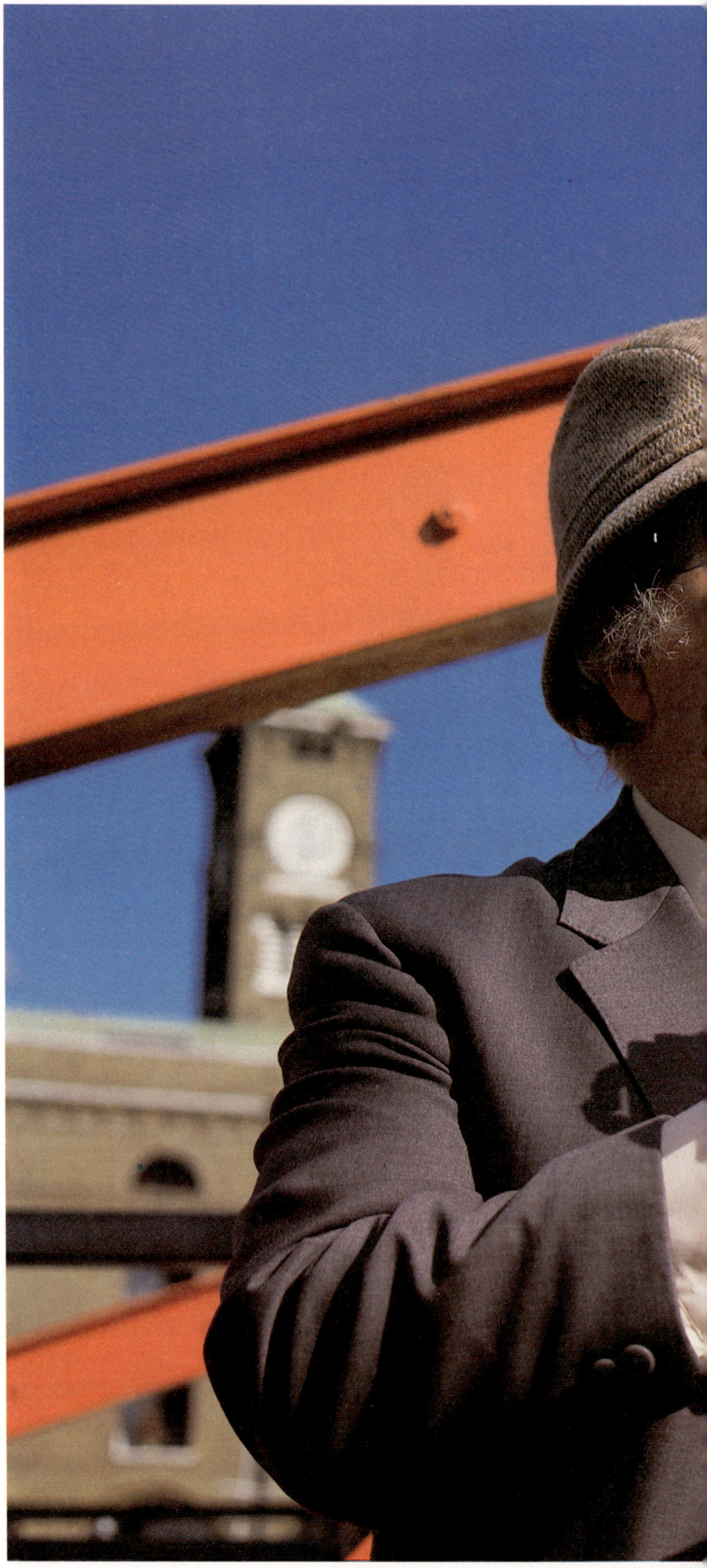

Tourism is people - I think that this is the most important thing to remember, and I always keep it in mind when I am shooting travel or holiday pictures of any kind. Even if I am using professional models, I try to involve them with genuine locals - I'll get them to ask the way from a passer-by, or to talk to an old fisherman mending his nets. Getting people to look natural is important. I have to set pictures up sometimes, but they must not look staged, or people will not identify with them. From my point of view as a professional, I want the people who see my pictures to feel involved because this will encourage them to visit the places I'm photographing - after all, that's what I'm paid for - but amateurs should always have the same aim in mind. If your holiday pictures really show what it is like to be somewhere, people will be able to identify with them, and they will be interested in them.

Apart from people I'd say that the other important points are studying your subject from all angles and in all lights. Try to imagine what the light will be like at another time of day, or even at another time of year. And do try for something a little out of the ordinary: shoot early morning mists and always look for reflections - on a car, in a pool, even on a Guardsman's cuirasse. As far as my own work is concerned, one year I'll go to the Lake District, for instance in the springtime, then another year I'll go in the autumn when the colouring and light would be entirely different.

Finally, always be alive to details. I find that no matter how often I go back to a place, there's always something else to see - gargoyles and carved pew-ends in churches, old street signs and milestones, trees in bloom, and so forth. Because of my job, which involves supplying pictures all over the world to illustrate articles on Britain, I'll sometimes use up a whole roll of film on a couple of details. I'm not suggesting you do the same - after all, you don't need twenty pictures of the same thing - but I do suggest that you shouldn't be afraid to use film: you always regret missing the pictures you *didn't* take.

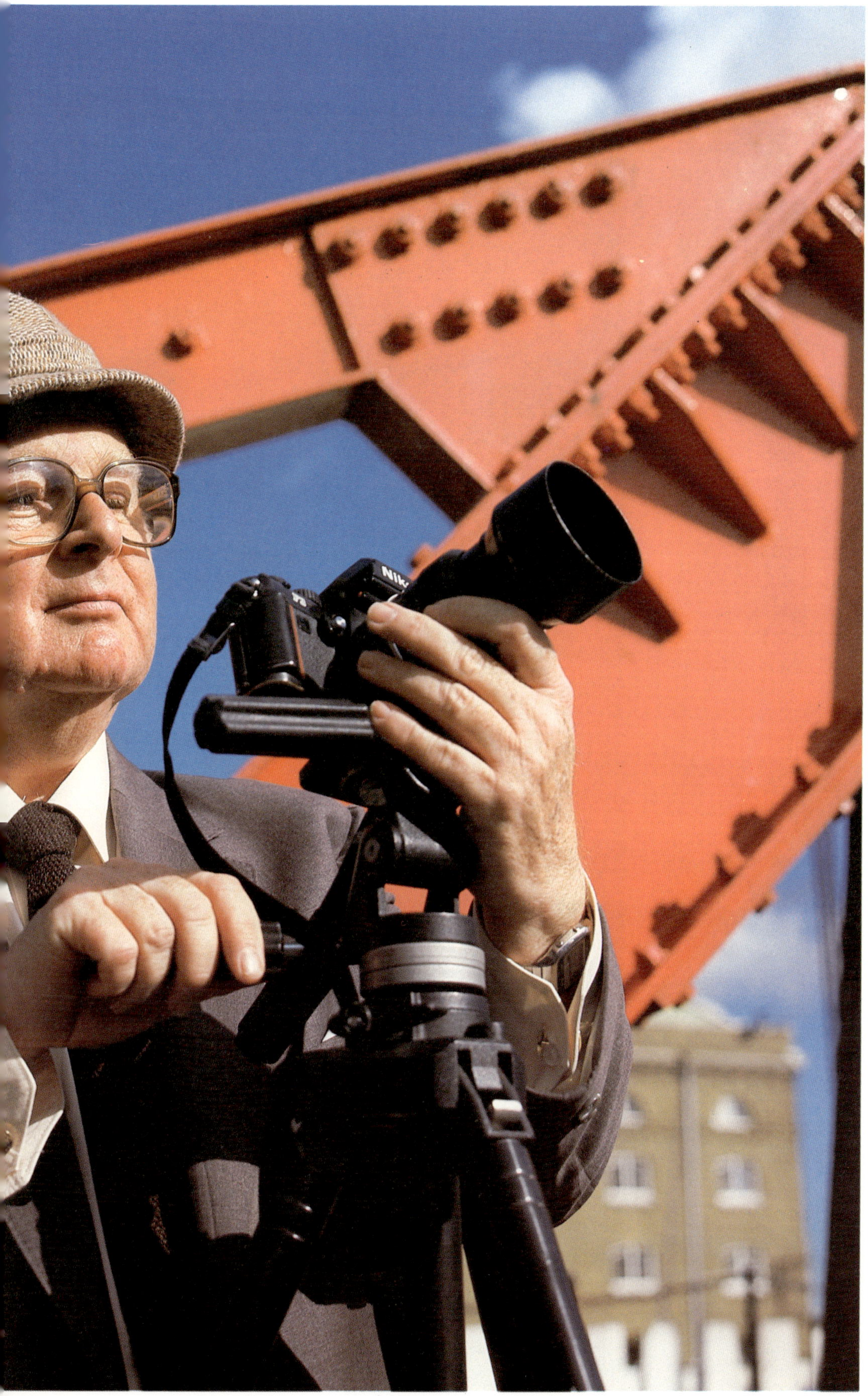

Barry took up photography in the late 1930s, using an old Leica of his father's, but he says, 'before I could really get under way, World War II intervened and I found myself in the Air Force 'for the duration''.

During the war, the Air Force put his photographic talents to good use - mainly on aerial photography. After the war he worked in advertising and publishing, but did not really enjoy it. In 1952 he saw an advertisement for a six-month temporary job with the old BTHA, the forerunner of the British Tourist Authority - he's been with them ever since. As Chief Photographer of the BTA his pictures are used world-wide in their work of promoting Britain overseas, whilst his work for the ETB promotes tourism inside the British Isles.

Barry seldom takes holidays - he likes his work too much and says that Britain is 'a wonderful country to photograph and to travel in'.

Ray Daffurn

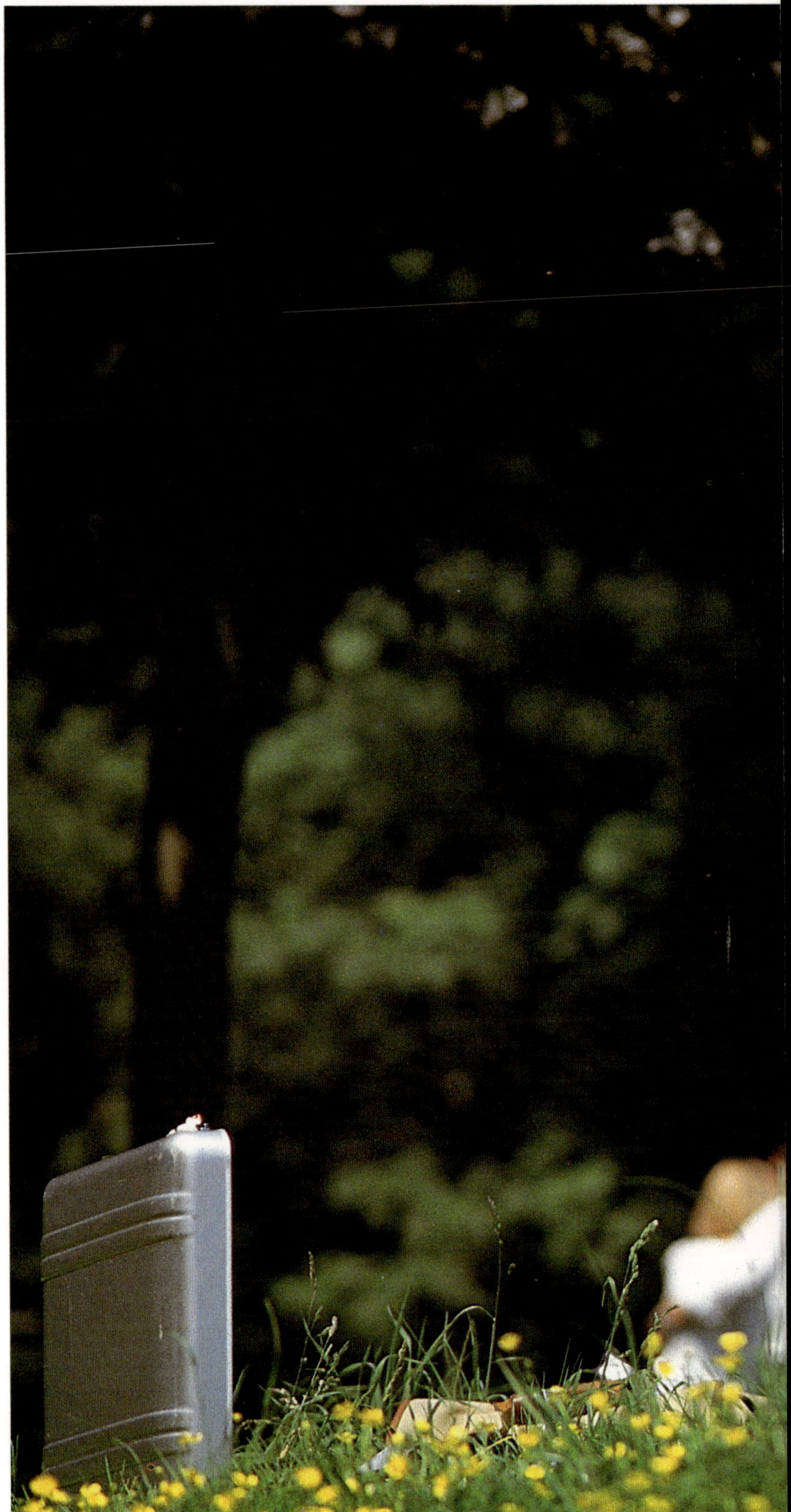

The very nature of travel photography - the erratic hours, the travelling to unusual places and the bizarre situations that can arise - seemed to fulfill my restless nature. I was lucky enough to win a contract early on in my photographic life, which enabled me to travel extensively around the country. This planted the seeds of thought that I could happily exist with the nature of travel photography and remain untied to a traditional 9 to 5 job.

Subsequently the majority of my photography has been related to travel and holidays. It is difficult to say whether my life is now one everlasting holiday or just constant work. I certainly spent a lot of time taking photographs on holiday before I was ever given any money for it, and now when I take a break from commissioned work and go off on holiday, I invariably take photographs which I know I will be able to sell when I return home.

Through my work I have learned the importance of researching a place prior to the visit and as a result am usually able to see more of a city or village than would normally be possible in the time available. It is possible, for example, to arrive at your destination knowing what the weather is going to be like for your stay, whether there are any places of unusual interest off the beaten track, any special events taking place or simply the fastest way to get from A to B. When time is short, which is usually the case, these things can make the difference between a good or bad shoot.

When I arrive somewhere, I try to spend some time walking about the places I will be photographing, assessing where the sun will be at certain times of the day, so that I can plan a route which will enable me to shoot with the light in my favour. This means that when I do start shooting, I am prepared with the right lenses and equipment. Ultimately this exercise saves a great deal of time and frustration.

I hope that this book will be of real help to you and show you the value of taking a little more care with your holiday photographs. Not only can photography provide you with lasting memories of places visited, but it can encourage you to look more carefully at an environment, it´s people and their lifestyles. I'd like to leave you with the thought that your camera will feel a good deal lighter about your neck if you feel the film contains some good pictures!

Ray studied photography at Ealing for three years and although he has rarely pursued it, he specialised, towards the end of his course, in cinematography.

When he left Ealing he took a job as one of six photographic assistants at Vogue Studios, working on 'House & Garden', 'Wine & Food' and naturally 'Vogue' itself. Location shoots as well as working in the studios were part of Ray's work and his enjoyment of location work led to his interest in travel photography.

From Vogue he moved to his own studio, concentrating on advertising and public relations work; one of his

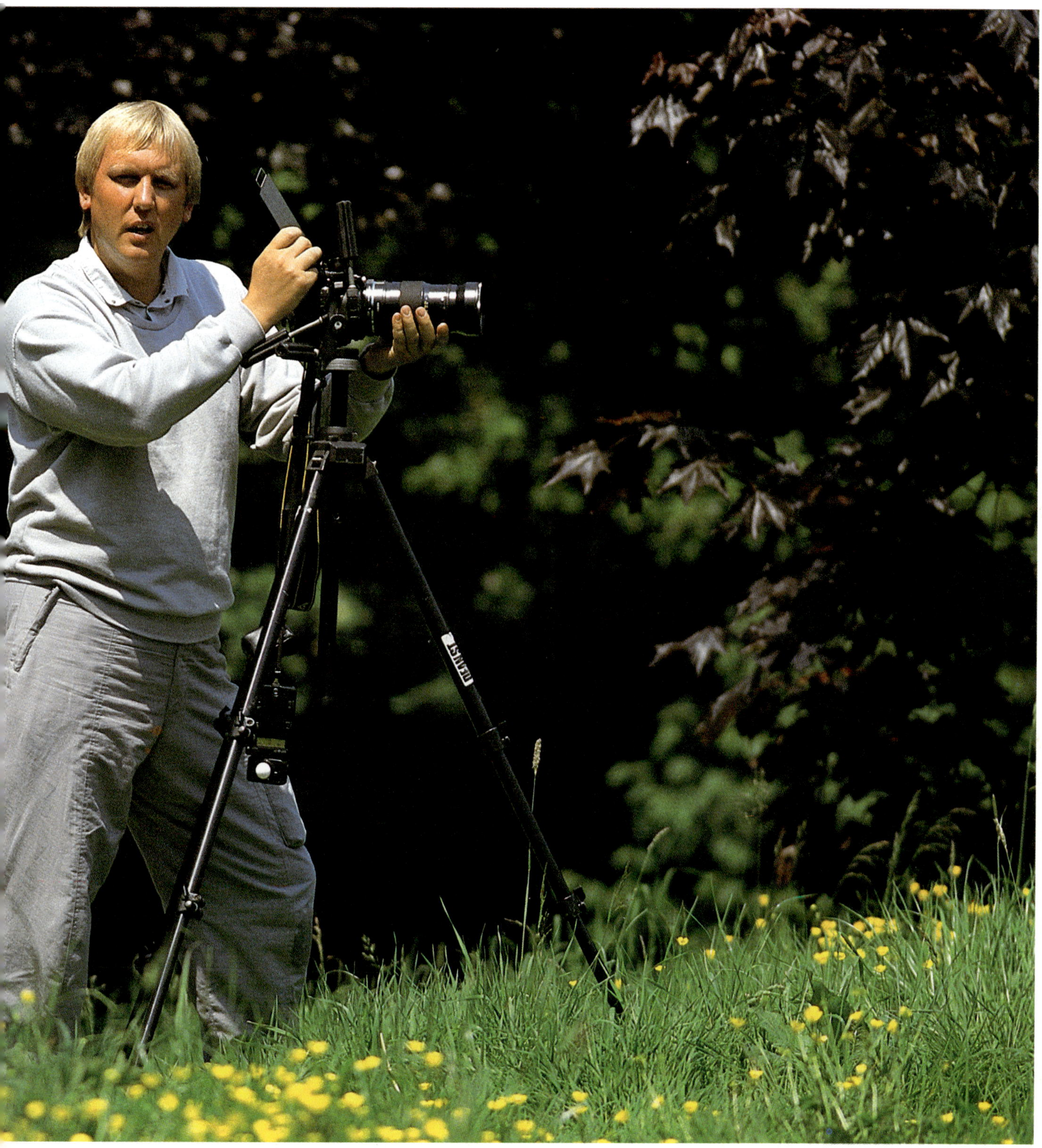

largest clients were Martini Rossi, for whom he worked not just on drinks and still life, but also on sport including motor racing, golf and fencing. Working on location helped his interest in travel and holiday photography to develop.

In addition to his hectic life as a travel photographer, Ray also runs his own photo library, has a publishing company and a software company. The application of computers in relation to photography and laser discs is an area where he is becoming increasingly well known - where else better to store those holiday pictures?!

Mike Busselle

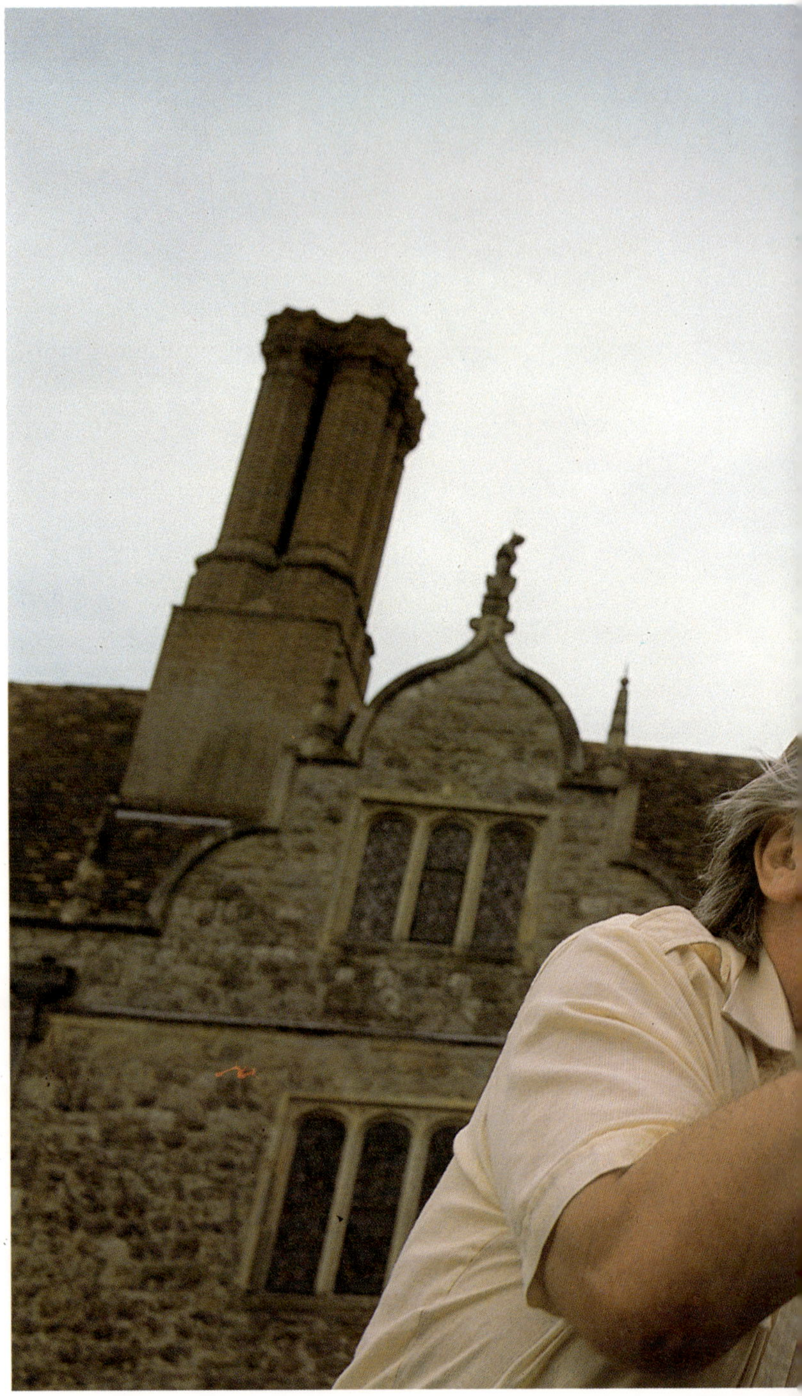

There's quite a difference between the kind of photographs which I take professionally, and the sort which I take for myself. On a typical holiday shoot, the client has paid a lot of money for the models, and he wants you to shoot those models, so you do; but if I'm shooting for my own sake, whether they are 'happy snaps' or for a book, I shoot a lot of landscapes without any people in them. Then, after a spell of pictures without people in them, I find that I'm ready to go back to shooting models again. I like having the choice, because each is like a break from the other. In fact, I like all kinds of photography: the only sort which I don't do much of is still life.

I agree with what Colin Molyneux says on page 12, about luck: a frightening number of my best pictures are ones that I shot almost casually, but it's also true that fortune favours the prepared mind: I've been lucky, but I've worked to make myself lucky. How do you do that? By keeping your eyes open! If I'm on a tight schedule, I'm constantly looking for pictures even as I'm driving along, though I prefer to be able to get out and walk about more; this is one of the reasons I enjoy working on books for the National Trust.

The most useful single lens that I own is probably my 80-200mm zoom, but after that I must admit that I do use two rather specialised lenses. They are called 'shift' lenses, and they allow you to duplicate (to some extent) the effects you could get with the old wooden cameras or with modern monorail cameras - mainly, photographing buildings without getting that 'falling over backwards' effect. They are expensive, and very few amateurs use them, but they are rather fascinating. If I couldn't afford those, I suppose I would use a wide-angle - something like 24mm - as a back-up to my zoom.

I also use filters. A pale straw-coloured 81A 'warms up' pictures and makes them look sunnier: a polarising filter increases colour saturation; and a graduated grey filter can make skies stronger. Of course, I don't use them all at once, or even all the time: as far as I am concerned, a picture should look completely natural, no matter how much work you have put into it. If you can see that a filter has been used, the picture doesn't look natural, and you've failed!

Mike is a noted photographic writer as well as a professional photographer specialising in advertising and travel. He came into photography by what he describes as 'the normal amateur route' - a box camera at the age of eleven, then progressing by stages to

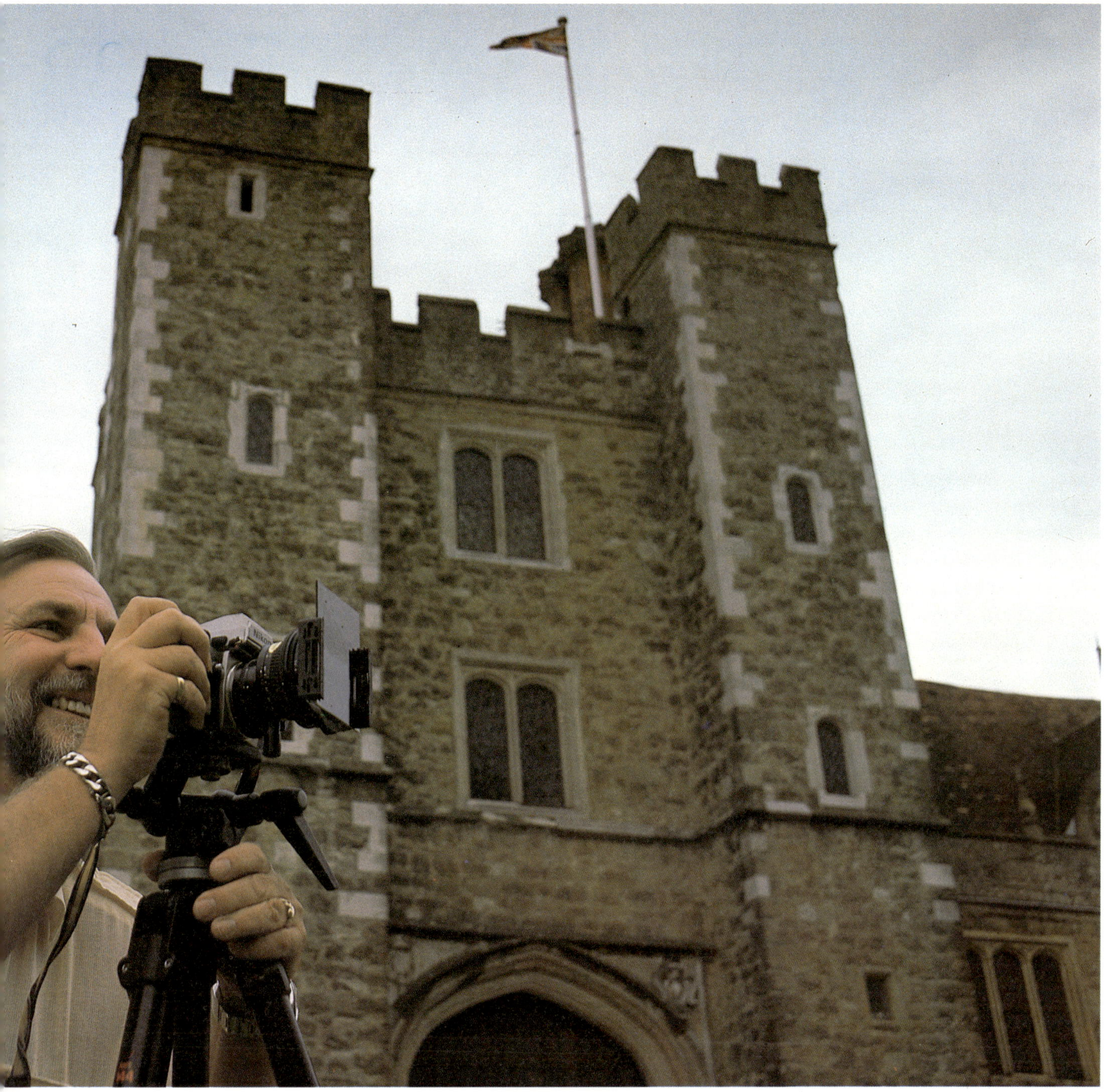

taking pictures of the neighbours and their children, and so forth. He did consider nuclear physics as an alternative career, and even worked in it for a year before deciding finally that photography was for him. His advice to would-be professional photographers is not to be too proud, or to aim too high; his own first full-time photographic job was in a film processing lab. Like the other photographers in this book, he takes pictures as a hobby as well as for a living.

CHAPTER TWO

Memories

Just as our grandparents' family albums are an endless source of fascination, today's holiday snap is tomorrow's cherished memory.

'Memory' is a magical word. If we ask ourselves what 'our memories' are, all kinds of things come flooding back. We remember weddings, state occasions, falling in love, falling out of love, journeys, friends, meals, places... and holidays.

What makes holidays different, though, is holiday photographs. Over the past hundred years or so, it has become increasingly common to carry a camera on holiday; nowadays, most of us automatically pick up a camera, or sling it round our necks.

What is really fascinating is that we can look at our own pictures of last year's holiday, or at circular Kodak pictures nearly a hundred years old, yellowed and faded with age and showing complete strangers, and recognise the same thing: the need to say, 'Hey! Look at me! I'm here, and I'm on holiday!'. Old family albums - even other people's family albums - are always intriguing for this very reason, and in a sense, this book is a plea for a return to the family album: not necessarily a massive leather-bound tome, but a series of albums we can look back on with pleasure. And, of course, our children and grandchildren will be as fascinated by those albums as we are by our grandparents' pictures.

We take our photography so much for granted today that it is amazing to realise just how recently simple, cheap colour photography was introduced; a quick history lesson makes illuminating reading.

It was in 1888 that George Eastman coined the word 'Kodak'. He wanted a word that was hard to mispronounce in any language, so that it would be recognised the world over, and apparently he liked the 'firm and unyielding' sound of the letter *K*. Shortly afterwards came the famous slogan, 'You press the button - we do the rest'. From the era of glass plates, photography moved into the era of film - the era where it still is today, and where it will remain until some electronic refinement of the video camera can begin to match the quality we take for granted on the cheapest conventional camera.

Over the years, photography has been getting easier and easier. Those old Kodaks took 100 circular pictures on a single roll of film, but they had to be returned to the factory for the film to be developed and the camera to be reloaded, and they needed bright sunlight in order to get any sort of image at all. Nor were there any enlargements: all Kodak pictures were 'contact prints', the same size as the negative, so that if you wanted a bigger picture, you needed a bigger film. If you wanted (say) 5 × 7″ pictures, this meant that your camera had to take 5 × 7″ film!

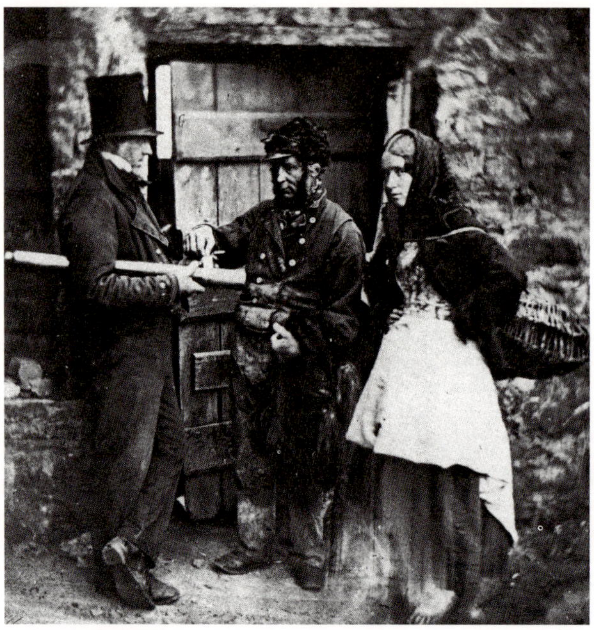

If the fisherfolk having their picture taken appear to be a trifle stiff in their pose it isn't surprising, as in 1854 when this picture was taken, the slightest movement during the long exposure necessary could cause problems.
In this picture the woman must have moved because as you can see there is a blurring around the area of her skirt and foot.

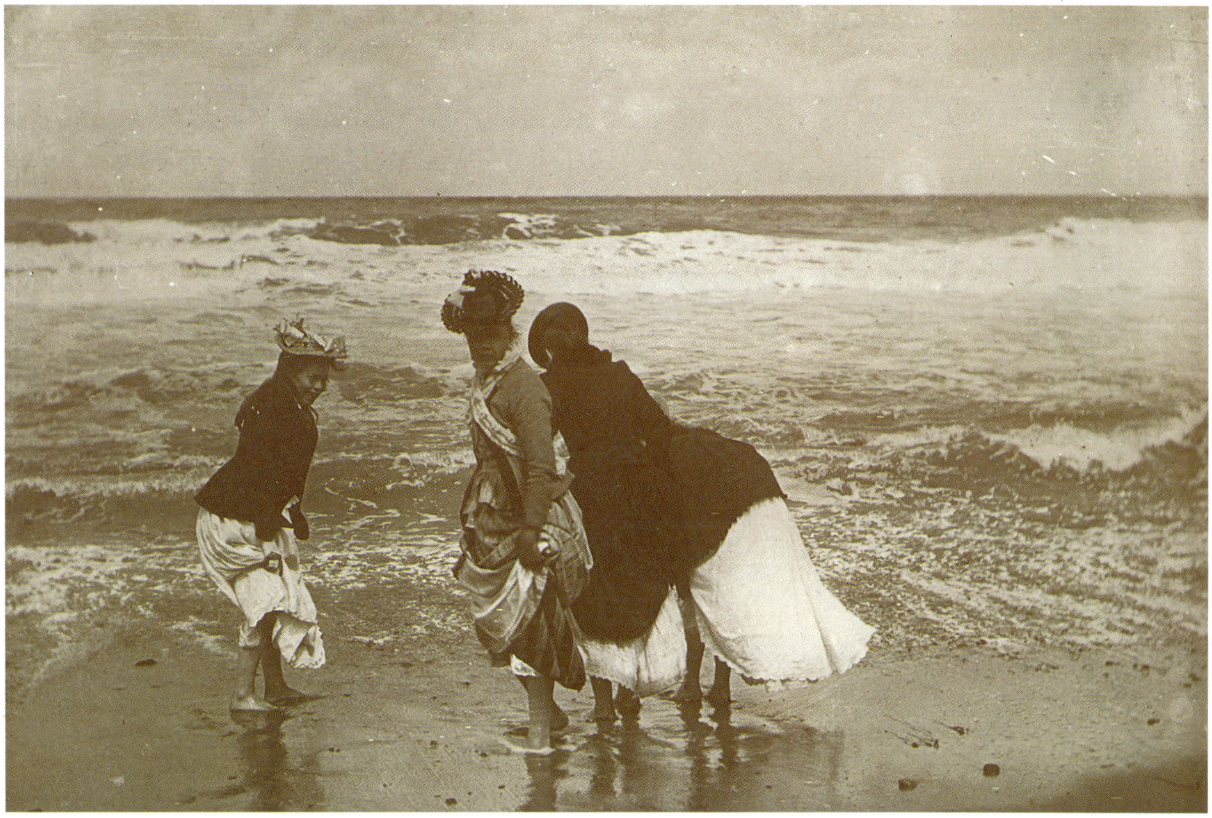

Before the 1880s, most photographs tended to be either of the nobility and gentry - Queen Victoria was an enthusiastic photographer - or carefully-posed pictures of the 'lower orders'. A few pioneers like Paul Martin were already challenging this convention in the 1880s(above). But when The Kodak (as Kodak cameras were first advertised) came out, the era of 'the common photographer' had arrived.

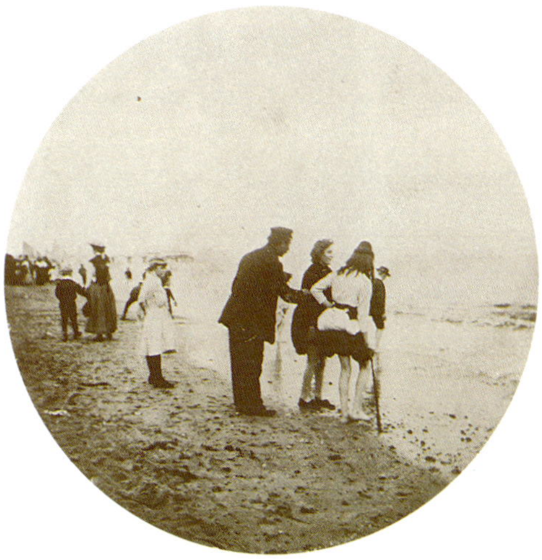

When you consider how long it can take to finish a 36-exposure film, it is amazing to think that early Kodak cameras took 100 circular pictures on a roll. The whole camera had to be returned to the factory for reloading, and for the pictures to be developed and printed.

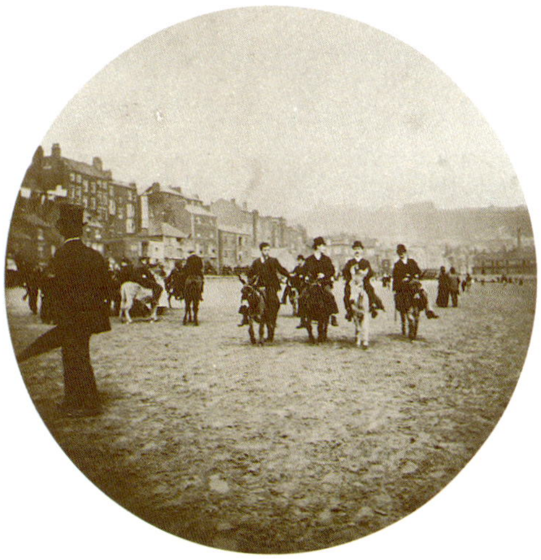

Bowler hats and donkeys - a wonderful 1890s combination, captured on a Kodak camera again.

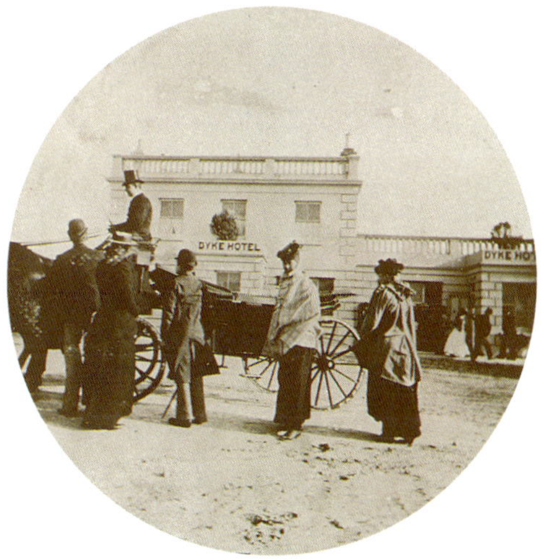

One wonders where the Dyke Hotel is, and who the ladies and gentlemen in the foreground are. Even pictures of total strangers can be fascinating, and if they are pictures of your relatives, in your family album, they are even more intriguing. Imagine how your pictures will be received a hundred years from now.

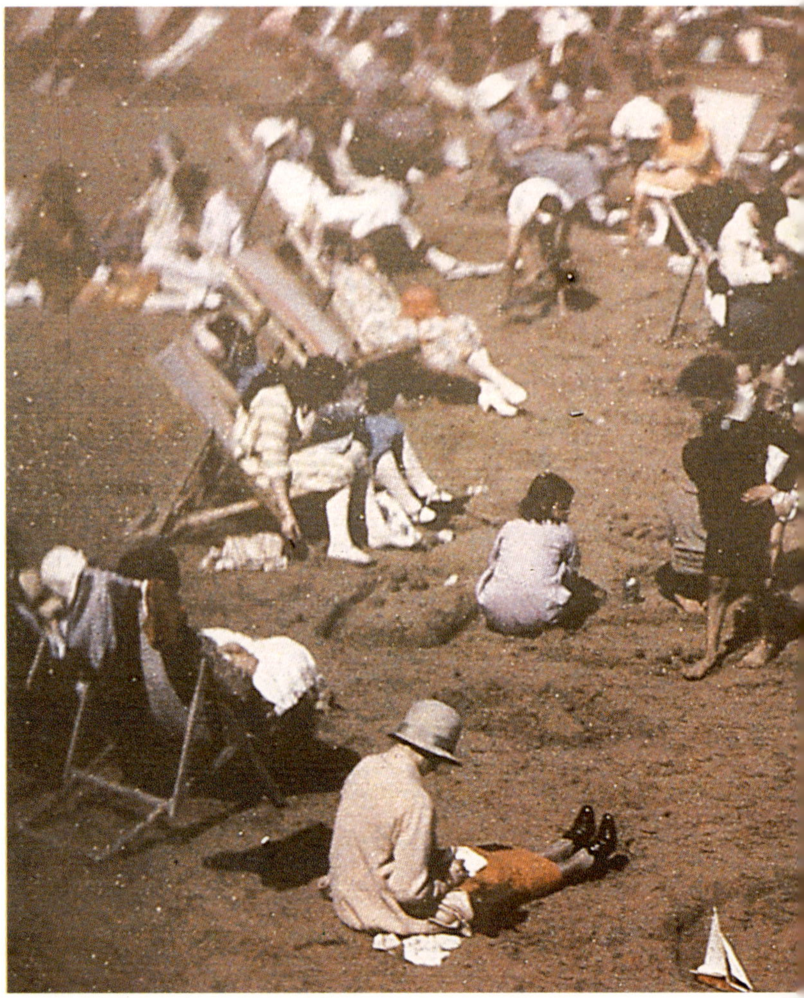

In the 1890s, Kodak introduced what they called 'cartridge loading', which was what we now call 'rollfilm'. Many people nowadays may never have loaded an old-fashioned box camera, with its fiddly roll of paper-backed film, but it is an intriguing thought that the modern 120 film size which is still widely used in professional cameras was introduced in 1902, and that the packing has hardly changed since - though the films themselves, and the cameras which use them, have grown very much more sophisticated.

Even the 'cartridge loading' Kodak cameras were still tied to the old 'contact print', and it was not really until the advent of the Leica in 1925 that enlargements - that is, big prints from small negatives - became commonplace. Then, diehard users of the big, old cameras scoffed at 'postage stamp size negatives'. What would they think now, if they could see 110 and disc cameras, with their negatives no larger than a finger-nail?

In those days, of course, everything was in black and white. It is true that various colour processes were invented even in the 19th century, and that James Clerk Maxwell successfully demonstrated a cumbersome system of colour photography as far back as 1861, but the first really successful commercial colour system was the Lumiere Autochrome of 1907. It used dyed potato starch grains to make up the colours, and still relied on glass plates rather than rollfilm. It was also very expensive! In 1936 came Kodachrome, but that was only for slides, and only in a limited number of film sizes: 35mm, the now obsolete 828 'Bantam' size, or sheet film. The vast majority of amateurs continued to use box cameras and were left out in the cold, with no easy way to get colour prints. Both Kodak and Agfa developed colour print processes during World War II, but it was not until after the war that they became widely available.

Even then, it was a long time before they became affordable. In 1963, for example, it cost 22/- (£1.10) to buy a 20-exposure Ilfacolor print film, and another 30/- (£1.50) to have postcard enprints made. A quarter of a century later, the price had risen by about 50% - but the price of a car had risen 1000%, the price of a pint of beer by 1500-2000%, and the price of a house by 2000-3000%. No wonder so few of us have colour pictures from the 1950s in our albums!

But difficulty and expense were never an absolute bar: they just meant that we (or our parents, or grandparents, or even great-grandparents) took fewer and fewer pictures; and correspondingly, the pictures were treasured more. The family album was an institution; now, we tend to take pictures as if the camera were a machine-gun, and we are hard put to find the prints a few weeks later, never mind a couple of decades on. As we have already said, this book is a plea for a return to the family album; but now, with modern techniques, we can create pictures of a standard that our grandparents (or even our fathers) never dreamed of, and use them in ways that would be unimaginable to them.

If we look back over the near-century of popular photography, though, we can see a number of underlying factors which have remained the same in the holiday photograph. They are as important now as they were then, and it is worth looking at them in some detail.

First, they are very personal. Nowadays, we may find the old-fashioned clothes and voluminous bathing costumes comical, but if we look at the faces of the people in the pictures, there is an immediate bond across

continued on page 24

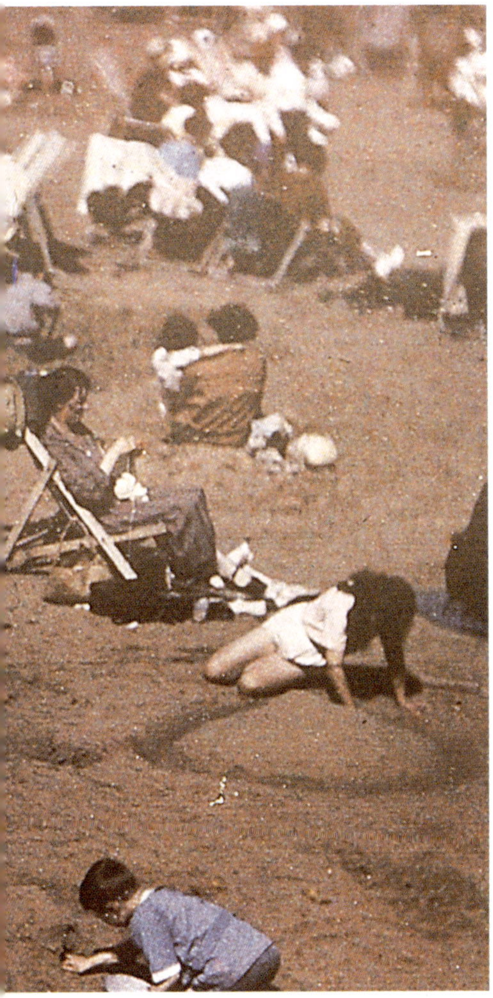

Colour photography has been around a long time - this dates from 1910 - but it was only after World War II that it became readily available for family snapshots and holiday pictures.

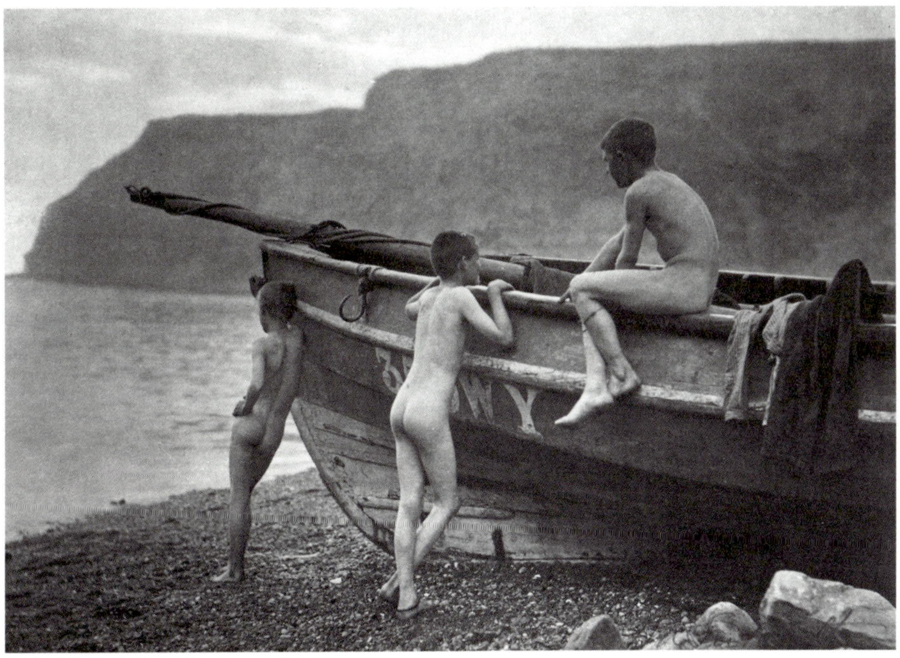

This apparently casual shot was almost certainly a re-creation of a scene that had caught the photographer's eye: in 1885 when this was taken, snapshots were not easy. Exposures were long, cameras were large and clumsy, and (as can be seen from the out-of-focus background) focus had to be spot-on.

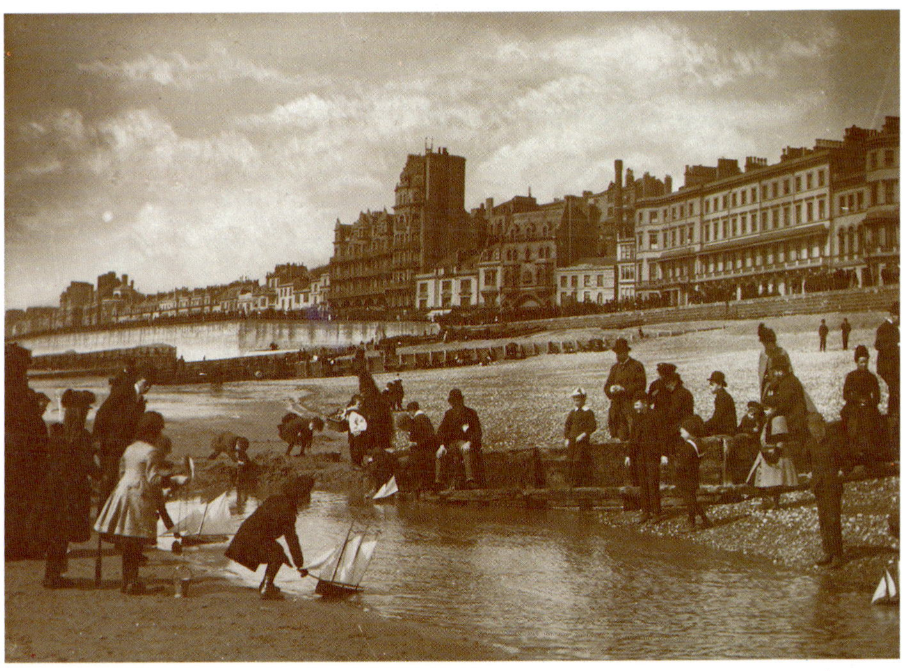

Paul Martin was one of the great pioneers of the snapshot. Working in pre-Kodak days (this was taken in 1885), he used a 'detective' camera to capture everyday scenes.

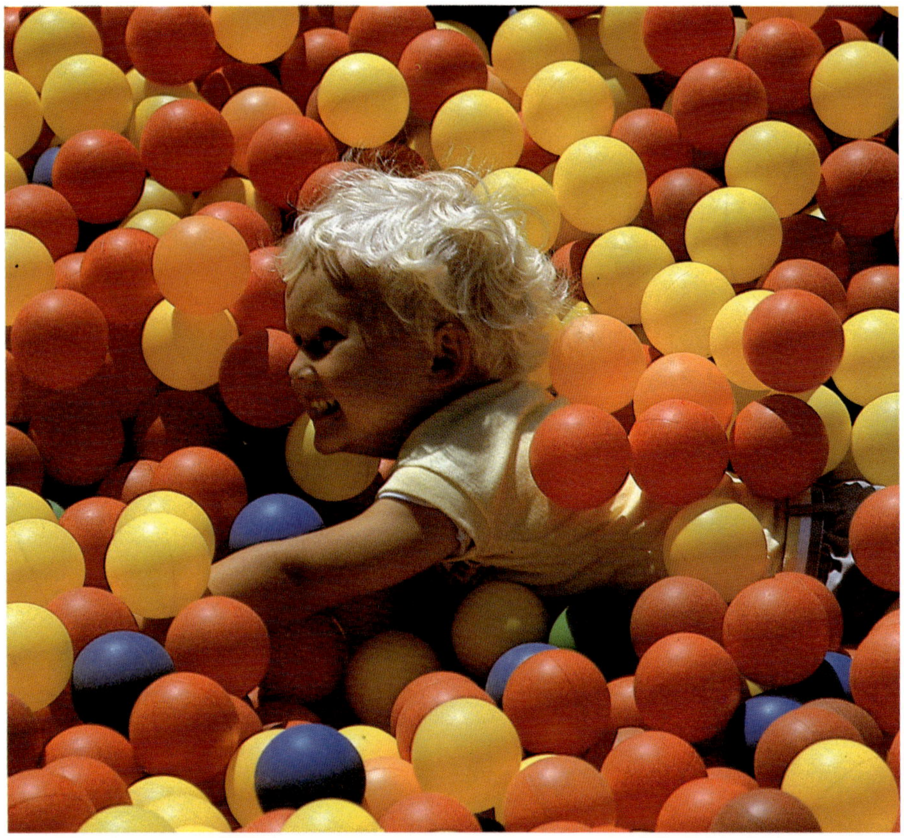

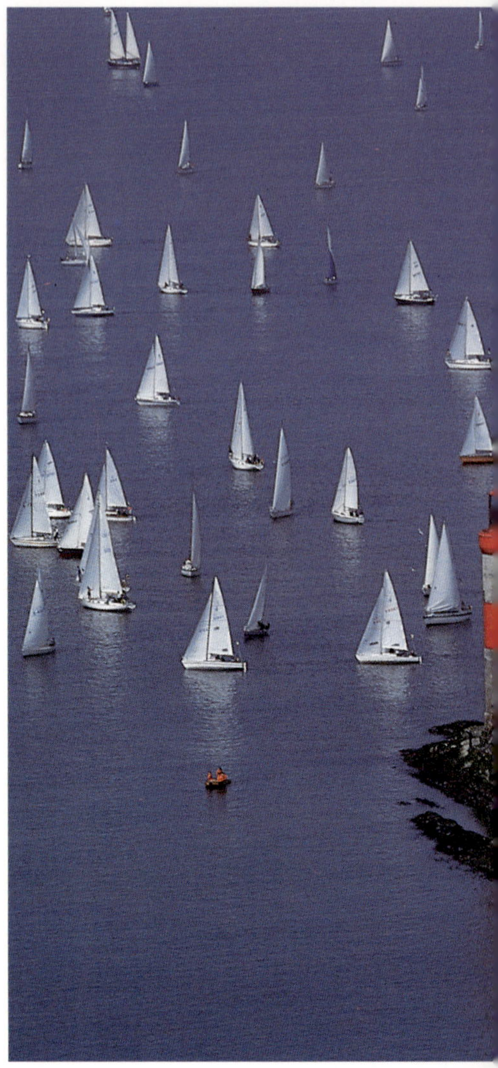

Some images are so eye-catching, so unforgettable, that you would never forgive yourself if you failed to capture them on film. The only way to get spur-of-the-moment pictures like this is to have your camera out of its case and ready for action at all times.

the years. This bond is often completely lacking in the more formal pictures of the day - the grand portraits of the aristocracy, the working people in their Sunday best, the middle classes trying to look important - but it is usually there in those casual, happy snap-shots. Of course, if we know who the people are - Great-Aunt Eugenia, Uncle Harold (aged eight), there is an additional fascination.

Second, they are very typical of their time. The clothes, the surroundings, and even the photographic processes used, all give the period away. Unless we are students of costume, we may not be able to date them precisely, but we can easily identify them as products of their time.

Third, like the majority of holiday snaps today, they are unpretentious. Oh, the girls may be trying to look prettier than they are, and the men more handsome, but it is all in a very jokey sort of way: no-one is terribly worried about What Other People Will Think. They are not photographs for their own sake; they are photographs as a slice of life, pictures taken incidentally to some other activity, whether it is a day at the sea side, a picnic, a trip to the zoo or a donkey-ride.

These three characteristics are typical of the snapshot, and if we are honest, we have to admit that most of the pictures which are most important to us are nothing more than snapshots. Much as we may admire the work

A meal of crabs in Scarborough (right) is a memorable event - so why not photograph the fish stand where they sell the crabs? Most people are delighted to ham it up and pose for this sort of picture, especially if you have just bought a crab!

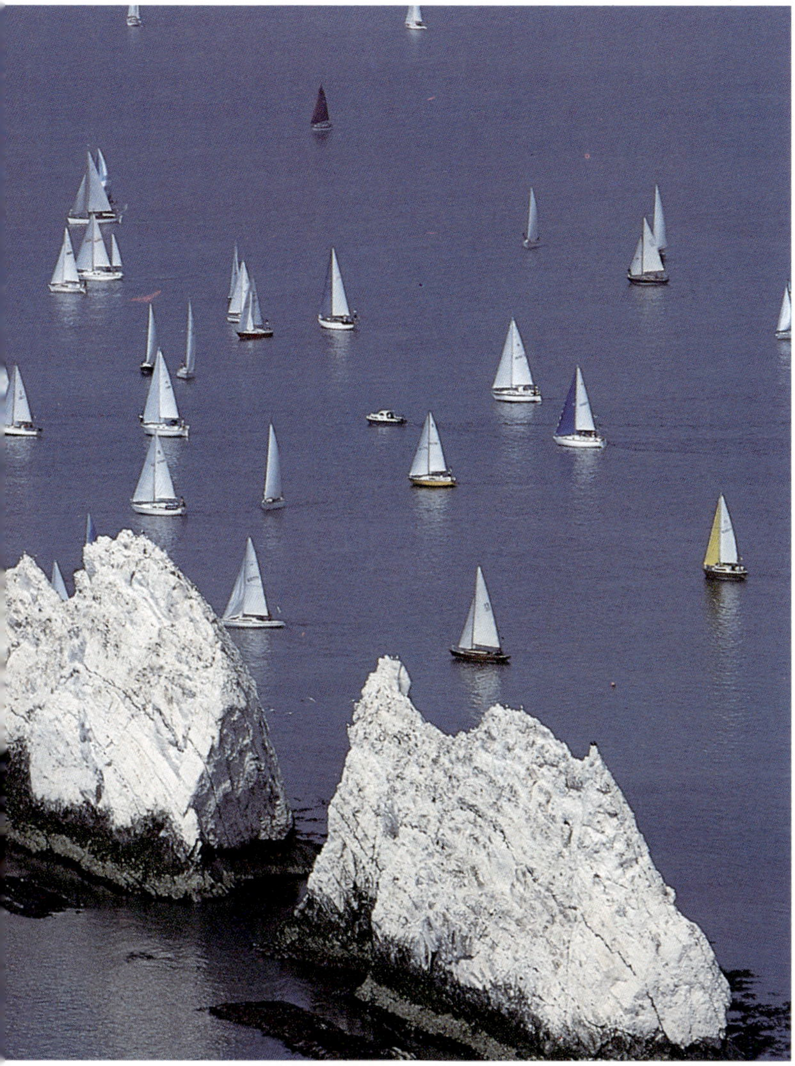

Think of the questions that you ask when you say 'Do you remember...?' Do you remember when the sea seemed full of boats? A photograph will help you to remember.

of the great photographers, whether our tastes run to Ansel Adams or David Hamilton, the pictures which we value most are pictures of our friends, our family, and ourselves, at times which were important to us, or simply when we were happy. Most of the others are of places which we thought were beautiful or interesting, and which we tried to capture (however unsuccessfully) on film.

The great advantages of modern cameras and films are that we can record far more of these moments, and that we can do so with a greater certainty of success - indeed, with a fair hope that we can produce a picture with some artistic merit as well! In fact, the greatest single advantage of modern cameras and films is that almost anyone can produce pictures that are technically first-class. This leaves us free to concentrate on the content of the picture, rather than on the technicalities of taking it.

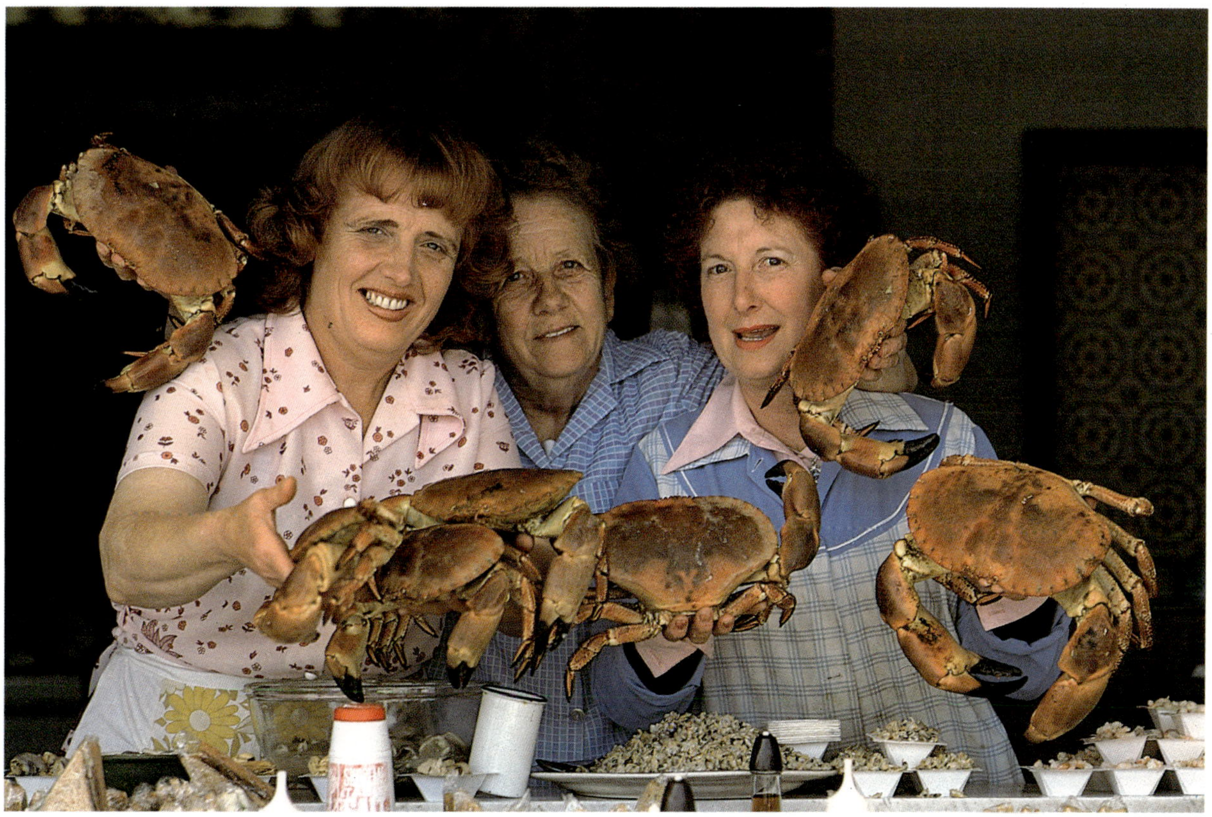

The knotted handkerchief as protection against the sun is alive and well and living at the British seaside. Little vignettes like this can be found in many places, and are well worth photographing.

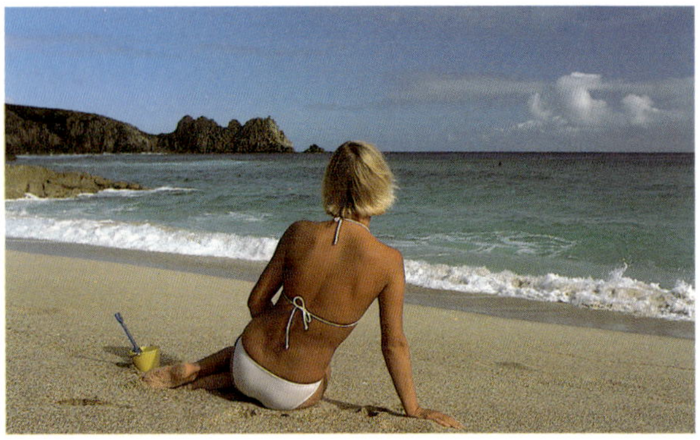

Most of us would have been tempted to show the girl's face - but doesn't the back view, with her looking out to sea, make a much better picture? The bucket and spade by her feet add a touch of humour, too, which makes this a very attractive picture indeed.

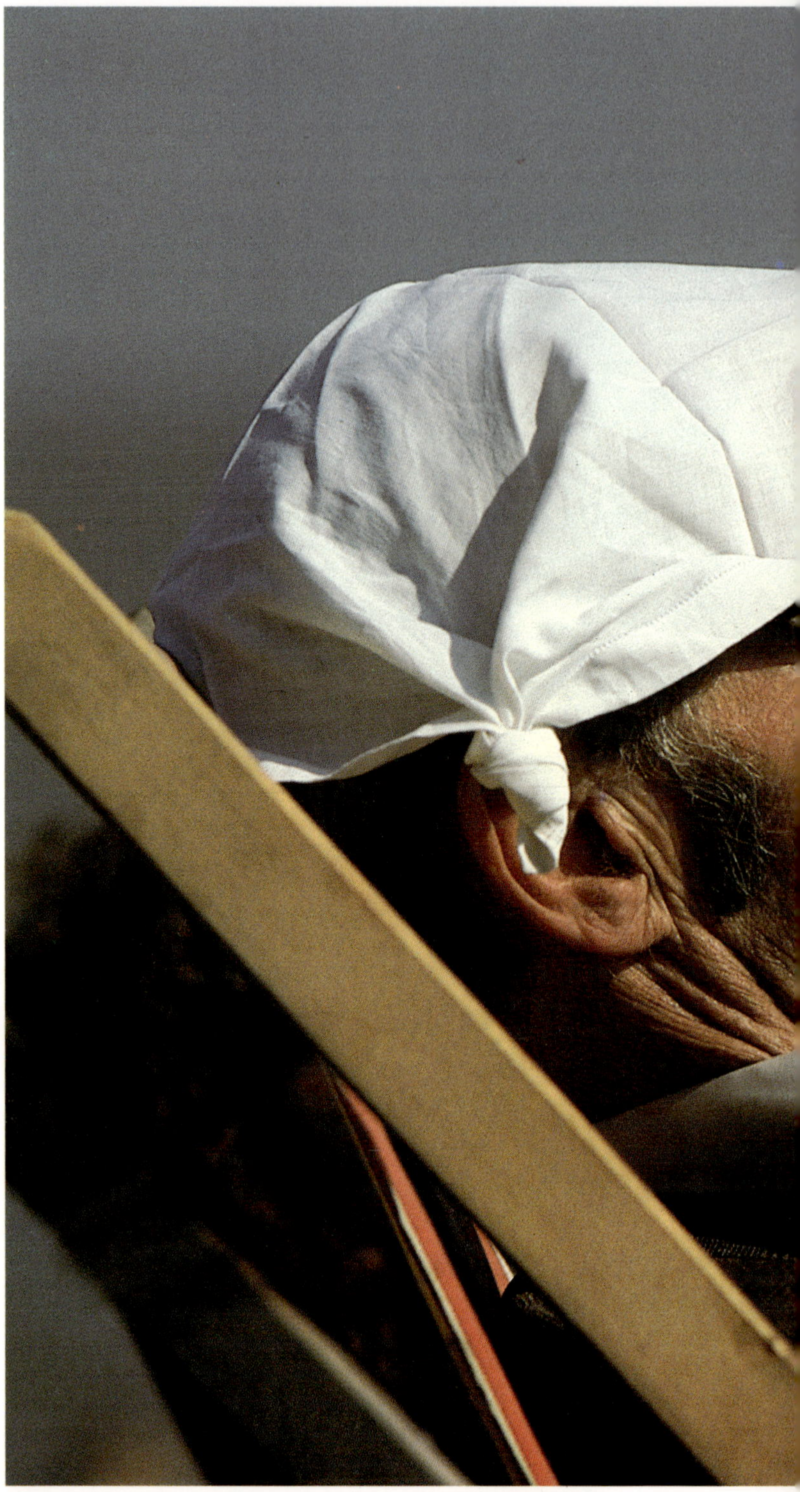

The next chapter, called 'The Golden Rules', deals with a number of 'tricks of the trade' which are second nature to professionals, and which can be applied whether you are using the most expensive camera or the very simplest. Because it is a book about holidays and memories, rather than about cameras and lenses and film, the chapter that deals with equipment and technique is at the very end of the book. But there must be a reason why people buy more expensive cameras, so before we go on to the next chapter, it is worth taking just a very quick look at precisely what it is that you gain (and what you lose) if you buy a more complicated and expensive camera.

The first advantage is *versatility.* Unfortunately, versatility and simplicity are often mutually exclusive, so if you want a camera that is both versatile *and* simple to use, you will need to spend a good deal of money. It can be done, but it will not be cheap. In any case, cameras are subject to the law of diminishing returns. The very cheapest cameras will take 80-90% of the pictures that most people want to take on holidays. Buying a mid-range amateur camera, especially a single-lens reflex (see pages 118-119) brings that up to 95-99%. Only if you want to take photography really seriously will you need to spend any more. Also, watch a so-called 'serious amateur' with two or three camera bodies, a battery of lenses, and a separate light meter. Often, he will spend so much time fiddling around with his equipment that he misses the picture!

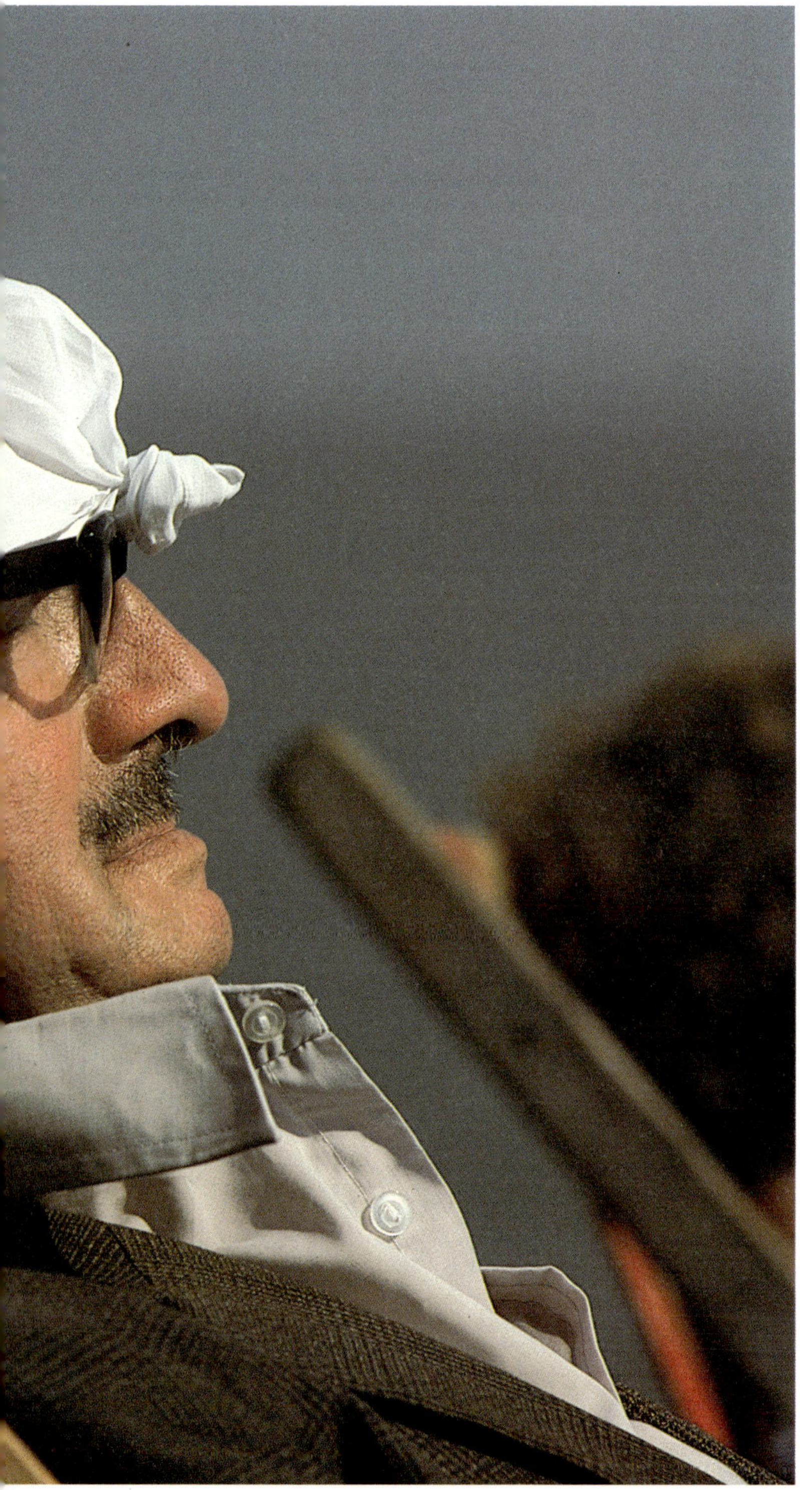

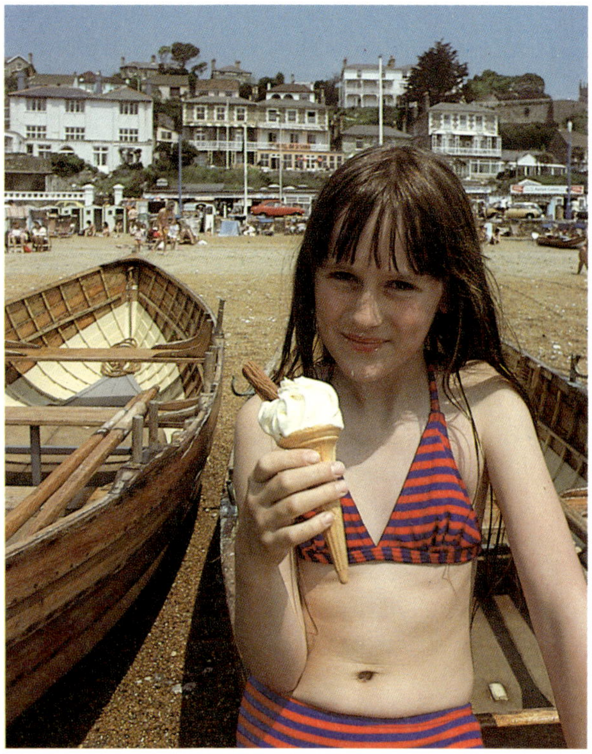

A picture for the family album, though not necessarily one to show to strangers. When she gets married and has children of her own, you will still be able to recall that day when she was just a little girl with an ice-cream cone. Her children will love to see it too!

The second thing that you get for your money is *sharpness* - the ability to show fine detail and texture. Here, you do need to spend a little more than the absolute minimum if you want pictures with good detail, but you still don't need to spend very much: a reasonable-quality 35mm compact camera (see pages 116-117) should deliver colour prints which are indistinguishable from those taken on very much more expensive cameras. This is no longer quite so true if you shoot colour slides, because the films themselves can show finer detail, and hence the differences between good and very good lenses become detectable; but with prints, it is generally not worth worrying about.

The third thing that costs money is *durability*, but unless you put literally hundreds of rolls of film through your camera each year (as most professionals do), this is not worth worrying about either. Any camera should be good for at least a couple of thousand rolls of film, and even at a roll a week, that is forty years photography!

In other words, don't worry if you haven't got the latest all-singing, all-dancing, bells-and-whistles camera. If it will take pictures at all, this book will show you how to take better pictures with it. As soon as we've finished with our Golden Rules, which are common to all picture taking, we shall look at how to take pictures of the typical sights and views of Britain - probably the most interesting and varied country in the world for the photographer and holidaymaker.

CHAPTER THREE

The Golden Rules

Four simple rules, easy to learn, can make all the difference to your holiday photography.

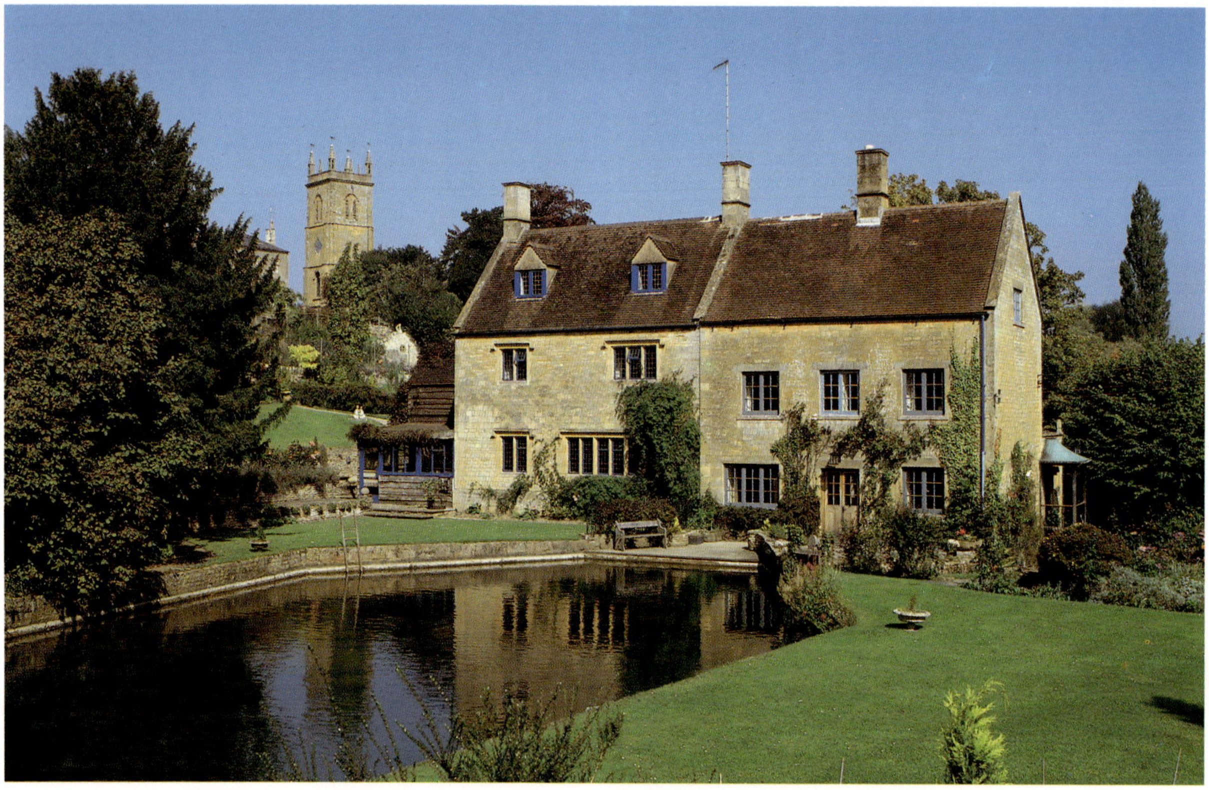

This is an attractive picture, but not as satisfying as it might have been. On close examination, the canes in the foreground prove to be the problem: they are too obtrusive, and it is not possible to crop them out and still get an attractive image. What would have been ideal was a still higher viewpoint (see pages 34-35, DETAILS MAKE THE PICTURE).

There are no such things as absolute rules in photography. For every 'rule' that you can find, you can also find at least one photograph which breaks that rule and still succeeds as a picture. But having said that, there are certain guidelines which are so useful that we have lumped them together under the title, 'The Golden Rules'. We do not say that you can never break them; we do say that if you follow them, the vast majority of your pictures will be the better for it. They are all second nature to professionals, who will only break them if they have good reason - and it takes a lot of practice before you can confidently say that you do not need the 'rules' any longer.

There are only four golden rules in this chapter, each with a double-page spread to itself, but before we look at them in detail, it is worth summarising them. They are:

- WATCH AND WAIT
- CHOOSE A CLEAR SUBJECT
- BE CAREFUL WITH THE DETAILS
- COMPOSE THE PICTURE CAREFULLY

The first one - WATCH AND WAIT - is in many ways the simplest. All that it means is that you should not be content to raise your camera to your eye and take a picture just because you like what you see. WATCH the picture in the viewfinder carefully, and do not be afraid to WAIT until it is exactly what you want to capture.

CHOOSING A CLEAR SUBJECT is in many ways the same as the advice above, to WATCH. If you want to photograph (say) a little girl paddling at the seaside, then photograph just that: do not include half the rest of the beach, but concentrate on your chosen subject.

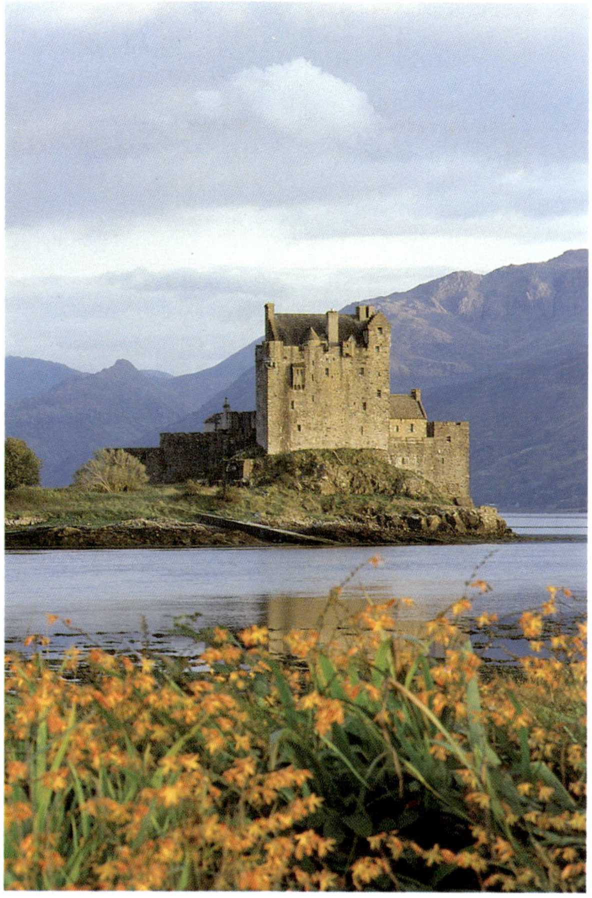

BEING CAREFUL WITH THE DETAILS is something else that distinguishes the typical snapshot from the successful picture. We have all seen pictures where a telegraph pole grows out of somebody's head, or where a picture of a beautiful garden is ruined by a brightly-coloured ice-cream wrapper (or film box!) in the foreground. Move a few feet to one side or the other, or get your subject to move, and the telegraph pole no longer sprouts like a unicorn's horn; pick up the wrapper and put it in the rubbish bin, and you will have a better picture as well as having done a small but useful public service.

Finally, COMPOSING THE PICTURE CAREFULLY is the most contentious of our 'rules', because composition is a matter of personal, aesthetic judgement; but although it is possible to produce a completely 'empty' picture while still following the rules of composition, it is also true that the majority of successful pictures conform quite closely to the old-fashioned rules. Do not be afraid to break the 'rules', but do not be afraid to use them either, because most of the time they really do work.

One of the traditional 'rules' of composition is that the main subject looks best on the intersection of lines which divide the picture into thirds vertically and horizontally, like a noughts-and-crosses board (see pages 36-37, COMPOSITION).

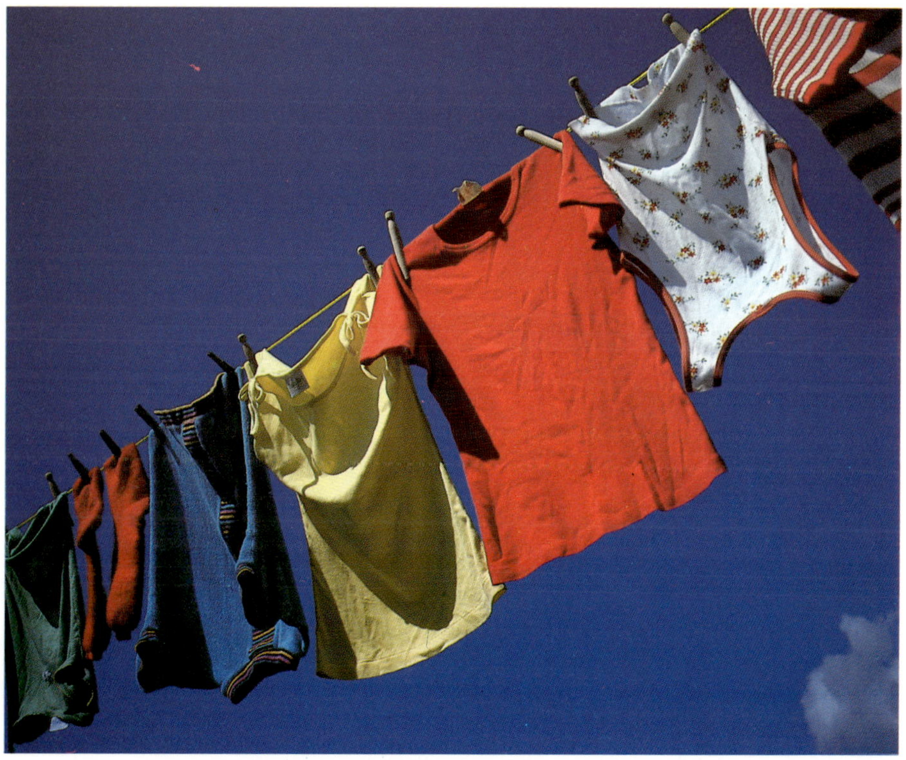

At first sight, there is nothing very holiday-like about this picture. But the clothes are all holiday-type clothes, and the bright colours contrasted against the deep blue sky speak of holidays - even if it is only an afternoon at the beach. By coming in close, and showing only the clothes, the line, and the sky, the photographer has made it abundantly clear what the picture is about (see pages 32-33, PICKING A SUBJECT).

Watching and Waiting

The first 'golden rule' is so simple that it seems almost impossible not to do it: *watch and wait. Watch* what is in the viewfinder, and *wait* until it is exactly what you want. But this is not as easy as it might seem.

Watching means a number of things. It means watching what is going on: if you practice, you can imagine every instant as if it were a frame in a movie. BLINK! - and you have captured the frame. You can slow the action down in your mind, sometimes, as if you were literally a slow-motion camera. Other times, you may shoot half a dozen pictures to get exactly the one you want, as fast as you can press the button. The thing to remember, though, is that you are the real camera: the machine you are holding in your hand is just a way of getting the picture (which already exists in your mind's eye) onto the film.

Watching also means watching the shapes in the viewfinder. We all know that it is easier to judge the composition of a picture when you are holding it in your hand than to try to judge it in the viewfinder, so try to imagine that what you see in the viewfinder *is* the picture, instead of a part of the scene all around you. Ignore the sounds, the breeze, the people who are standing beside you: think of that image in the viewfinder as if it were already a photograph. You know what shapes convey different moods - a swirl for action, level, horizontal lines for calm and peace, great masses and angles for majesty - so when you see them, press the button.

Watching with this kind of intensity may take some concentration, but it is not really difficult, and it works just as well with an old box camera as with the most expensive Nikon or Canon. *Waiting* is a part of the same thing. You need a person, or a car, in the picture to give it scale? Wait, and one will come. You need the sun to come out from behind a cloud? Wait, and unless the weather is really bad, it will. You need a skater, a powerboat, a small boy kicking a stone, a bird in the sky, to convey the spirit of the place? Wait, and if they really are characteristic, they will come.

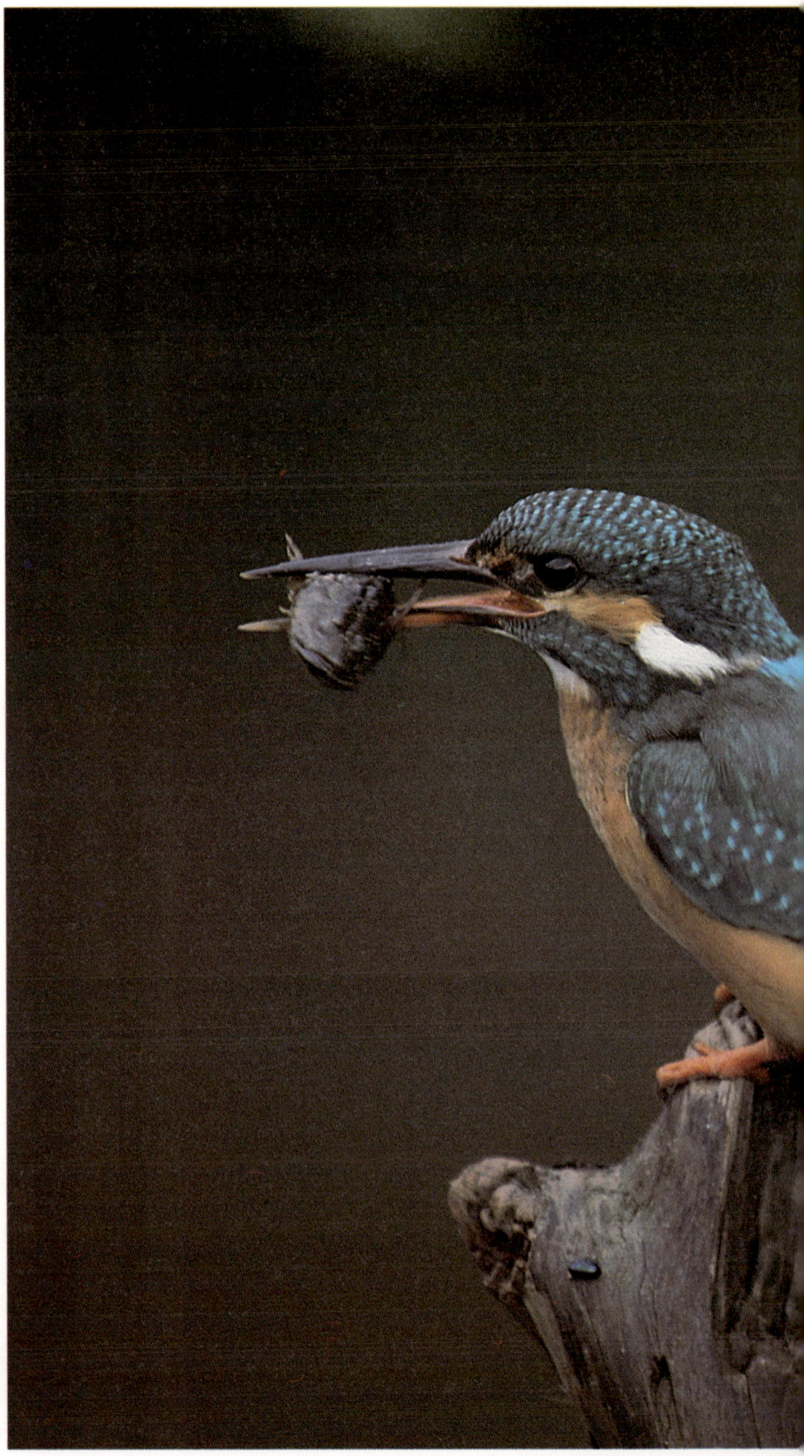

Patience is the only possible approach if you want to get good pictures of wildlife, but it can pay off, as this beautiful picture of a kingfisher shows. You need to approach the fishing site as quietly and slowly as possible, and then to wait until the bird's initial nervousness has been forgotten.

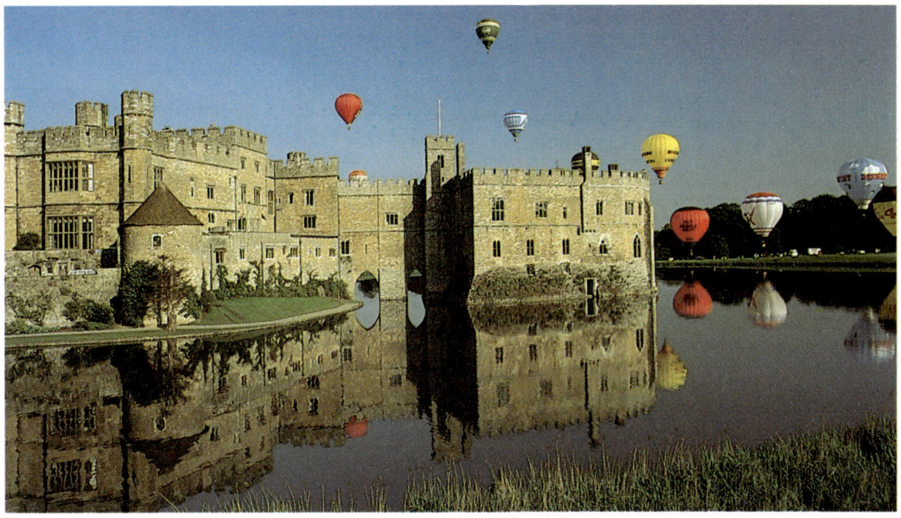

These two pictures show the value of picking your time. The time while balloons are being inflated is always interesting, as the huge bags fill with hot air, but you need to arrive early to get this sort of shot. In the other picture, where the balloons are being launched from a field beside the moat, a little forethought and a short walk has enabled the photographer to show the castle, the moat, and not just the balloons but their reflections in the water.

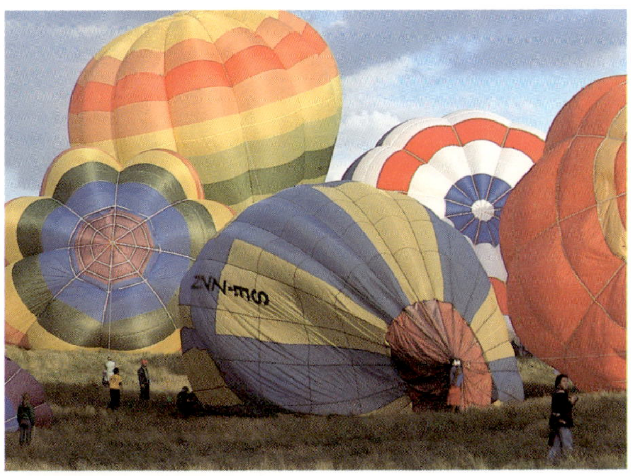

Although you are unlikely to frighten a sunset away, you may need just as much patience as you do with a more timid subject like a kingfisher. The reflections of the setting sun from the clouds are what really make this picture, and they were only there for a few minutes.

Picking a Subject

The second 'golden rule' may sound even more obvious than the first: you have to know what you are photographing in order to be able to photograph it! But once again, things are not what they seem...

Take a second look at the pictures you admire - at pictures of your own, and at the pictures in this book. Then compare them with the pictures that 'didn't quite make it'. One of the most common faults in pictures that 'don't quite make it' is that it is not really clear what they are about: the subject has got lost, because there is too much else in the picture.

It is true that there are plenty of 'busy' pictures which are fascinating to read - and you do 'read' them, like a book. The more you study them, the more they repay study. But it is also true that there are many pictures where (to parody the song) 'there's a whole lot of nothing going on'. There is the traffic around Trafalgar Square; there is Nelson's Column itself; there is someone feeding the birds; there is an itinerant peanut vendor; there is an old-fashioned British 'bobby'; but what are we actually supposed to be looking at? None of them is doing anything particularly interesting; if you are really unlucky, the one thing which actually catches your eye is a dog lifting his leg against a lamp post!

Now compare that sort of picture with a professional picture of the same scene. It concentrates on a particular

Of the three pictures on these pages, this is the most recognisable one of Trafalgar Square. It is, however, a classic example of 'less is more': instead of trying to show us the whole square in detail, it uses underexposure (set the film speed dial to 2-4 times the recommended film speed - see page 124) against an evening sky to create an instantly recognisable image.

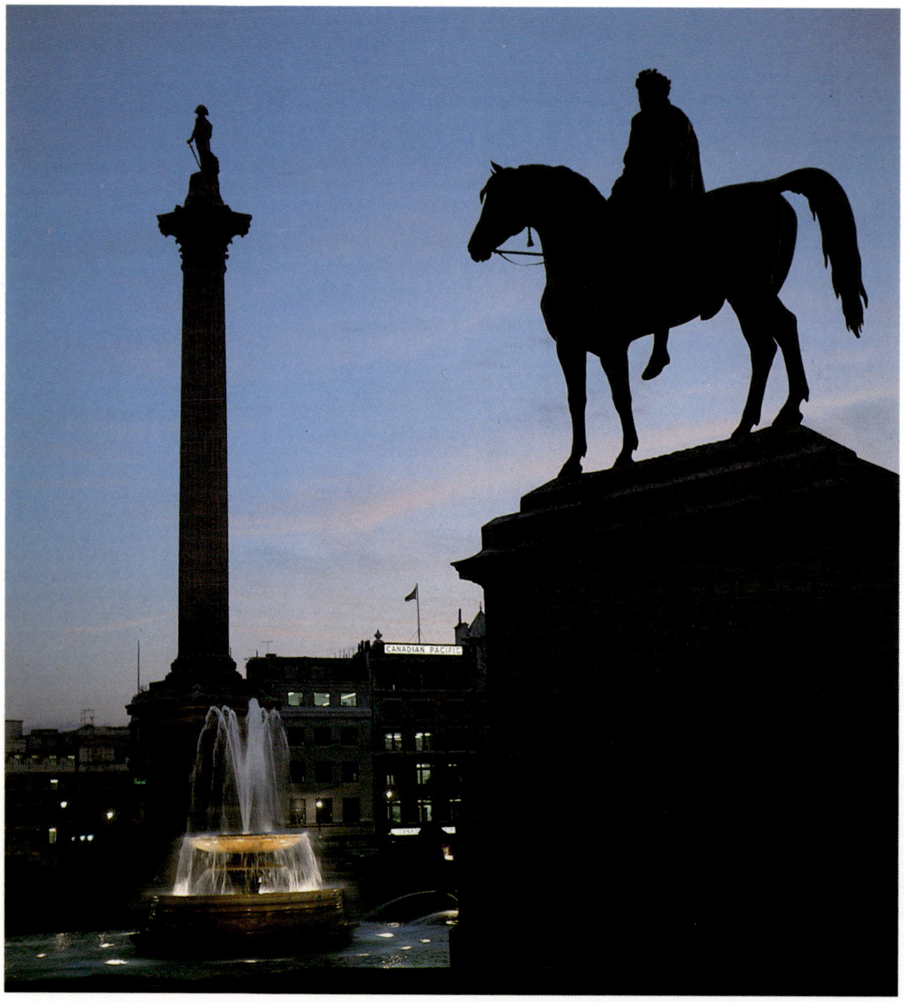

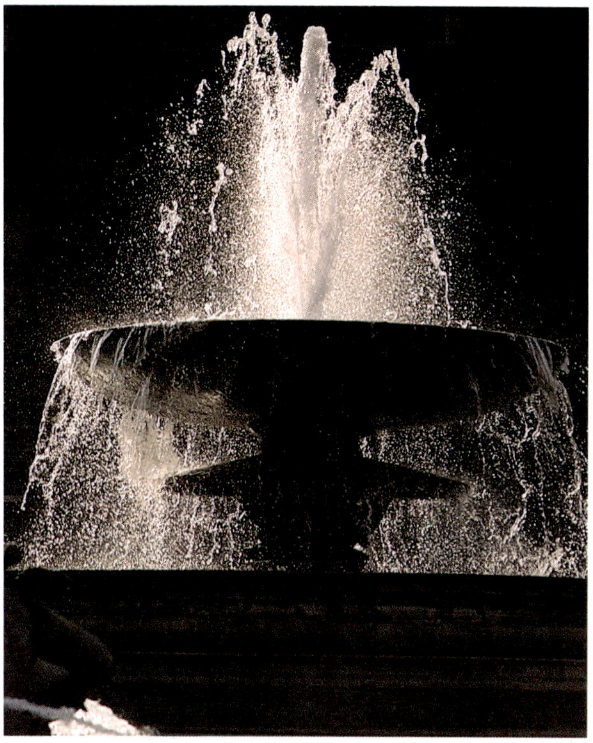

aspect: the girl feeding pigeons, or the big red bus, or the Column, or the policeman, or whatever. The other things may still be going on in the background (or the photographer may have chosen to make other pictures out of them), but there is no doubt what is the *main* subject, the focal point of the picture if you like.

The simple way to obtain this effect is to get *closer* to your subject. Admittedly you can go too far, and frame your subject so tightly that it could equally well be in Trafalgar Square or Red Square, but this is only something to worry about after you start doing it; look at the pictures for an example of what we mean. In any case, it is amazing how little information the brain needs in order to work out context. *Part* of a bus (preferably the front, with the destination board, or the side, with an advertisement) will set the scene in London; the base of Nelson's Column, plus the pigeons, will set it in Trafalgar Square. If you practise, you can use this 'power of suggestion' anywhere - especially if you follow the previous advice, to *wait* and to *watch.*

This is Trafalgar Square again, but there are no real clues to tell us so - we only know because the photographer tells us that it is. As a single souvenir, it is less effective than the other pictures, but as part of a slide show, or as a picture in its own right, it is certainly very attractive. The dramatic effect of the water against a dark background was achieved by underexposing (as described for the silhouette picture), but shooting the water back-lit by bright sunlight.

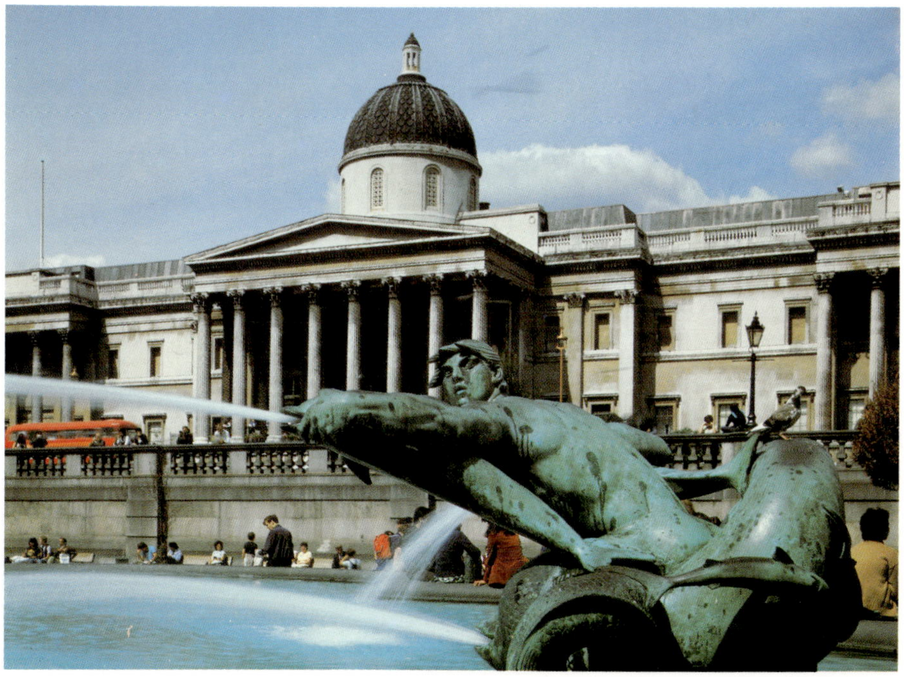

By concentrating on the fountains in Trafalgar Square, the photographer has drawn our attention to a detail most of us might never notice. The big red bus and the National Portrait Gallery in the background do, however, establish clearly where we are.

Details Make the Picture

Most amateurs are amazed at the number of pictures which a professional will take of a single subject. Surely, they feel, anyone could get good pictures if they shot that much film, if only by the law of averages.

Well, yes and no. It is certainly possible to take too many pictures, but it is also true that details which went unnoticed when you shot the picture can make the difference between a great shot, and one that is flawed. This is why so many professionals take extra pictures, in order to rule out such misfortunes as the one we described in the last section, a dog lifting his leg against a lamp post.

But although details can spoil a picture, they can also 'make' it. Examples of details which can transform a picture might be the expression on someone's face, or a figure crossing a dark doorway at just the right instant, or a wave breaking around a child standing in the shallows on the beach.

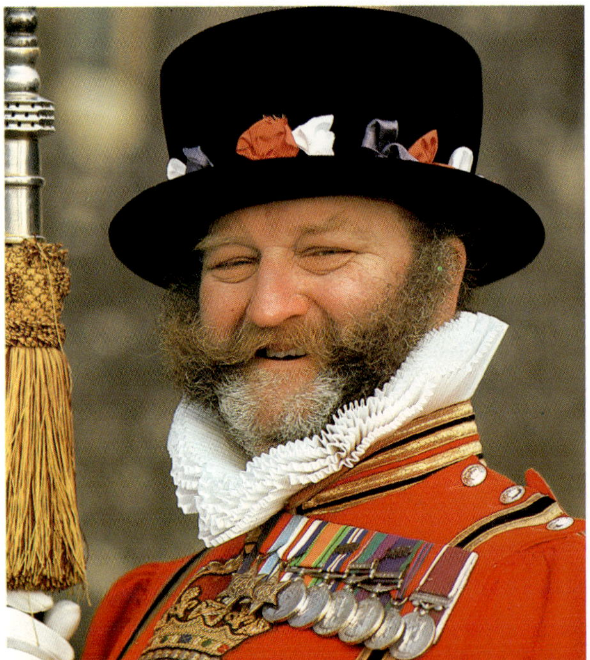

Often a close-up is more effective than including all of the subject. However, you do need a camera which is capable of focusing at close distances. A medium telephoto lens such as a 105mm or 135mm is ideal for this type of picture as you can fill the frame without having to get close to your subject.

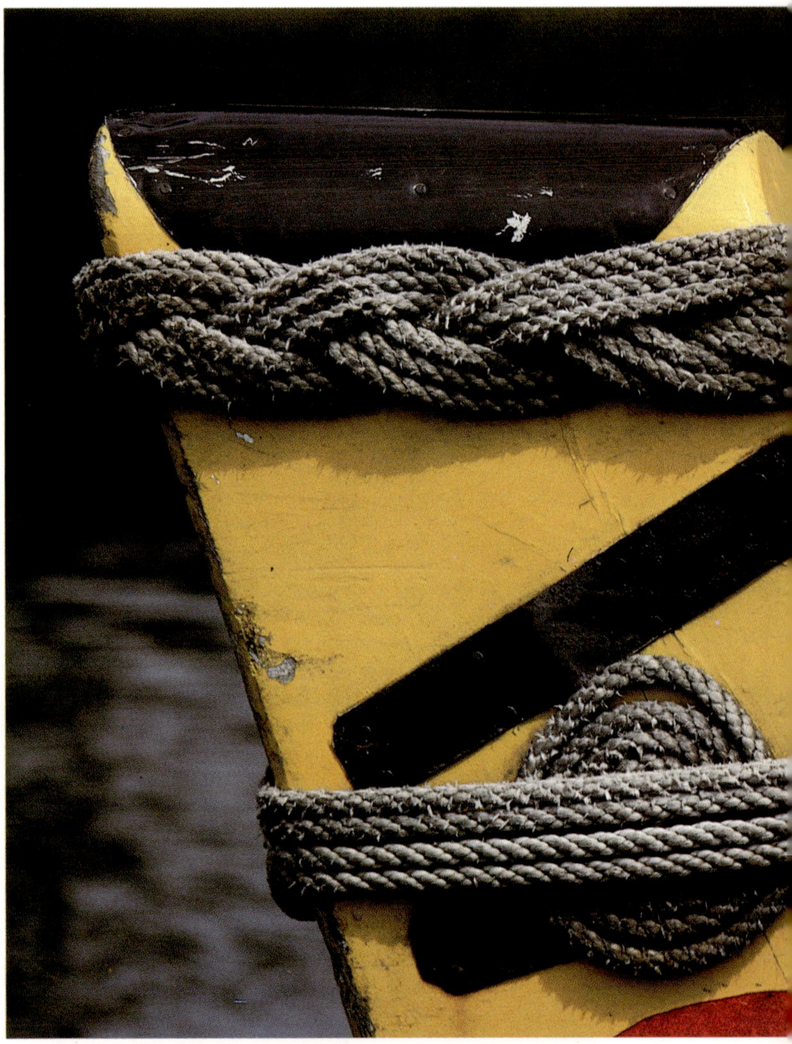

In order to make the best use of details (or to leave out the ones you don't want), you can do two things. One is closely tied to the point we made before, about *watching:* if you see our friend the dog, wait; if you see an ice-lolly wrapper or cigarette packet in the foreground, go and put it in a bin. If part of a building is obscured by scaffolding, try to pick an angle where it is least obvious - and so forth. The other thing you can do is what the professionals do: if you are not sure of the very best angle, take two or three pictures of the same subject. Film may be expensive, but it isn't *that* expensive!

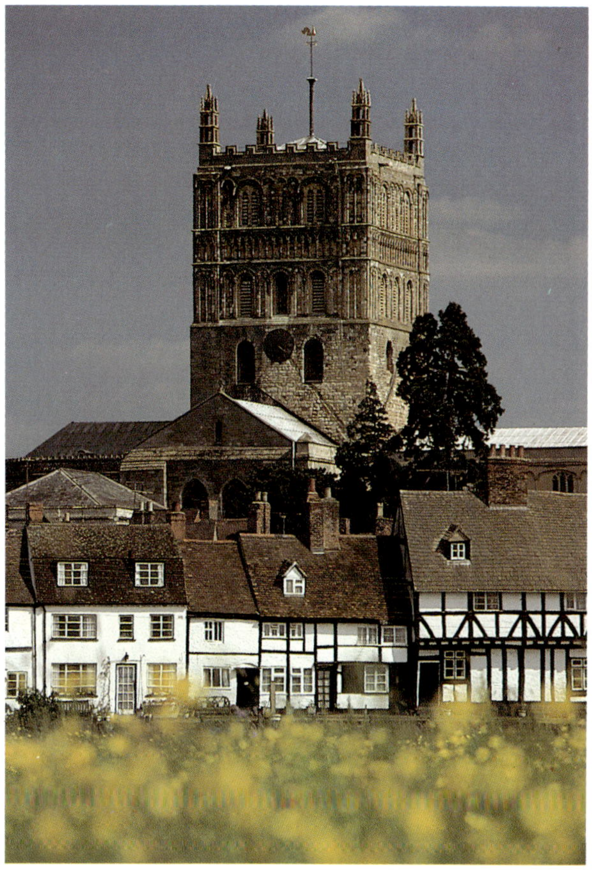

The church tower in Tewkesbury makes an attractive picture - but it is virtually impossible to get a good, close shot. By standing well back, you can have it rising majestically from the half- timbered houses, and by choosing a low angle you can add foreground interest to complete the picture; it would have been all too easy to have a dull, asphalt foreground.

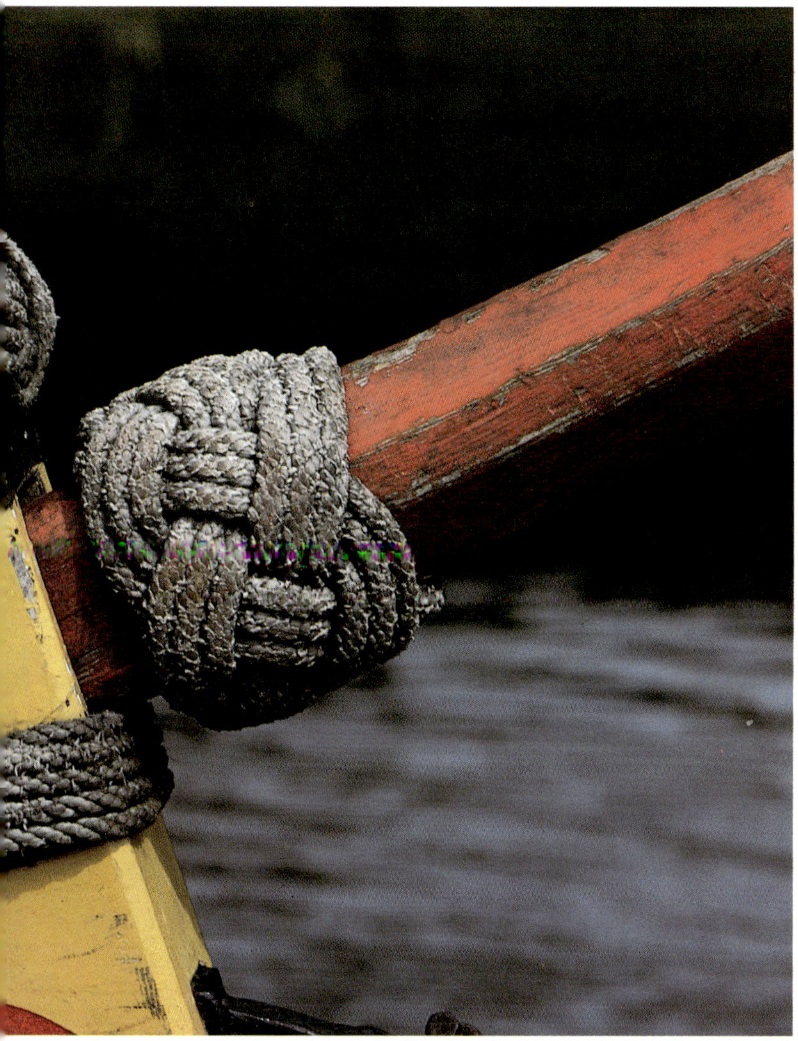

This tiny detail of a canal boat says more about the whole subject than would seem possible. We all know the kind of bright paintwork to be found on these boats; here, the photographer's eye has used a detail to sum it up. As with the picture of the fountain on page 33, this picture can either stand alone as a good photograph, or for a part of a picture story about canal boats.

The trouble with both approaches is that things which seemed insignificant in the original scene suddenly leap out at you when you see the finished picture. Telegraph poles sprouting from people's heads are the classic example, but others are huge and obtrusive sign-posts, building work of various sorts, graffiti, large empty expanses of grass or asphalt in the foreground, and overhead wires, power cables, and telephone lines. All you can do is to train yourself to look for these negative elements, and to try to choose viewpoints where they are concealed or at least insignificant. The only consolation is that it gets easier with practice!

Composition

'Composition' is something of a dirty word in some photographic circles, because of the way that certain rules used to be raised to the status of a religion, and a picture which did not follow the Rules of Composition was automatically disregarded by the self-appointed pundits in the camera clubs and magazines. Even so, the old 'rules' are excellent general guidelines, though you should never be afraid to break them if you can get a better picture that way. These are the most useful ones:

The *Rule of Thirds* states that if you mentally divide a picture into vertical and horizontal thirds, like a noughts-and-crosses board, the principal subject will always attract the most attention if it is at the intersection of two of these lines, and the result will almost invariably be more pleasing than if it is dead central. Why? No-one knows - but it works.

The technique of using a gentle curve - a path, or a river, perhaps - to 'lead the eye into the picture' is known in composition as *'the S-curve'*, though it is not necessarily particularly S-shaped. Once again, this technique works surprisingly well.

Closely related to the S-curve is the *frame*, where you use an overhanging bough, or an archway or doorway, to frame the principal subject. It can be overdone, but if you don't do it, you may find that your picture just 'peters out' towards the edges.

Positioning the horizon is an important part of composition: if it is bang in the middle of the picture, it will cut it in half. It is usually much better to have it distinctly above half-way or distinctly below half-way up the picture.

Balance is one of the harder things to convey, but basically, if you have all the masses in a picture at one side, it will look lopsided. A small 'counterbalance' on the empty side will repair matters.

Stability is another awkward one, but at its simplest, it is concerned with the grouping of the main elements or shapes in the picture. For example, if they are grouped in the form of a triangle resting on its base, the impression will be one of calm: if it is resting on its point, the impression will be one of instability, or looming. If you find the concept of 'shapes' slightly awkward, try putting your eyes slightly out of focus as you look at the picture; then, you see the 'shape' rather than the subject

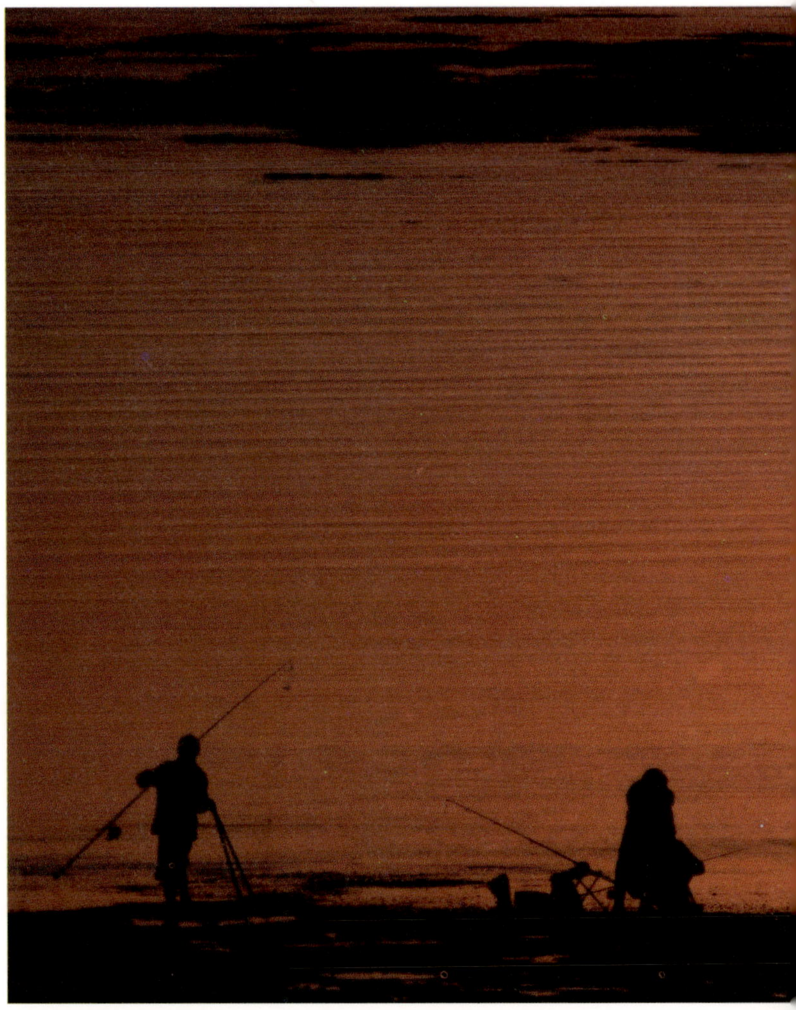

Finally, the dominant line of the picture affects its mood. *Vertical lines* generally convey strength, massiveness, and durability; *horizontal lines* generally convey calm and repose; and *diagonal* lines are 'dynamic'. This is the most disputable of all the 'rules', but it still works most of the time.

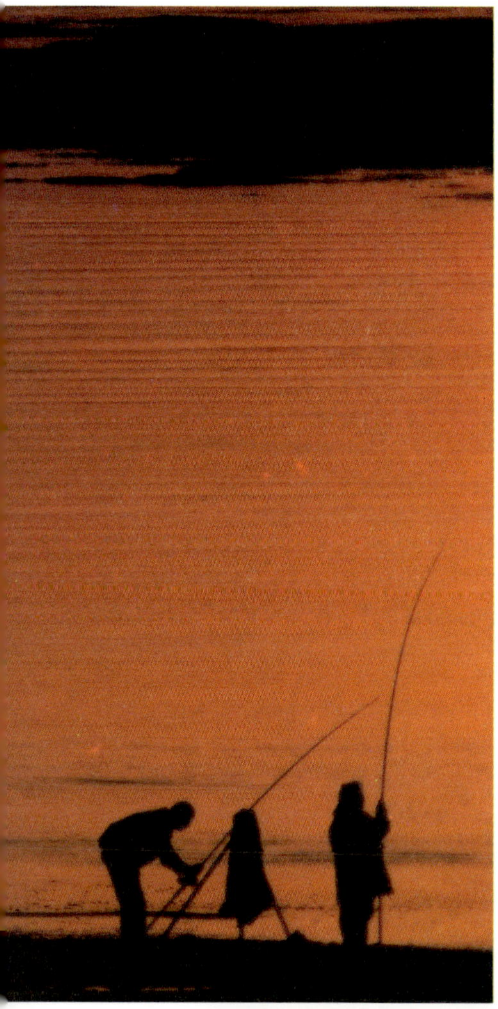

Composition is often illustrated best in silhouettes, where shapes are shown substantially without colour. Here, the big, empty sky illustrates the importance of not 'chopping the picture in half' with a horizon. Imagine how the picture would look with more foreground...

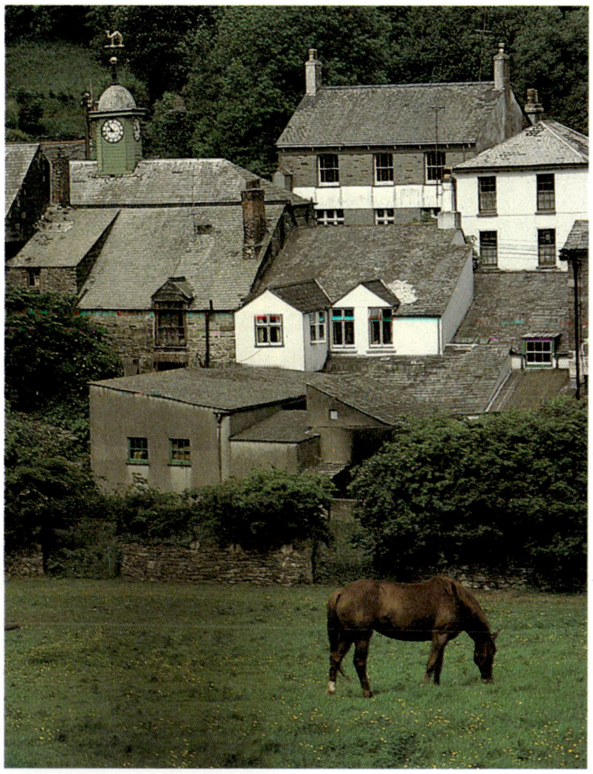

Put your finger over the horse in this picture; suddenly, the image is far less satisfying. The horse provides a 'focal point' for the picture, and is placed more-or-less on the 'intersection of thirds' (see text). It also occupies a foreground which would otherwise be fairly empty.

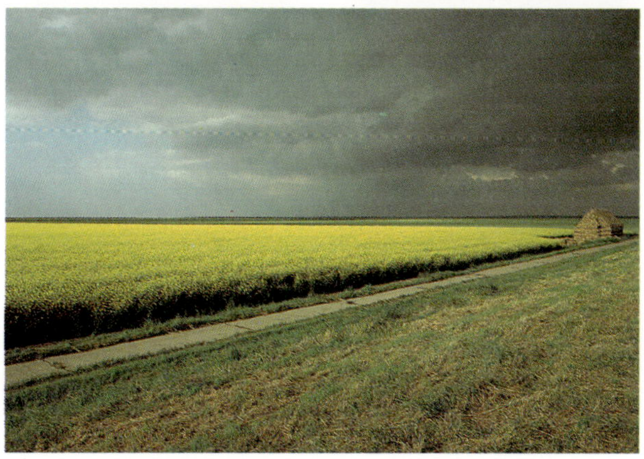

The Rule of Thirds is broken here and yet this picture provides a dramatic and successful image from simple graphic elements. The horizon is central and the haystack is placed in a position which would be expected to destroy the balance of the picture. However, the strong, convergent, diagonal pathway needed the haystack to restore visual equilibrium. The dark clouds enhance the vividness of the yellow rape field, whilst continuing to fulfil the rules of balance and composition.

CHAPTER FOUR

At the Seaside

Look beyond the sun, sea and sand for some really memorable photos that will last longer than your holiday tan.

The seaside is the classic place for a holiday: a time away from the cares and worries of work, away from the day-to-day routine of home, where everyone's aim is to enjoy themselves. Nowadays, we may take our holidays in all kinds of places - but the spirit of the seaside, the spirit of fun and of getting away from it all, is what we are usually after.

There is much more to the seaside than just the beach, of course. There are usually amusement arcades, often with some sort of fairground rides; there may be donkeys; there are the promenades, where the more mature holidaymakers take a stroll, and the younger ones go in search of the opposite sex; there are the eating places, from up-market restaurants to take-aways, hot-dog stands, and candy-floss and ice-cream vendors; there is the distinctive architecture of the Victorian and Edwardian periods when most of these resorts were built; often, there are illuminations of some kind; there are new friends to be made in the hotel or on the beach; and, of course, there is the night life. *All* of these subjects can be photographed, and if you try to show the multi-faceted nature of a seaside resort you will usually end up with much more interesting pictures than if you just confine yourself to the beach. In this chapter, we have given some of the more obvious subjects pages to themselves, but here in the introduction is the place to urge you to photograph *everything* that you can. The cost of a couple of rolls of extra film is nothing, at least compared with the overall cost of the holiday, and successful pictures can enable you to enjoy your summer holiday all the year round.

Just two words of warning. First, cameras are valuable, and it is not a good idea to expose would-be thieves to too much temptation. Most hotels and boarding-houses will accept responsibility *only* for those valuables which are handed over into their possession: they will not take responsibility for things left in rooms, nor are they legally obliged to do so. Second, buy your film before you go, or at least buy it from a camera store in the town that you visit. Films bought from kiosks are often out-dated, usually overpriced, and will often deliver awful quality because of the extremes of heat to which they have been subjected in the shop window or cooped-up kiosk.

Children are not the only attractions of the seaside. There is the opposite sex, often revealingly dressed, and there is the beauty of the beach itself, especially late at night or early in the morning when there is hardly anyone about. Look at the picture of the girls with the beach umbrella in the light of what was said on page 36 about composition.

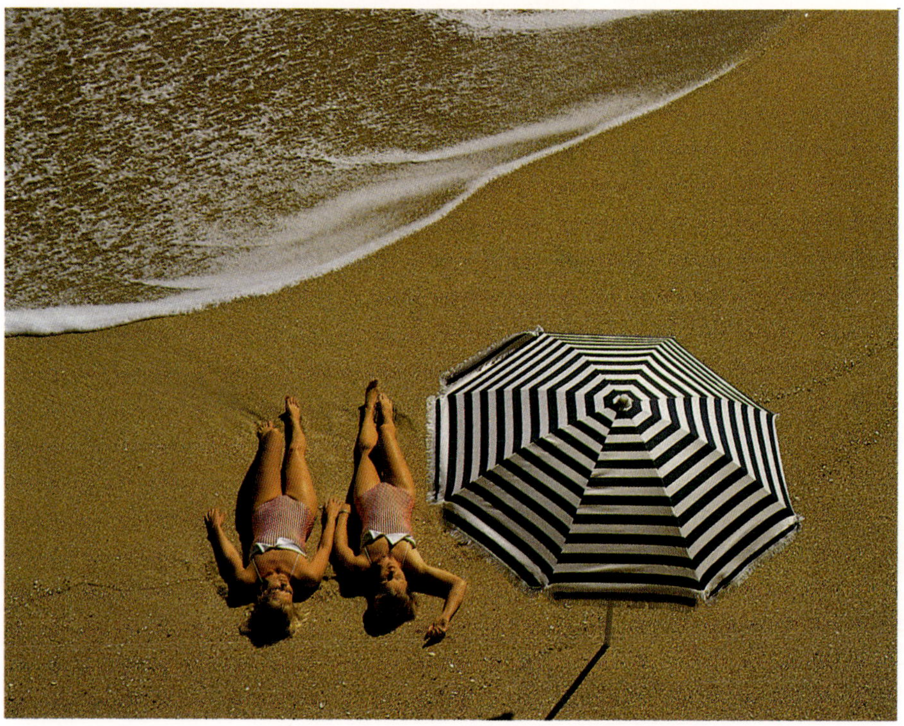

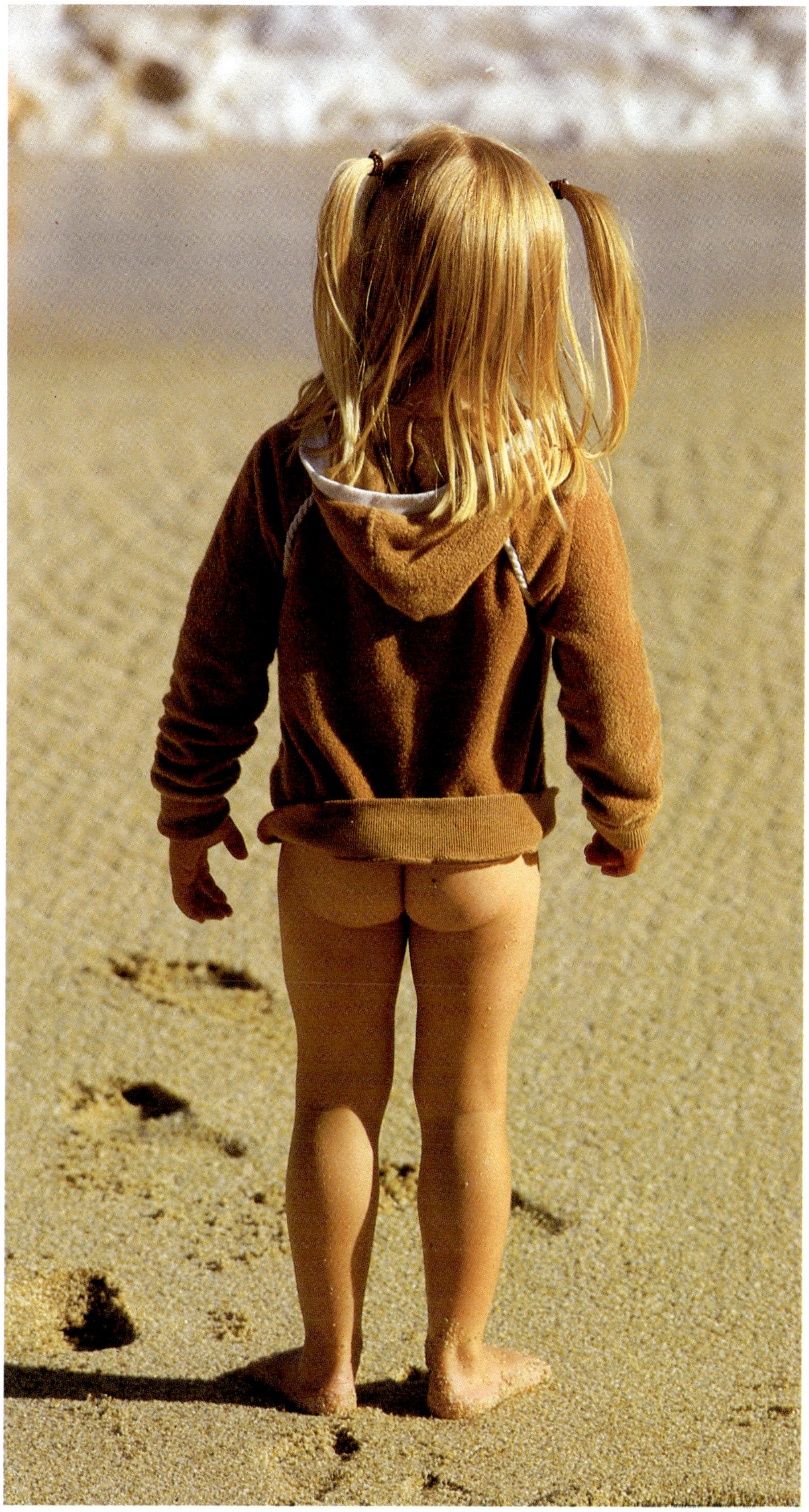

The seaside is very much a place for children of all ages, from a little sunbather to a teenager who still remembers what it is like to be a little girl. Children are perennially irresistible subjects, but you need to come in close and get a neutral background to make it work. Here, although the background is neutral, the horizon encroaches somewhat. One of the hardest lessons to learn, but an important one, is to look at the whole frame in your camera and not only at your subject. An otherwise perfect shot can be ruined by background confusion.

On the Beach

When you are photographing people on the beach - whether they are family, friends, or strangers - one of the most important things to remember is to have them *doing* something. A child absorbed in building a sandcastle makes a much better picture than one that is waiting stiffly to have its picture taken, and if your wife or girlfriend is sunbathing, you will get a much better photograph if you attract her attention just before you press the button than if you photograph her just lying still, or if she is deliberately posing. Of course, this means working unobtrusively, without telegraphing your intention to take a picture, so it is a good idea to pretend to be about to photograph something else, and then suddenly to whip round and take the picture you want.

Concentrate too on the things which are unique to the beach, things that a child may be seeing for the first time in its life. Do not forget candy-floss and ice-creams, and make the most of the graphic possibilities of brightly-coloured beach towels.

Apart from looking after the camera, the main technical difficulty with beach photography is likely to be the tremendous brightness range of the subject: if the sand is correctly exposed, the shadows are likely to be a featureless black - including the faces under beach hats - although the sand should throw back enough light to stop them being complete 'black holes'. The professional way around this is to use *fill-in flash,* which means firing the flash at the same time that you take the picture, even though it is brilliantly sunny: the flash lightens the shadows, without affecting the background. Not all cameras can be used this way, but if you can switch on (or attach) a flashgun without automatically switching the shutter speed to 1/30 second, you should be able to do it. At least try a couple of experiments, with and without the flash, to see if you can make this work with your camera.

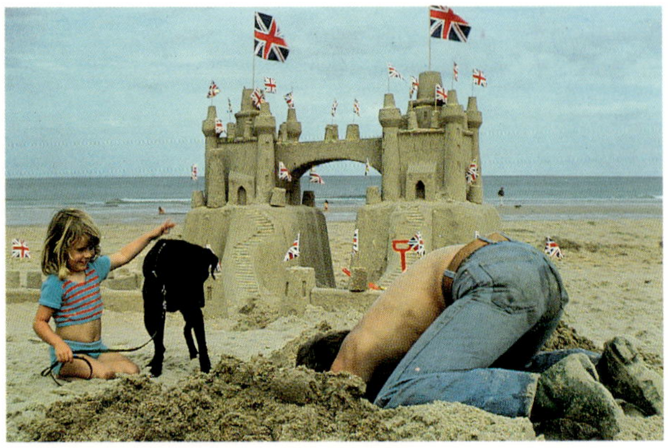

One of the dangers of taking pictures on the beach is that you can get so involved in the subject itself that you put your camera down: the temptation is to start watching the Punch and Judy show(right), or to join in the building of a sandcastle (above). Quite apart from the risk of theft, the likelihood of sand getting into the works makes this very rash indeed.

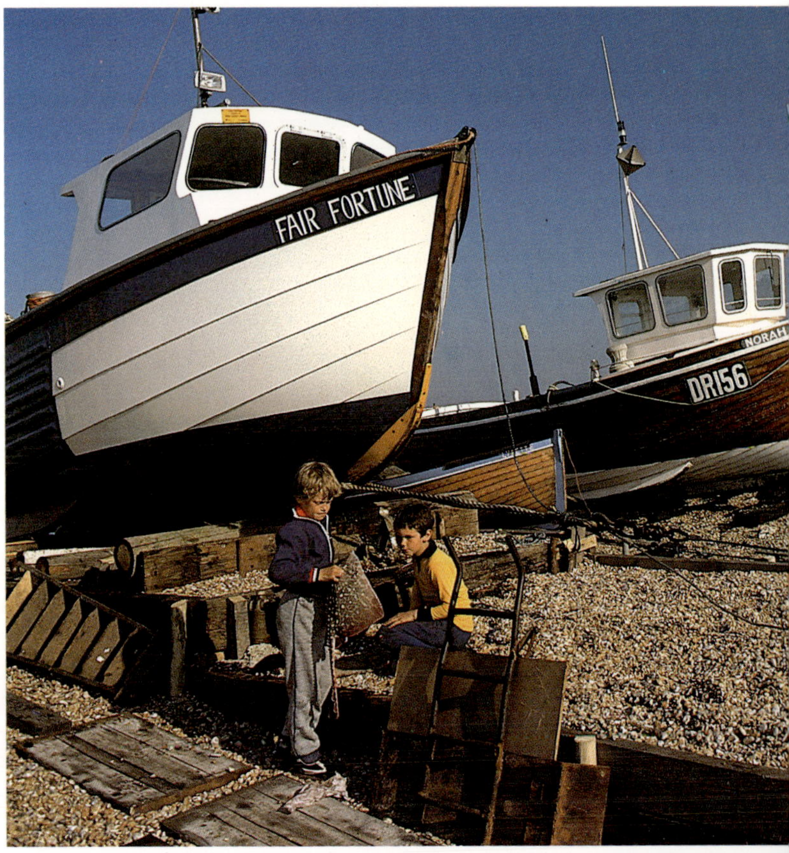

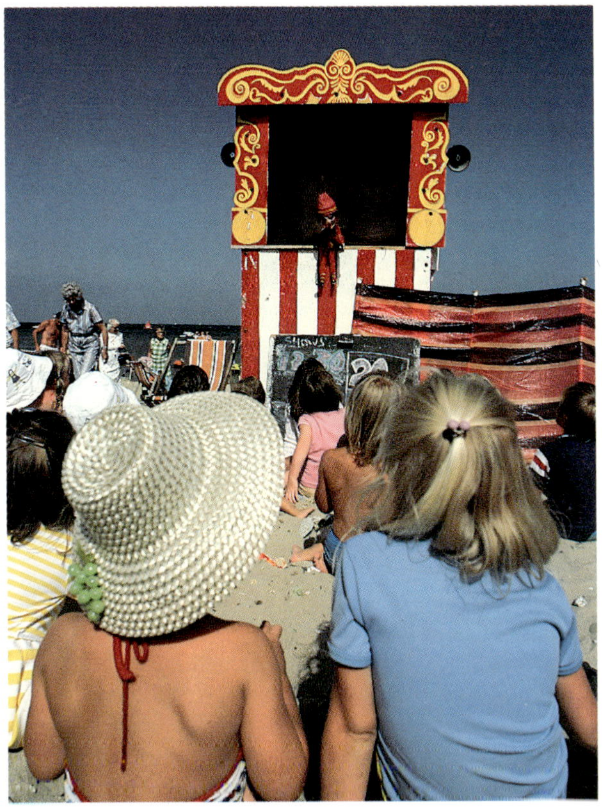

We said that looking after the camera was important, because sand, sun and salt water do not mix with precision machinery. Sand is extremely abrasive, and if it gets into your camera it will not just scratch the film: it can also mix with the camera's own lubricants to form a grinding paste which will both accelerate wear dramatically and clog up the works. A camera which has a bad dose of sand in the works might as well be scrapped, because it will cost more to repair than it is worth. The best protection is a self- sealing plastic bag, which is far more sand-proof than any conventional camera case.

Leaving a camera in the sun (or in the glove compartment of a car) is dangerous because it 'cooks' the film, spoiling colour rendition, and can also evaporate internal lubricants or cause the lens elements to separate. Electronic cameras may stop working altogether if they are overheated.

Salt water is even more dangerous than sand. If you drop your camera into the sea, you might as well write it off, as once again it will almost certainly cost more to repair than it is worth. But even if you do not drop it into the sea, salt spray can corrode the outside, and (if you are unlucky) the inside as well. Keep the camera in a bag when you are not using it, and wipe any spray off the outside as soon as possible after it happened - but pay particular attention to the lens: an ultra-violet (UV or Skylight) filter will protect the lens, as described on page 122. You should also follow the instructions given there for cleaning, as trying to dust off the lens with a towel or T-shirt is likely to do more harm than good, and result in irreparable scratching.

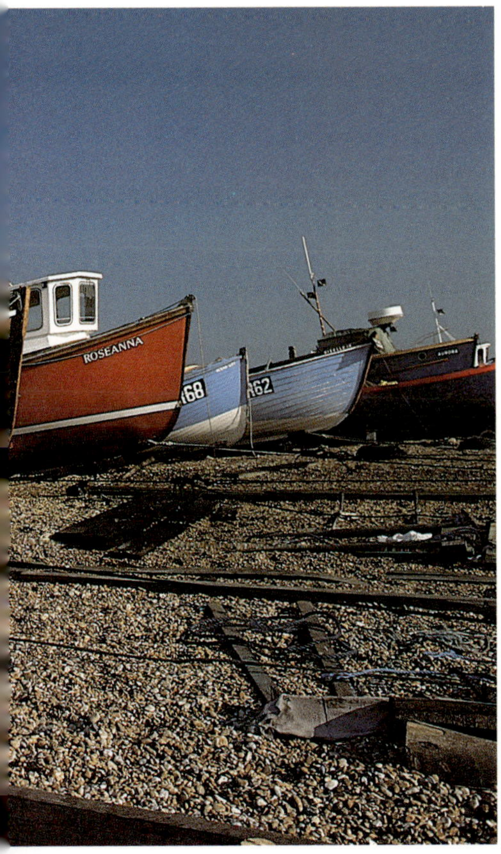

Dramatic angles, whether looking up or looking down, are always effective; and the wide-angle lenses fitted to most compact 35mm cameras are ideal. Photographers with interchangeable-lens SLRs (see pages 118-121) should use 35mm or even 28mm, rather than the 'standard' 50mm or a telephoto zoom, to obtain these effects.

Rainy Day Blues

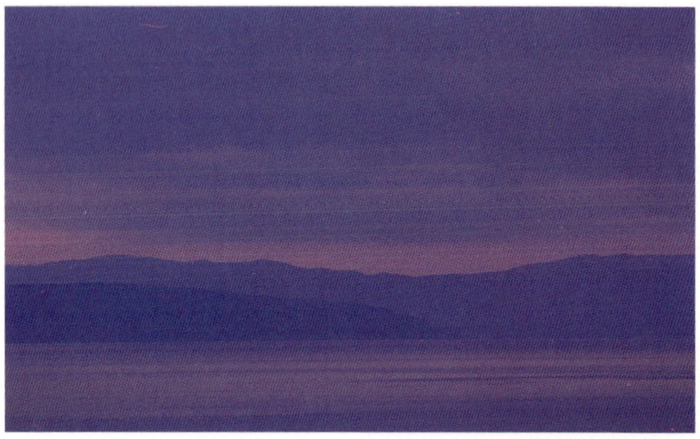

This picture was taken immediately after the storm had moved on from the hills. By choosing an area of the sky which has cleared and by subtle use of a light blue filter, the picture evokes a feeling of cool twilight.

Into every life, a little rain must fall - and sometimes, it seems that it all falls during the holiday season! Even so, there are still plenty of possibilities for pictures, and no matter how bad things may seem at the time, they will give you something to laugh about when you get home.

To begin with, there is the humorous aspect. You can usually find wind-and rain-swept posters advertising seaside shows; if you can get somebody walking past with an umbrella, so much the better. There are always a few people, too, who don't seem to realise it's raining: they still wear their shorts, T-shirts, and Kiss-Me-Kwik hats in half a hurricane. They, too, provide light relief.

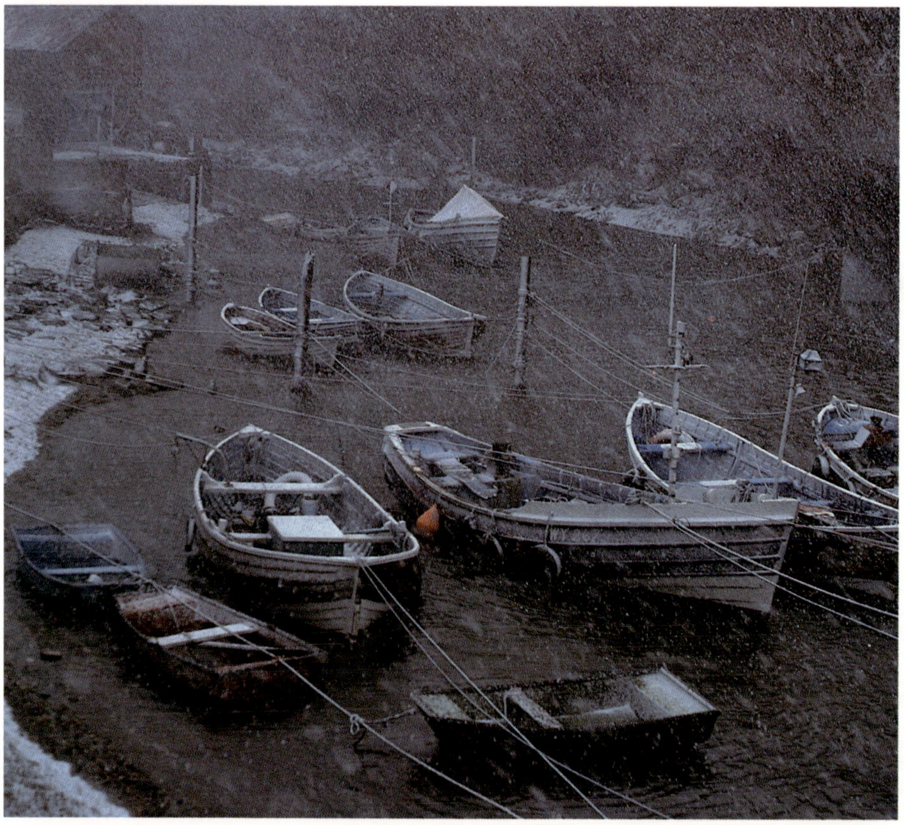

Even in the worst conditions, there are pictures to be taken. You need to be determined, and even though you may be freezing, you still need to pay attention to composition. Here, the boats in the foreground give a real feeling of depth, as does the diminishing perspective of the frozen river. The almost monochromatic colour and the driving snow reinforce the impression of bleakness.

Secondly, there are the indoor activities - the amusement arcades, the pier, and so forth. People are often driven together by adversity, and the British weather can be pretty adverse when it wants to be, so if you load your camera with fast film (see pages 124-125) or use your flash-gun, you can get all sorts of people enjoying themselves indoors.

Thirdly, stormy weather can give some wonderful lighting effects. Dramatic skies contrasting with a shaft of sunlight can make a superb photograph, and when the rain is over, the lights at night reflected in the puddles and on the wet streets provide some very attractive pictures.

Finally, even if you do not want to take any pictures, you can spend the time profitably by scouting out possible new locations, whereas if it was sunny, you would probably never bother to explore the place at all! This may sound a bit too much as if we are putting the best face on a bad job, but all of the photographers in this book could point to occasions when bad weather turned out to be a blessing in disguise.

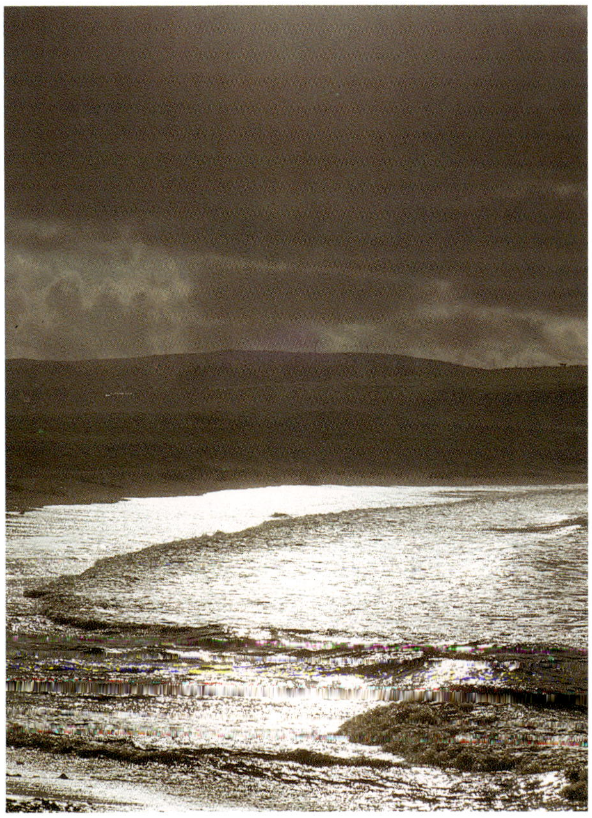

If you are ready with your camera, the sun can be caught breaking through the clouds during a lull in the storm. Sunlight in contrast with grey clouds is usually highly spectacular, as seen above, with the highlights standing out against the heavy grey 'backdrop'. Although such pictures present technical problems, it is important to think fast and act quickly because such moments pass rapidly.

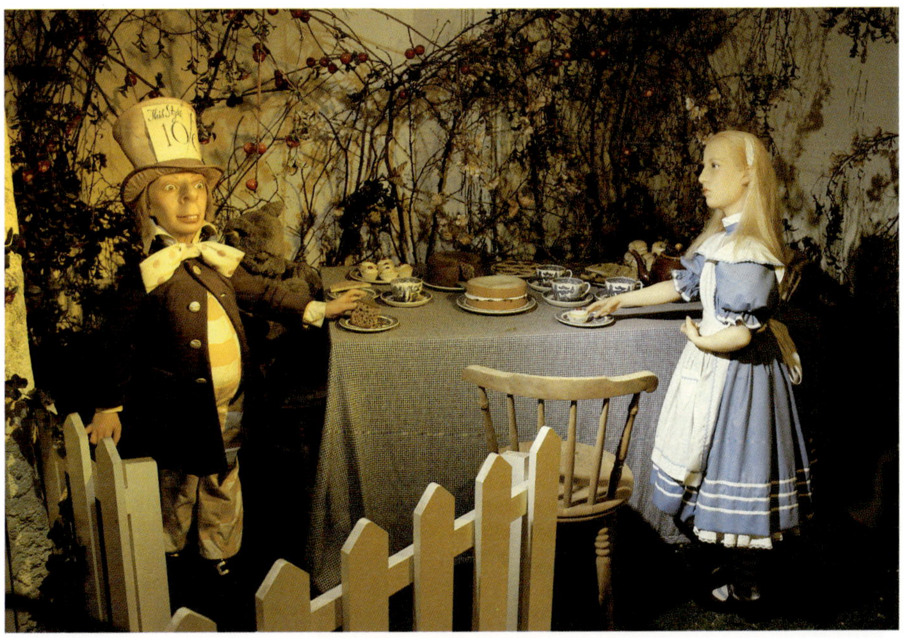

When the rain forces you from the beaches, there are usually plenty of other things to do. This interior picture of Alice in Wonderland at Gt. Yarmouth's House of Wax was taken from a tripod with available light to avoid camera shake. The artificial light can sometimes prove problematic but in this case adds to the 'fantasy' atmosphere.

Night Life

'Night life' is a broad heading, but it includes two main types of subject. First, there are the outside shots in poor light or at night, showing illuminations, shops and arcades, and so forth, and secondly there are the indoor attractions such as discos, restaurants and parties.

For outside shots, flash is going to be useless because it will not reach far enough, so you will need to use *fast film* (pages 124-125). Indoors, you can try either fast film or flash, but fast film will usually give a more natural sort of picture. In any case, using flash is often inconsiderate towards other people, as it can destroy the atmosphere of (say) an intimate restaurant.

An old professional trick for outdoor 'night' shots is to shoot at dusk, when there is still some light in the sky, because this allows you to get the kind of rich, deep blue which you actually *see* and remember, rather than the dead black which the film records at night. This is particularly effective when you are photographing illuminations, arcades, piers, and the like.

Opinions differ about pictures of parties, discos, etc. One school believes that you should photograph them fairly *early* in the evening, before people are too drunk (or just plain silly!), and the other reckons that you get better pictures a bit later, when things have really started jumping. The truth probably lies somewhere between the two: you need to pick a time when everyone is relaxed enough to be having a good time, but not so relaxed that they are sliding under the table. An additional problem for the amateur is that he (or she) is likely to be a part of the festivities, whereas a professional would normally walk in 'cold', which makes it far easier to judge the picture.

One thing which is very difficult indeed is to convey the impression of a crowd at a party: no matter how many people are there, and how packed it seems at the time, photographs often fail to convey the mood. There are, however, three ways around this problem. One is to try and get as high a viewpoint as you can, and wait until the foreground is fairly well crowded. Another is to forget about the crowd, and concentrate on individuals or small groups of people; a few more figures behind them, out of focus, can suggest a crowd more powerfully than trying to get everyone into the picture. The third approach is rarely possible, but if you can do it, it can be very successful. It is to wait until there is a particularly energetic dancer, or someone showing off a party trick. Other people will then draw back to give the performer some space, so you have the best of both worlds: a strong centre of interest (the dancer or whoever) *and* a tight-packed crowd behind them.

Two techniques are combined here: shooting while there is still some light in the sky, and using a long exposure (a second or more) to turn the windmill's arms into a blur. Imagine how dramatic this could have been if the streets had been wet as well!

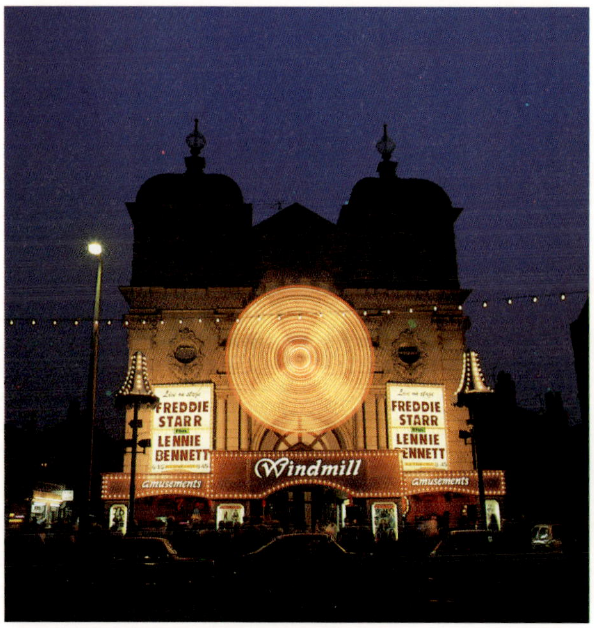

The circus ground and funfare are quite common to the seaside. The artificial light might give your prints a slightly 'warm' tint, but providing you hold your camera very still and use a fast film (p124) interior night photography using the available light can be highly rewarding. In this circus picture (right), although blur occurred, a real feeling of movement has been achieved.

This type of picture can be taken during the day of course, but then it may contain daylight as well as artificial light which would give the picture a different colour. If you used flash on a subject like this you would probably find that you ended up with no picture at all or that it illuminated just the foreground.

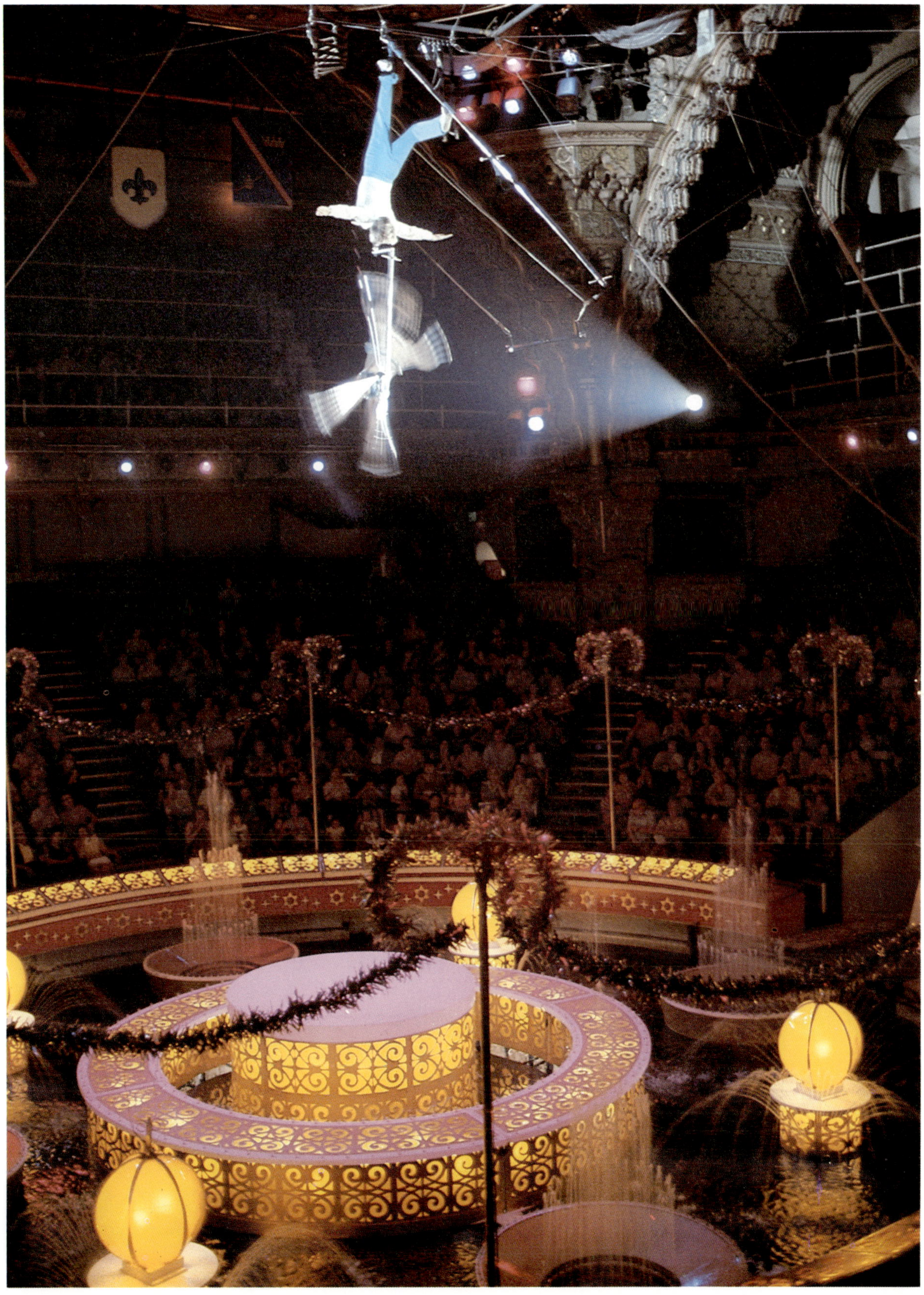

New Friends & Personal Memories

One of the great attractions of any holiday is that we meet new people - people from all walks of life, from different parts of the country or even from different countries, and people whom we would not normally meet. There are, however, two kinds of pictures of 'friends': first, pictures of people whom we may meet again, and secondly, pictures of local 'characters' or other people who are visually (and often personally) interesting, but whom we shall almost certainly never meet again.

The first sort is more difficult. Human nature being what it is, we always want pictures of our new friends. But if you look through your albums, you will no doubt find lots of pictures of people who are now complete strangers, sitting on the other side of a bar or restaurant table and staring solemnly at you like stuffed fish.

The second sort, surprisingly enough, is easier. There are two things to watch out for. One is clear pictures, and the other is good backgrounds.

For a clear picture, move in reasonably close, and make sure that the lighting is right. Unless you are very experienced, or just plain lucky, back-lighting is harder to handle than frontal lighting: if you can, have the light coming slightly from your side, rather than head-on, as absolutely flat lighting looks dull and unflattering.

Getting a good background is not really difficult, either: the old picture of a fisherman mending his nets may have been taken by every holiday photographer since Daguerre, but at least it tells you something about the man. If the attraction of the person lies in their features or clothes, and there is no real question of context, try to get as uniform a background as possible, without sudden changes of tone or colour behind the person. Be careful, though, of too-regular backgrounds (such as a brick wall) which by their very regularity can draw the eye away from the person, and can also make it look as if they were facing a firing-squad rather than a camera.

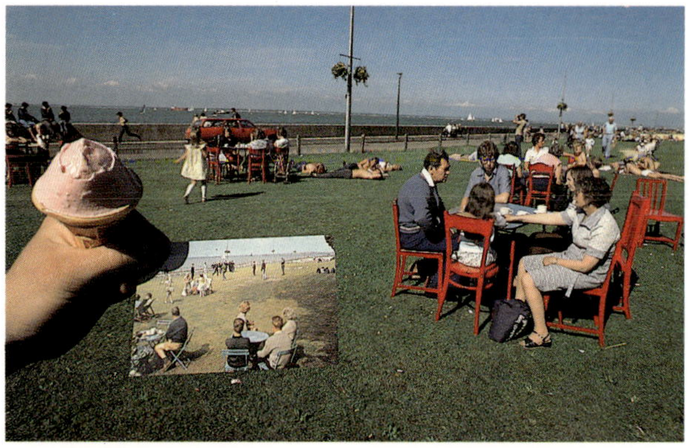

Just because pictures are personal, they don't have to be boring. The introduction of the 'mirror image' in this picture gives a very dramatic and unusual effect by showing two different views of the same sort of place. The photographer used an ultra-wide-angle 20mm lens (Page 121) in order to keep the postcard, the ice-cream cone, and the background all in focus at the same time.

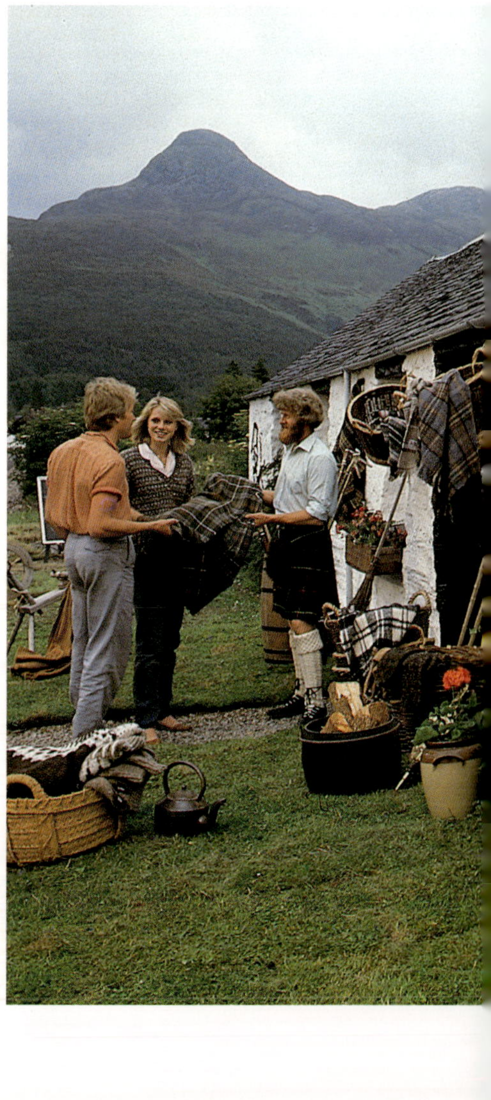

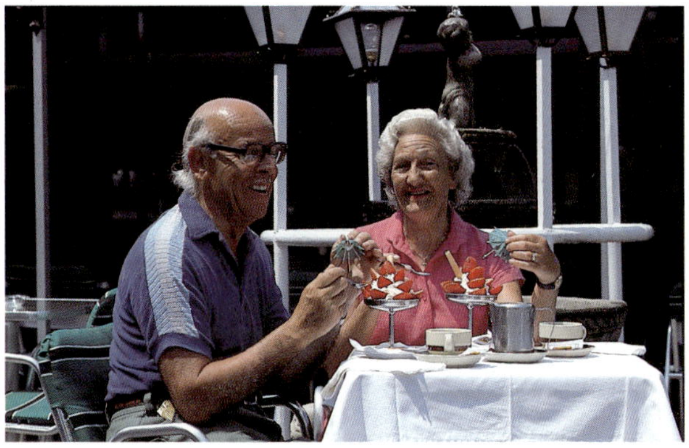

Preserve those special moments for the family album and make the picture complete by being in it yourself. Enlist the help of a passer-by to hold the camera.

As well as new friends, there are likely to be many other details which make your holiday truly *yours*. For example, you might have a particularly attractive hotel room, or there might be a pub where you spent several happy evenings. As pictures, photographs of these places would not necessarily amount to much, but as souvenirs, they can be invaluable. For the cost of a couple of extra frames of film, it is well worth recording these scenes.

It is impossible to make generalisations about this sort of picture, because by definition they *are* personal, but this is often the place for details such as a piece of ornate Victorian architecture, or for those little cameos which we see all the time and which strike us as funny, or just appropriate: an old man asleep in a deck-chair with a knotted handkerchief on his head (yes, it still happens!), a pair of young lovers entwined on the sand, a little child walking to the edge of the sea and then running back again when a wave comes in, half excited, half scared. Always have your camera ready for action, so that when the picture strikes you, you can photograph it.

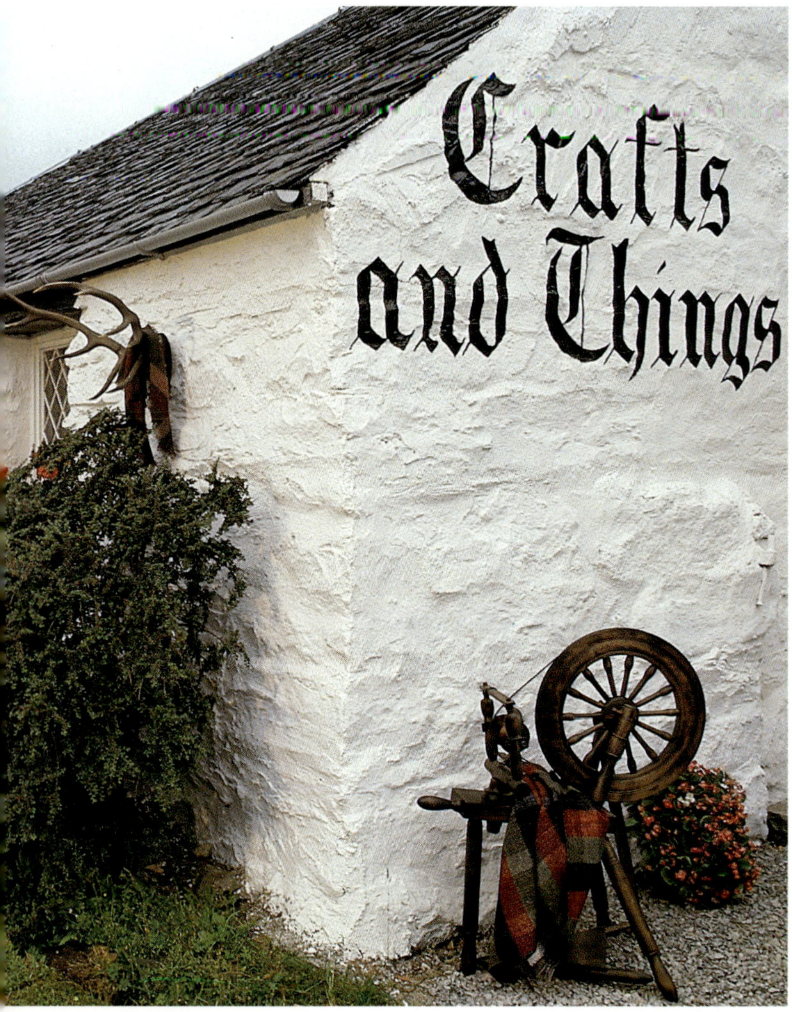

The daily excursion, so often available at the seaside, can offer a photographer the opportunity to veer from the traditional formats of portraiture. Pictures of friends can be far more interesting if they are doing something and if more of the surroundings are included in shot — as seen here with the photographers friends visiting a crafts shop.

CHAPTER FIVE

In Town

Britain is full of towns steeped in history: capture their moods by shooting individual pictures or going for a more ambitious photo-essay.

Most people go to the country to relax, to get away from it all, to see something different from their own city lives. But cities are (or can be) vibrant, exciting places, which offer a completely different kind of holiday. Even if you are a city-dweller yourself, you know how every city is different, and (as the old saying has it), a change is as good as a rest.

The first thing that most people do when they go to a city for the first time is to see the sights - some out of a sense of duty, because *everyone* goes there, and some because they really want to see them. Some sights rapidly pall - after all, how long *can* you stare at Buckingham Palace? - but others, such as museums, art galleries, parks, and even some streets and squares (think of Trafalgar Square, or Speakers' Corner) grow more and more fascinating with time.

Depending on how much time you have, you may wish to consider a tour; in many major cities, the municipal bus company runs a good, cheap one. That way, you can 'do your duty', and see all the obvious sights, and then settle down to enjoying the city properly. Of course, you can always decide simply to ignore the 'official' sights, but unless you know that you will be going back, that is never a good idea: there is always a slight feeling of dissatisfaction, of missing out on something if you do that. And, of course, most sights are worth seeing, which is why they became 'sights' in the first place.

If you just want a picture of a building (or whatever) with you in front of it, to prove you were there, then follow the old snapshotter's advice about keeping the sun over your shoulder and you will get a perfectly acceptable shot. But if you want something a bit more original, you are going to have to try a bit harder.

The professional approach would be to write out a list of locations and pictures - a 'shot list' - and to visit each location in turn. Ideally, you would scout the locations one day, armed with a pocket compass to work out (roughly) the direction in which the building was facing. East-facing buildings will have the sun on them at dawn, and west-facing in the evening, though you will also have to make allowance for shadows cast by nearby buildings. Indeed, in a narrow street, the best time to shoot may be noon, as this may be the only time when the light penetrates between the buildings. This sort of approach is a bit too rigorous for most people (though it is still worth bearing in mind), so let's look at some alternative approaches.

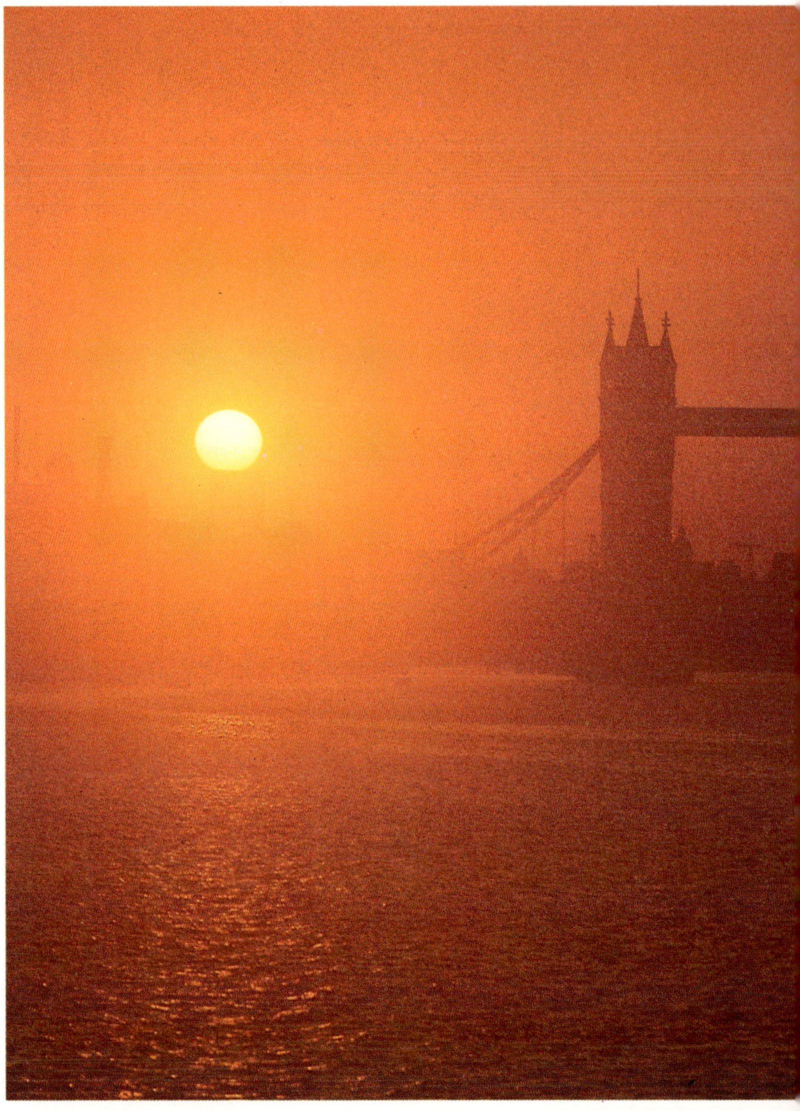

London's landmarks have been photographed hundreds of thousands of times. To achieve a photograph which you feel contains a really new perspective can be almost impossible. Making the most of your circumstances is important — here a simple orange filter transforms a dull sunset over Tower Bridge into an attractive and original picture.

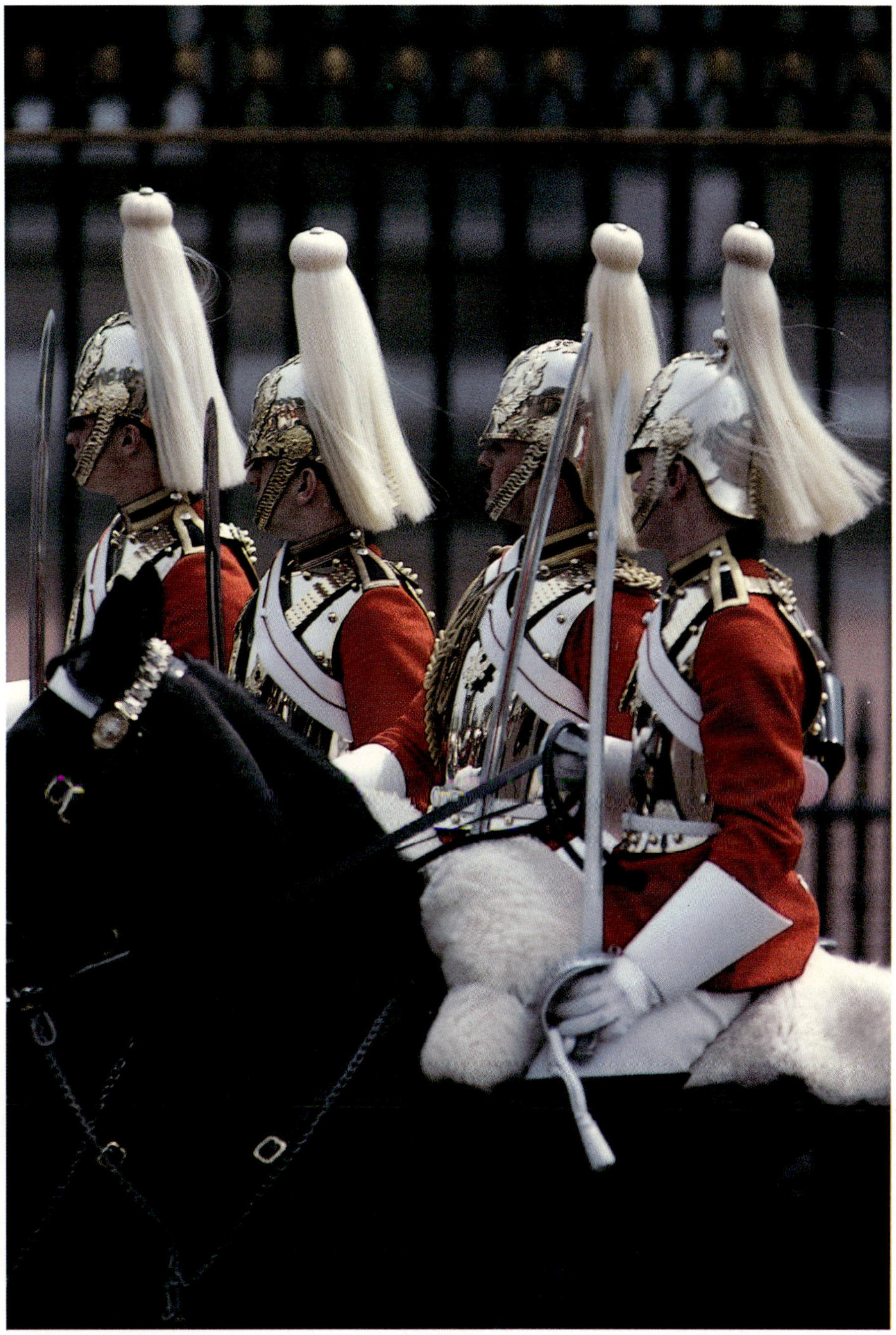

The lifeguards and horses on Horseguards' Parade are always a favourite subject - but by waiting until he had a clear shot and an uncomplicated background, the photographer here has achieved a picture which is far better than the standard tourist shot.

New Angles

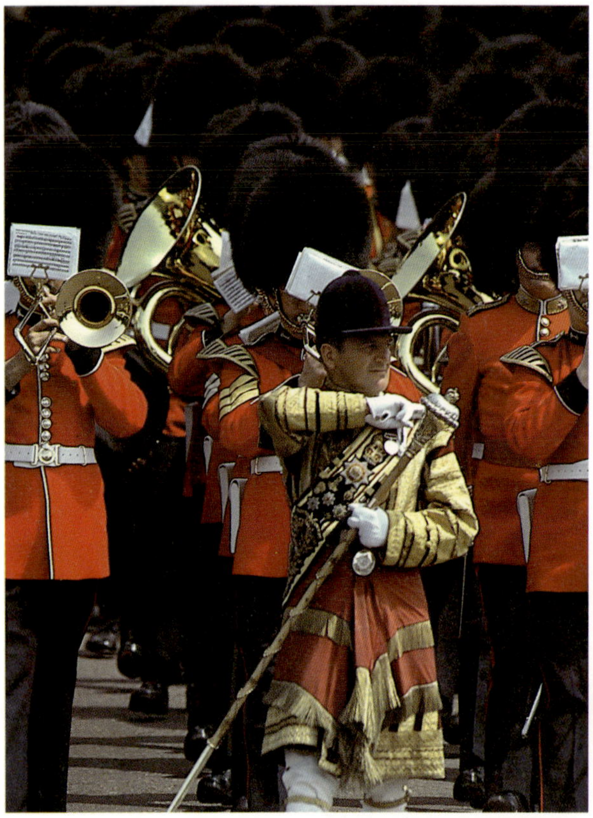

Instead of trying to photograph *all* of the sights of a city, which could take a month in London anyway, it usually makes more sense to try to get a few good pictures rather than a lot of ordinary ones. But what makes a 'good' picture?

Well, in addition to the four Golden Rules given at the beginning of the book, one of the most important things is to try to show the old, familiar subjects *in a new way.* This is not always easy, but there are a number of professional 'tricks of the trade' which you can try.

First, *try 'night' shots.* 'Night' is in inverted commas because, as we have already seen, you rarely shoot when it is completely dark but rather during twilight while there is still some light in the sky.

Second, *try new angles.* Try to get as high as you can, and look down on your subject; try a 'worm's eye' view, too, by kneeling or even lying down. Show the unfamiliar side of a familiar building; show it from a place that is difficult to get to.

As well as the more obvious shots, such as the Trooping of the Colour, (above) look for the more unusual but still typical details: the Chelsea Pensioners in their uniforms for instance.

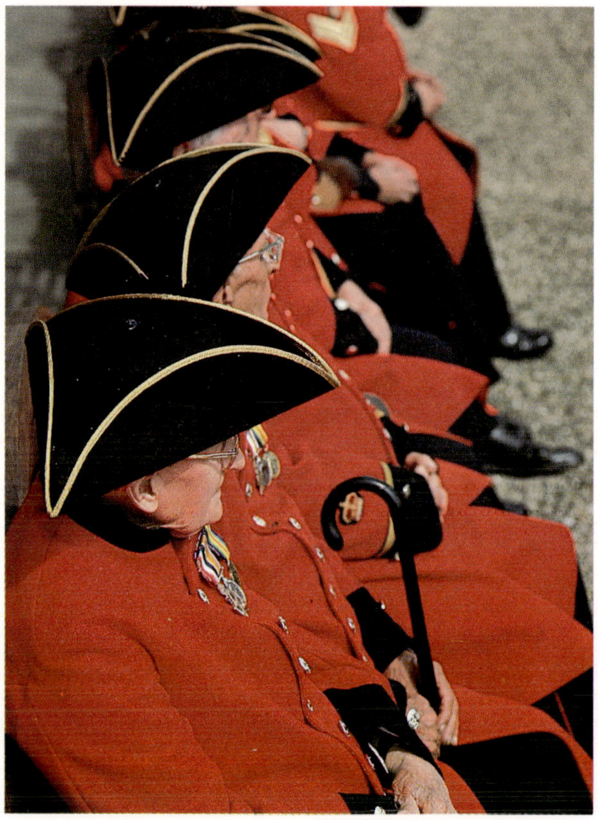

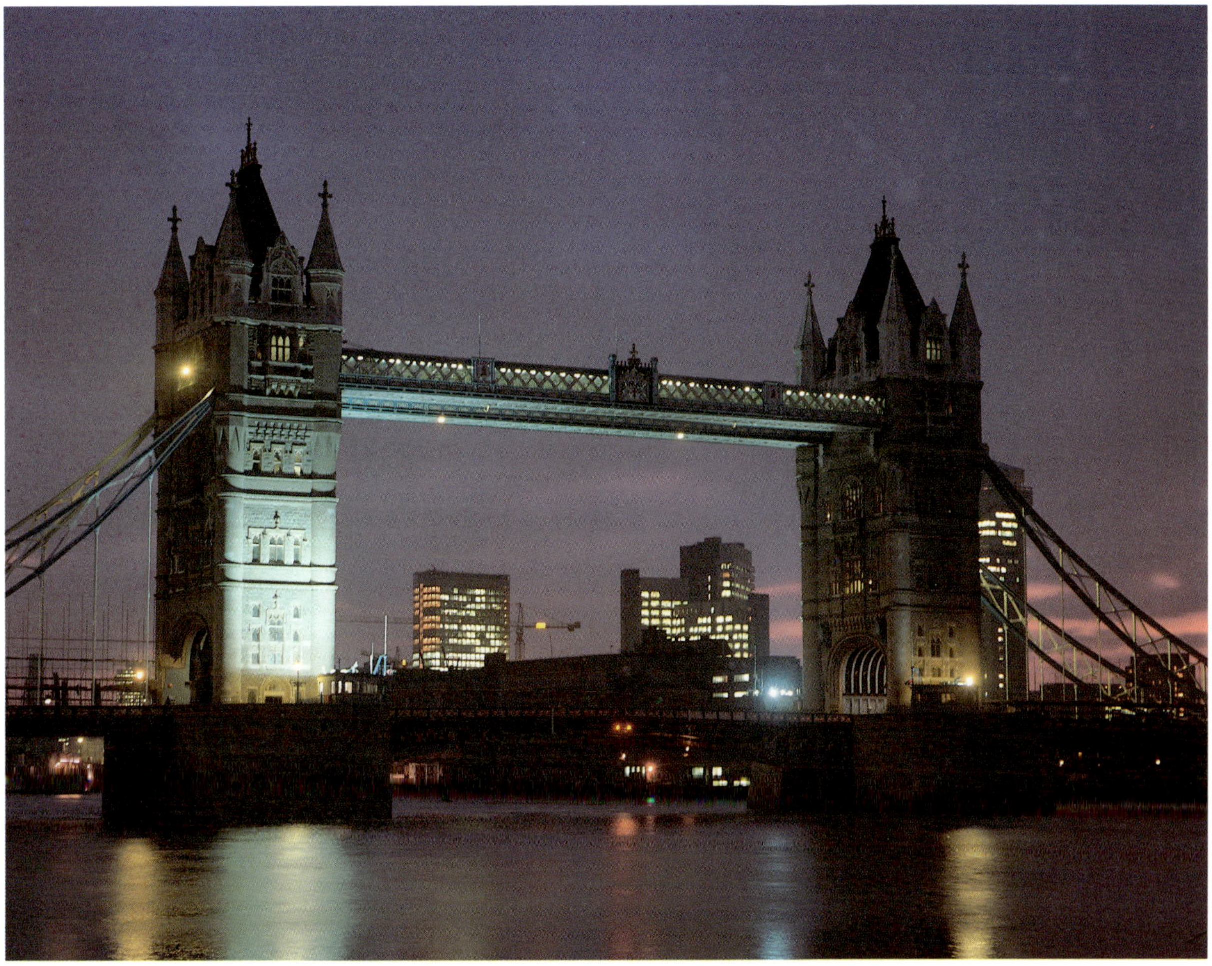

Familiar and well-known tourist subjects are difficult to photograph without becoming clichéd. A new angle can simply be the time of day, as shown here in this picture of Tower Bridge at dusk. The brief period when residual daylight in the sky can be balanced with floodlighting and reflections in the water can be extremely photogenic, combining elements of both day and night photography.

Third, *look for reflections.* The gaudy reflections of neon lights in puddles turn a rainy day into an asset rather than a liability, and there are countless other reflective surfaces, as suggested by Barry Hicks (see pages 14-15).

Fourth, *use frames.* In photographic use, a 'frame' does not have to surround the picture, though some, such as gates, will do so; it can be on two sides or even one side, so long as it gives some scale and depth to a picture. Imagine, for example, shooting Trafalgar Square with the distinctive silhouette of a helmeted policeman to one side.

Fifth, *go for details.* Often, it is the details which are most characteristic of a place: the destination board of a big red London bus, a close-up of the immaculately polished boots and spurs of a mounted horse guard.

Finally, *look for contrasts.* Look for a down-and-out in front of Harrods, an Arab in traditional dress tipping a doorman, a small boy standing to attention beside a guardsman. Some of these pictures will be funny; some will be sad; some will be curiously typical - but they will all make you think, which is a certain way to get people to react to your pictures.

A Personal View

As we have already suggested, it is important to realise that you don't *have* to see all the sights, just because everyone else does. If you already know the town, you can afford to ignore them anyway, and get on with photographing the town as *you* see it. If you are interested in a subject, why not photograph it? You may not go as far as Lady Lucinda Lambton, whose book *Temples of Convenience* documents the splendours of public lavatories, but why not concentrate on (say) pubs, or Tudor buildings, or brass name-plates, or even cast-iron man-hole and coal-hole covers, many of which have the most intriguing designs and patent claims cast into them. You could photograph the department stores, inside as well as out, or you could concentrate on the city's parks, or even on a single park.

When you do this, you are coming close to a *photo-essay*. As its name suggests, this is an essay which tells a story, or even argues a case, using pictures instead of words. If you find it hard to see how you can use pictures to do this, just take a typical example: the 'bag people' who are to be found in all big cities, often living rough.

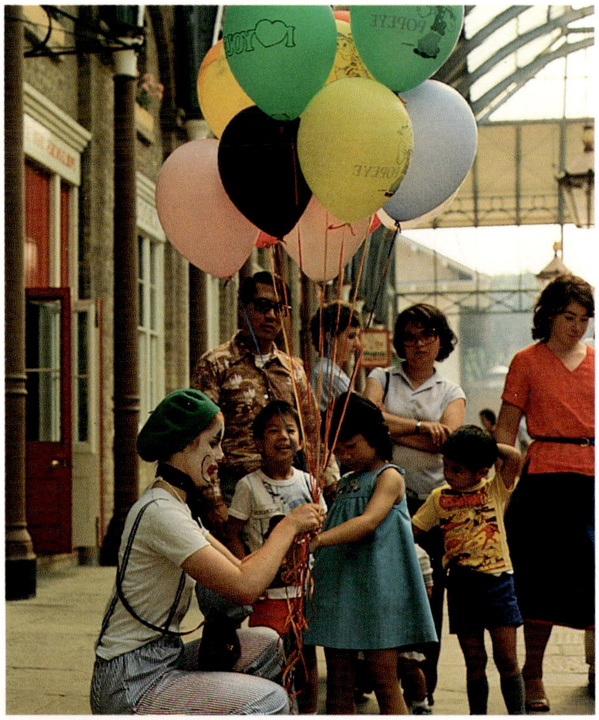

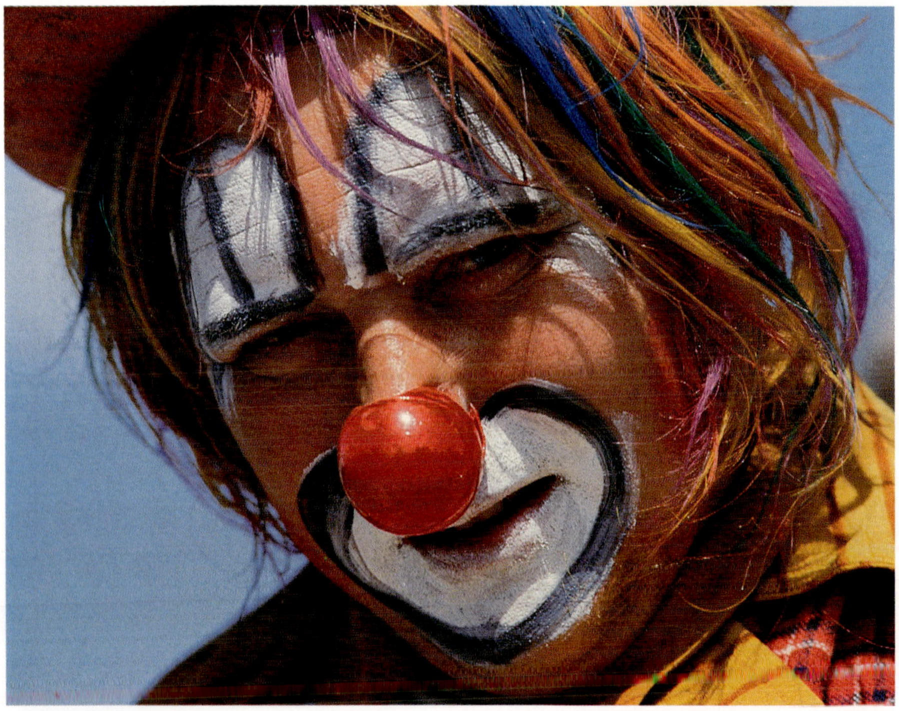

The restored Covent Garden is an attractive building in its own right, but what adds to it's appeal are the buskers, balloon sellers, jugglers and other street performers that it attracts. Some people prefer to concentrate on inanimate objects, while others are stronger on people.

The clown is a familiar sight, but by photographing him between acts, you can get a much more unusual and personal picture than if you simply photographed him in the middle of his act.

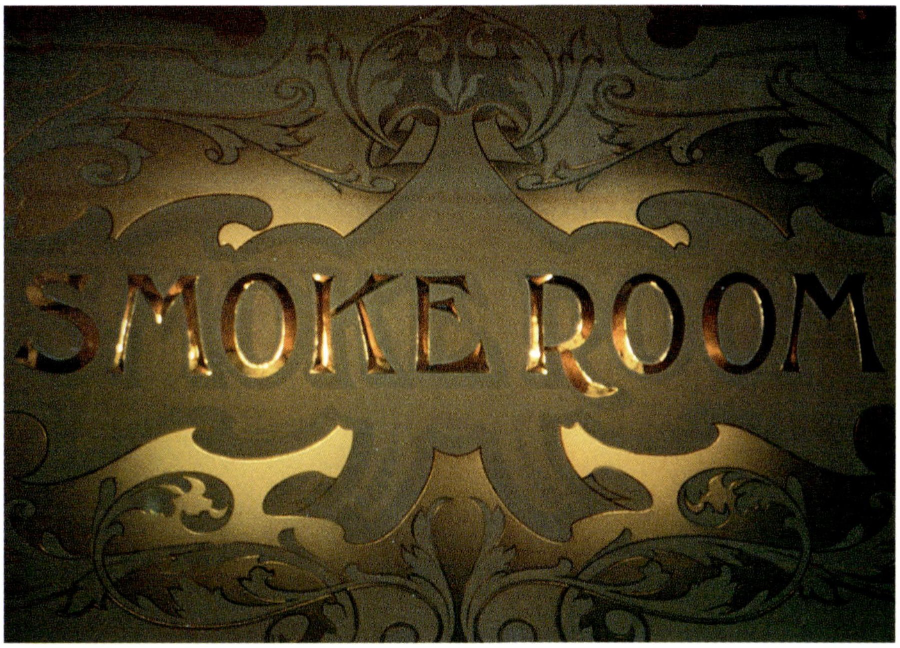

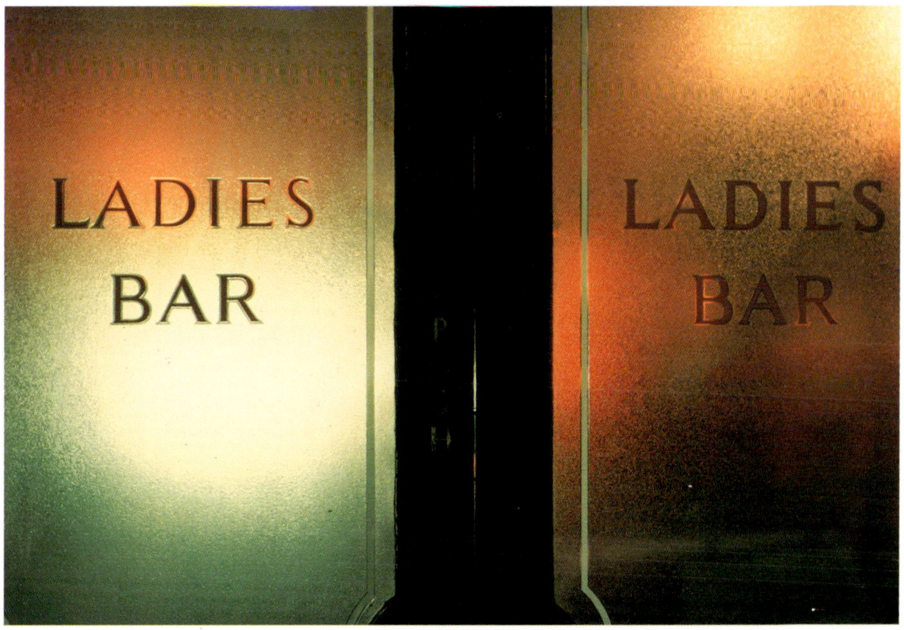

Shop and inn signs, engraved and gilded windows and the like are always a fruitful source of pictures; indeed, you could make a photographic collection of interesting, unusual, and attractive ones. Other possible topics for 'collections' include doors, churches, manhole-covers, piers... the list is endless.

Although photo-essays are traditionally associated with crusading journalism, there is no reason why you should not do a photo-essay about an altogether less controversial subject. A good example might be the uniforms from the past which still survive in London: not just military guards, but also commissionaires, Chelsea Pensioners, the attendants in the grander arcades, and so forth.

As an alternative to the photo-essay, for a really memorable picture, why not walk along a street such as Savile Row, stopping to take a picture every few yards so that the images overlap, and then assembling the prints into a long *collage* which shows the whole frontage of the street? This sort of collage can be a fascinating exercise, and (of course) you can do it vertically as well as horizontally, so that all the prints added together make up a much bigger whole, with a much wider angle of view, than any single camera with any one lens could make. You might shoot half a roll of film to make a single picture, but if you had 4 × 6″ prints made, the final result could be an impressive 18 × 24″ - though 15 × 20″ is likelier, once you have allowed for a bit of overlapping.

Outside London

Most of the examples which we have used so far in this chapter have been taken from London, because to most people (abroad as well as in Britain), London is the best-known city in Britain. But there is much more to Britain than London, and every city has its sights - though not everyone knows about them. To take an obvious example, Edinburgh's Royal Mile or Princes Street would be high on the itinerary of any visitor to the Scottish capital, but every city has its intriguing sights and associations. How many Britons, for example, know that the Mayflower Steps, from which the Pilgrim Fathers sailed, are in Plymouth.

Plymouth is also associated with Sir Francis Drake (who was Lord Mayor of Plymouth, as well as defeating the Spanish Armada), so you can see a lot of Drake memorabilia: the Drake Memorial, Drake's Leat (built to supply water to the city) and his country house a few miles outside the town. Another place worth seeing is 'New Street', which was 'new' in the sixteenth century, and then there is the cobbled Barbican, the old port area. But you would never know that any of this even existed if you were put down in Plymouth's rather uninspired 1950s city centre, which was completely rebuilt after unbelievably heavy German bombing in World War Two.

Each town has its surprises, and you only need to look for them to find them. For example, the sight of the

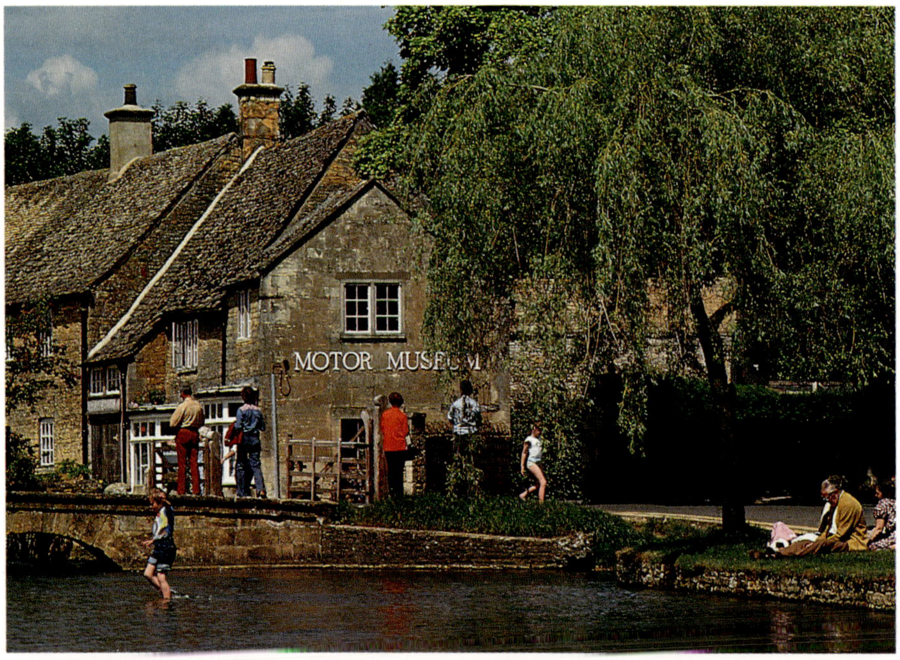

Bourton-on-the-Water is a typically attractive Gloucestershire village, but it is a matter of dispute whether the prominent words 'MOTOR MUSEUM' add to the picture or detract from it. As a personal souvenir of the museum, which is situated in an exceptionally attractive location, it is first class.

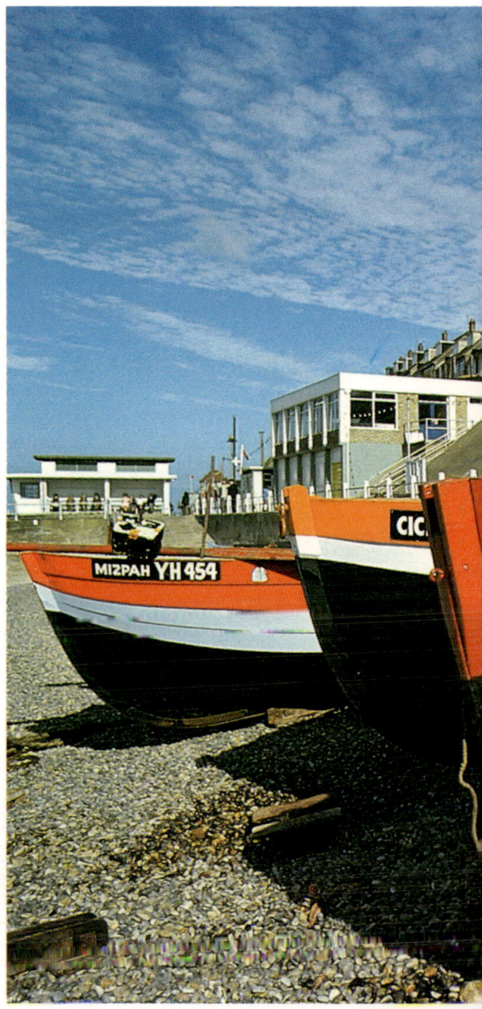

With Britain's maritime heritage, it is always worth exploring beaches and old harbours; looking at this picture you can almost smell the seaweed and hear the crunch of the shingle.

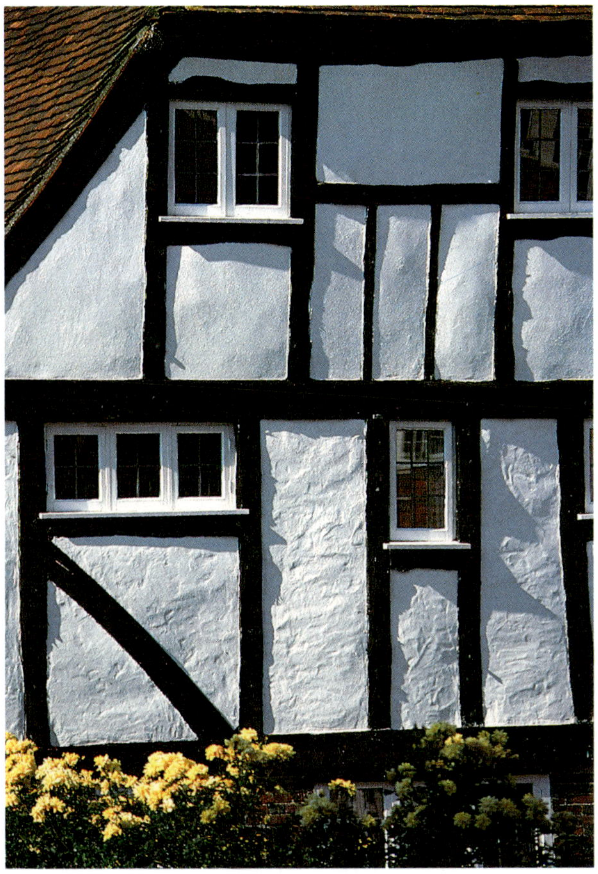

There are many half-timbered houses throughout Britain, in cities and towns large and small, and most of them make attractive subjects. This one is in Battle, East Sussex.

Minster apparently floating over the roofs of Lincoln is quite magical, and the state of preservation of York's city wall (or of Hadrian's wall, for that matter) is truly remarkable. And then of course there is Bath, the finest Georgian city in Britain, but still complete with its Roman baths!

Or take Canterbury, for example. Everyone knows about Canterbury Cathedral but not everyone knows that the old Norman town gate still stands at one of the main entrances to the city, and that twentieth-century traffic swirls around the eleventh-century masonry. About forty miles up the road are the Medway Towns (Chatham, Gillingham, and Rochester); this area is famous for its association with Charles Dickens, and Rochester Castle is also well worth a visit, especially when you reflect upon the fact that the stairs you climb to reach the top were laid by an unknown Norman mason over nine centuries ago.

This casual attitude to history, which is so typical of Britain, is one of the things which makes the smaller towns so fascinating to visit, and looked at in that light, the modern 'NO PARKING' sign, or the row of parked cars (or sometimes both!) against a row of mediaeval shops ceases to be irritating; it becomes a fascinating contrast between old and new, and an accommodation of one to the other. The important (and difficult) thing to do when photographing such a contrast is to show enough of the old without dwarfing the new, and enough of the new that it shows that the two co-exist, rather than being carelessly jammed together. Once again, shooting at dusk can be very effective: if you can find somewhere absolutely rigid to rest the camera, so that you can take a time exposure, the lights of the cars will record as streaks and blurs, while the massive old stone of the past stands unchanging in the middle.

Finding these 'in-between' towns is a matter of personal taste and experiment, but an excellent way to check them out is to take advantage of the bargain weekend and short breaks offered by many operators. These give you the opportunity to visit a place briefly and often at quite modest expense, and if you aim to shoot a roll or two of film across the weekend, you will be surprised at how it concentrates your photographic vision. For ideas on destinations, go to Tourist Information Centres, or to the public library.

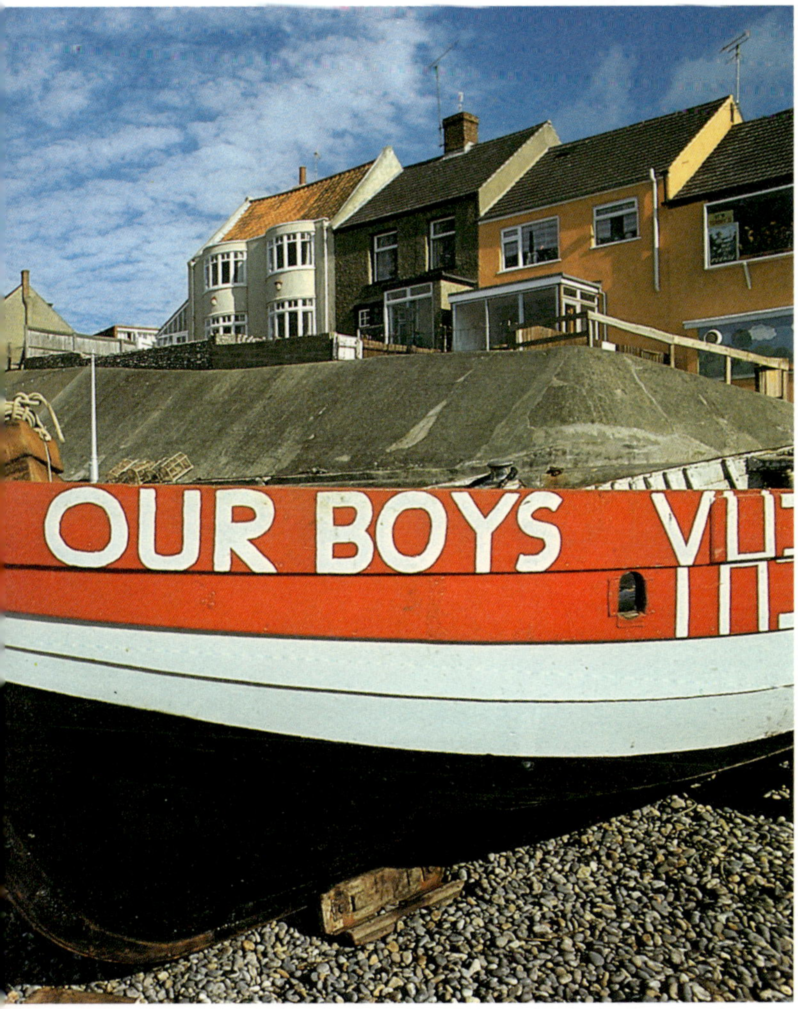

Museums

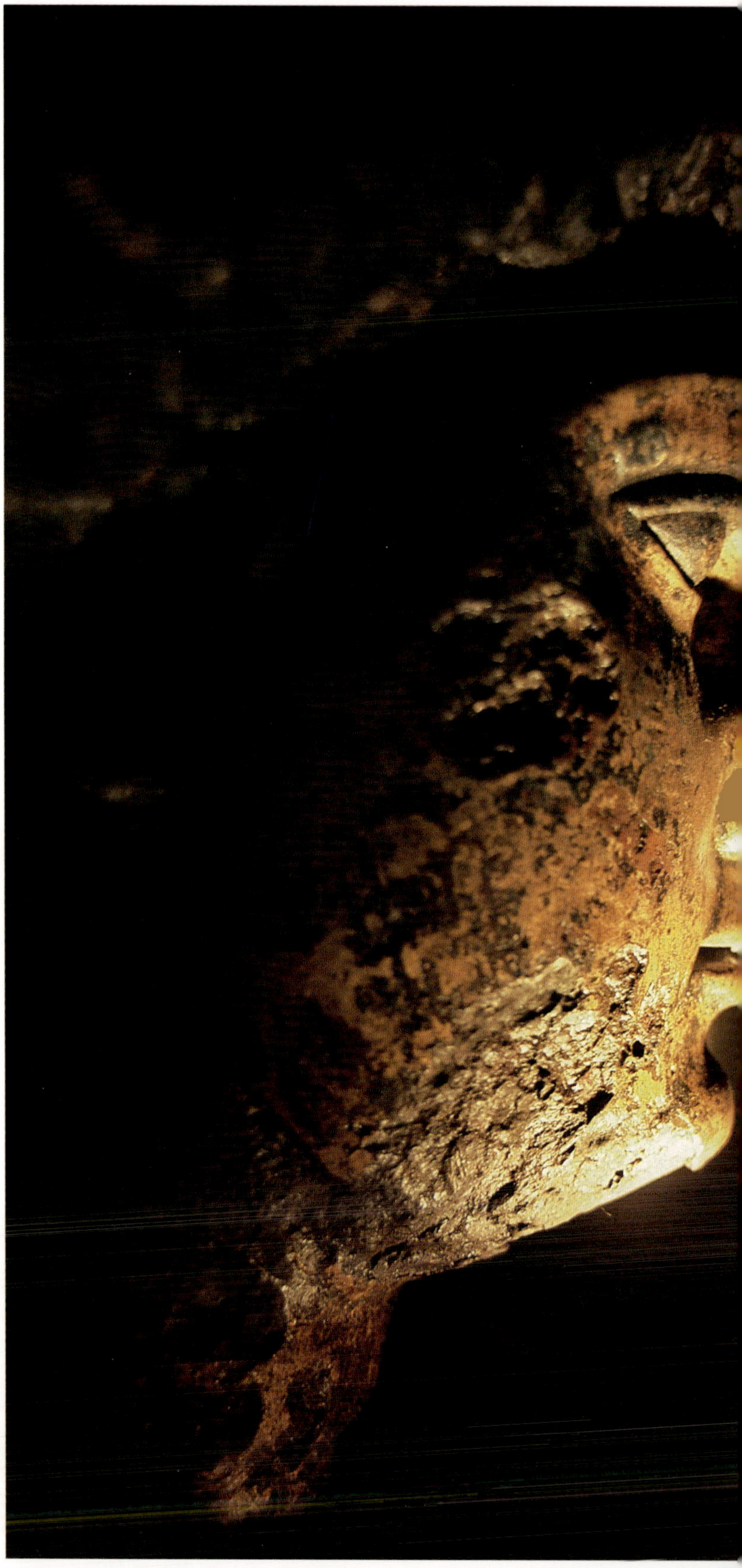

Some people love museums; others hate them. The truth is, though, that a museum can be a life-saver on a rainy day, even if you don't usually visit museums; and whatever the subject, Britain has some of the finest museums in the world.

Although most museums restrict professional photography, few object to amateurs taking pictures - but always ask before you do. In many museums, you will need a permit, which will either be issued for free or for a very small charge.

The two main difficulties about photographing in museums are first, getting back far enough to get your whole subject on the film, and second, the quality and quantity of the light.

The first difficulty is most easily solved with a wide-angle lens (see pages 120-121), but fortunately most compact cameras are fitted with a wide-angle as standard. If you have a camera with interchangeable lenses, use a 35mm or (better still) a 28mm, which will allow truly dramatic perspective, with the foreground looming large and reducing the significance of the surroundings - which, given how crowded most museums are, has to be a good idea. Alternatively, you can try focusing on details: the radiator of a car rather than the whole car, the driving wheels of a locomotive rather than the whole locomotive. If you are photographing things in cases, you can usually rest the camera against the glass for a long, shake-free exposure: a rubber lens-hood is useful, as it allows you to press the lens against the glass without risk of scratching. A word of warning: many autofocus cameras will not work through glass, so manual-focus cameras are more use.

The second difficulty is more of a problem. Beginning with *quantity*, you obviously cannot get a picture unless there is enough light, but the camera should warn you of this. Generally, if you are using a shutter speed of more than 1/30 second, you need some kind of support, even if you just rest the camera on a chair or lean against a wall. Not all museums allow flash, and even if they do, it will be useless for anything in a glass case because the case may reflect the light back like a mirror. As for *quality*, daylight should give perfectly acceptable results, and ordinary incandescent lamps (like domestic light bulbs, or spot lamps) will also be all right, but because of the colour of the light emitted by fluorescent tubes, you cannot really hope for much; a greenish or bluish cast is inevitable.

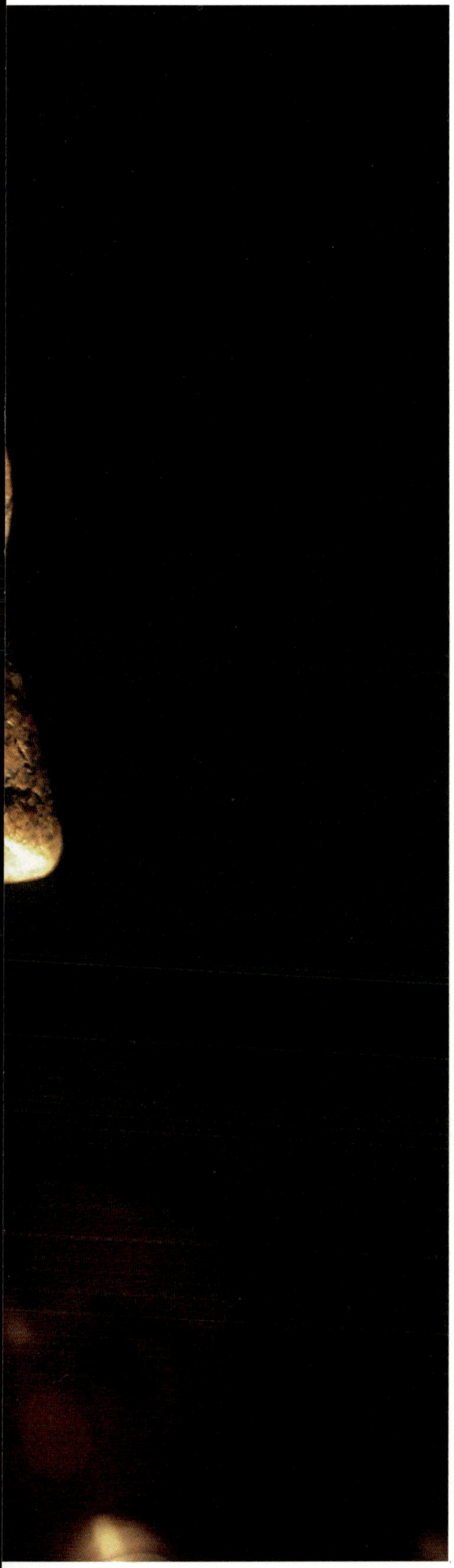

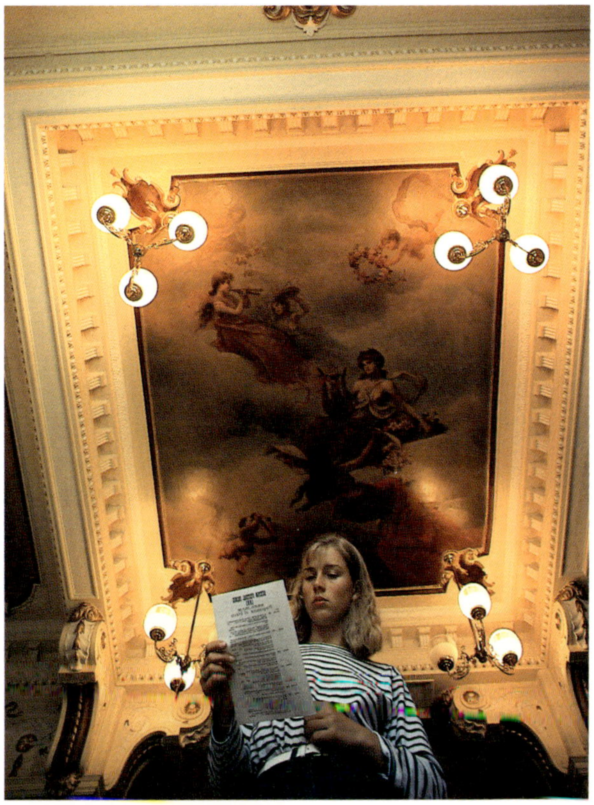

To get this unusual shot, the photographer laid the camera flat on the floor and aimed by guesswork - often an interesting technique.

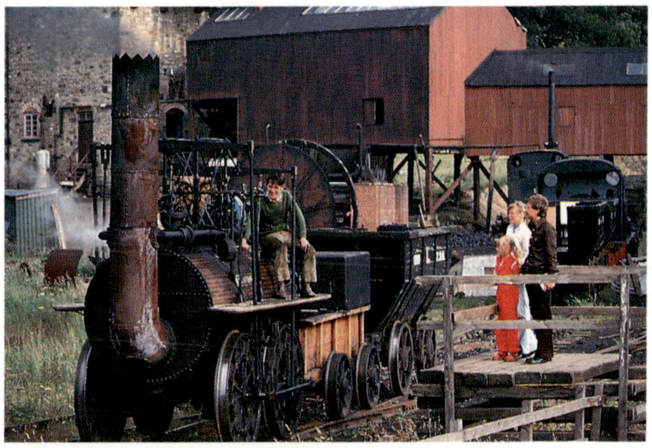

The sheer range of museums in Britain is astonishing, and many of them deal with the comparatively recent industrial past. You can study narrow boats (below), or even go for a ride on an antique steam engine. Outdoor industrial museums are becoming more and more commonplace; they are fascinating places to visit, and rich with subjects for photography. Often, museum exhibits are very dramatically lit (far left). If you can manage to find some means of supporting the camera, a long exposure (well within the capability of most automatic cameras) can give superb pictures like this.

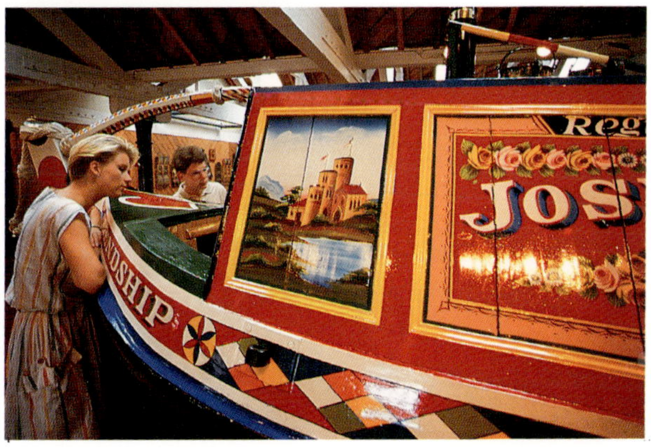

Nooks and Corners

We have already stressed the value of the unexpected, and of personal memories, and for most of us these are what make a holiday really memorable. This last section, therefore, deals with *how to find the unexpected.*

This sounds like a bit of a contradiction - how do you look for something when you don't know what you're looking for? - but it is actually quite easy. There are three ways of doing it.

First, use your eyes. Most of us may see the world around us, but we don't *look* at it: we only see enough to stop us bumping into things and falling off cliffs. Look up; look down; look for patterns and shapes and colours. Have you ever noticed how beautiful peeling paint can be? Then why haven't you photographed it? Have you ever noticed the extraordinary ornamental friezes and gargoyles which lurk above perfectly ordinary modernised shops? Have you never seen a pub which was just *perfect,* the way a pub ought to look, the way we all see a pub in our mind's eye? Where's the picture?

Second, use your legs. Instead of parking the car, walking straight to the 'attraction' which you're going to see, zipping round it, and going straight back to the car, try walking about a bit: creatively speaking, try to get lost. Only when you are lost do you start thinking about where you are going next: once you stop following the signs, you have to start looking at where you are, instead of where you are going to be.

Third, use your local Tourist Offices. They are there for everyone, not just foreign visitors, and it just doesn't make sense to pretend that you know all that there is to know about your native country: no-one does. The contributors to this book have a combined experience of photographing the British Isles which must be equivalent to about a thousand years of holidays for the average person, and even we are always finding something new.

When you find your nooks and corners, you are not always going to be able to photograph them successfully. We know: there are times when we can't photograph them either, even with all our professional equipment. But there will always be places to remember; and if you cannot go back to them in pictures, they are often the most rewarding places to revisit in your memories or in real life.

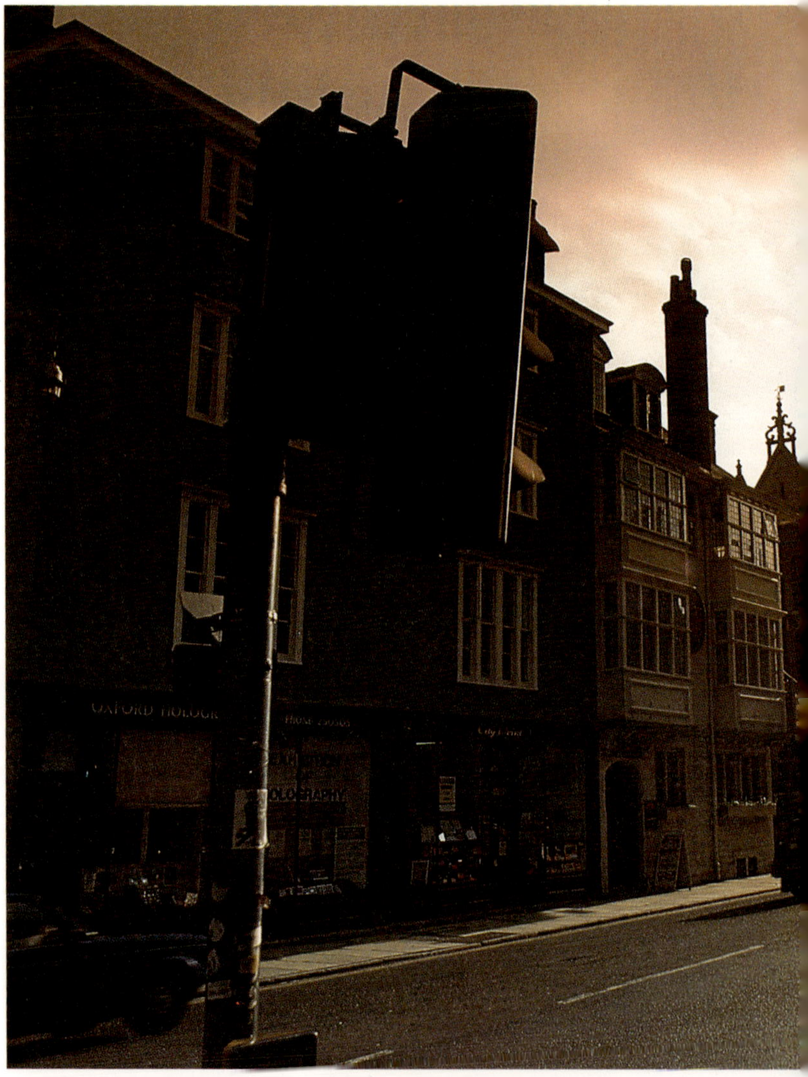

Our historic towns and cities provide a wealth of opportunity for exploration. This picture, for example, illustrates the wide variety of architectural styles and detail that can be found in a typical street.

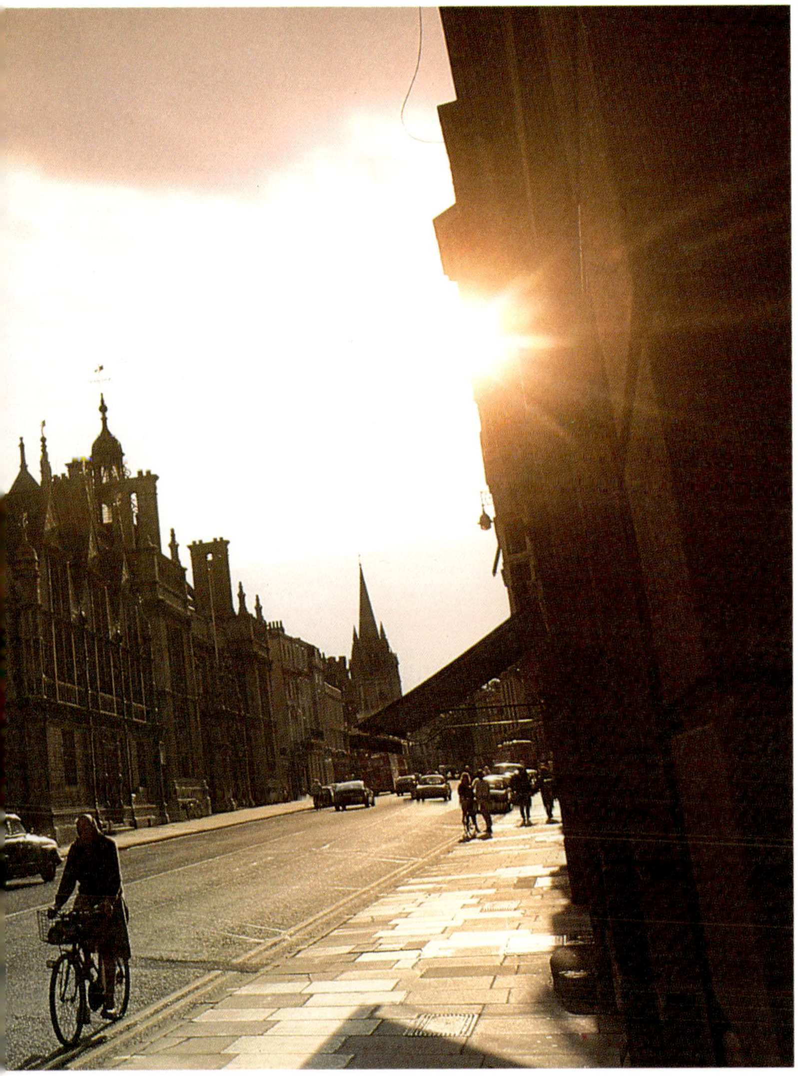

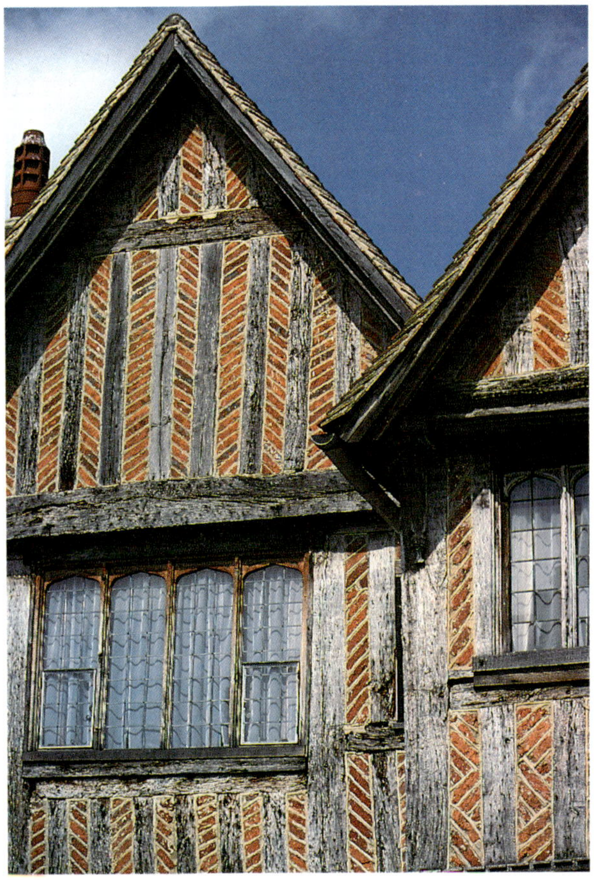

Kent is a happy hunting ground for the seeker of nooks, corners, and details. The brick-and-timber construction of this house in Charing is typical, as are the cottage doors from Sandwich (below).

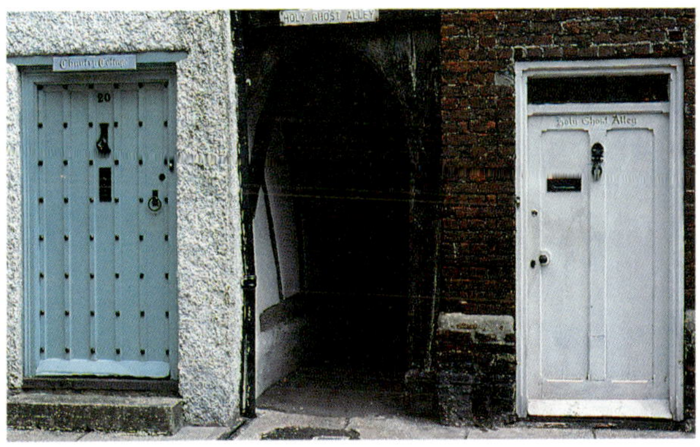

CHAPTER SIX

Country Life

Britain's countryside is as pretty as a picture - but not always that easy to capture on film.

The British countryside is famous the world over for its beauty. We may not be able to muster the majesty of, say, the Himalayas or the American West, but for pastoral loveliness our countryside has no equal, and for those who like the wild places there is still plenty of choice on the Yorkshire or West Country moors, or the Scottish highlands, to name only the most obvious.

Because the impact of man on the countryside has been so great in Britain, we have concentrated in this chapter on the way in which mankind has influenced the landscape, and only in the very last section (page 78) have we taken a look at the wild places. This does not mean, though, that we should hunt in packs, as visitors to beauty spots so often seem to do. Instead, we should try walking a little off the regular paths. Sometimes, there are unspoiled scenes of breathtaking beauty; at other times, we can get a new angle or perspective on a familiar view. The rewards are not merely photographic: the personal pleasure is likely to be much greater, too.

Many people will have the problem that they are accompanied by others who do not want to use their legs any more than they have to: children, in particular, seem to prefer to play in the car park, or near the ice-cream van, rather than a few hundred yards away in the peace and quiet. You have to accept that there is a conflict here between the time needed to get a picture - remember the Golden Rules about watching and waiting - and the demands of the rest of the party. How you resolve this conflict is up to you, but unless you are prepared to put in at least a little time looking for the right picture, rather than just snatching the obvious view, you cannot really expect any consistent success.

It is in the countryside, especially, that we should make the effort to watch out for details. Someone else's empty film box provides a garish yellow blotch on a green meadow; an electricity pylon towers over the landscape - but you can put the film box in a bin, and you may be able to hide the pylon behind a tree if you choose your position carefully. Usually, the most successful countryside pictures are the ones that evoke an age gone past, and disguise or obliterate the existence of the twentieth century, though you should also be alive to the possibilities of creative juxtaposition, such as a 'NO WAITING' sign over a stone horse trough.

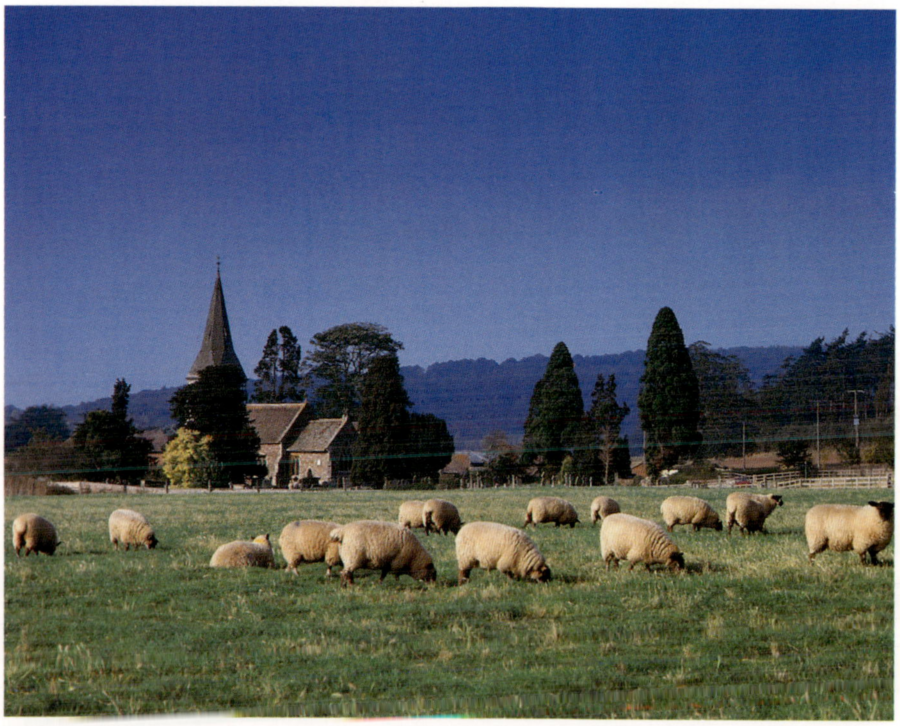

You can adopt many different approaches to photographing the country. In these two pictures (left and top right) you can see the difference between sheep in the meadow - a very calm, pastoral sort of scene - and sheep in a pen, which produces quite a different sort of mood.

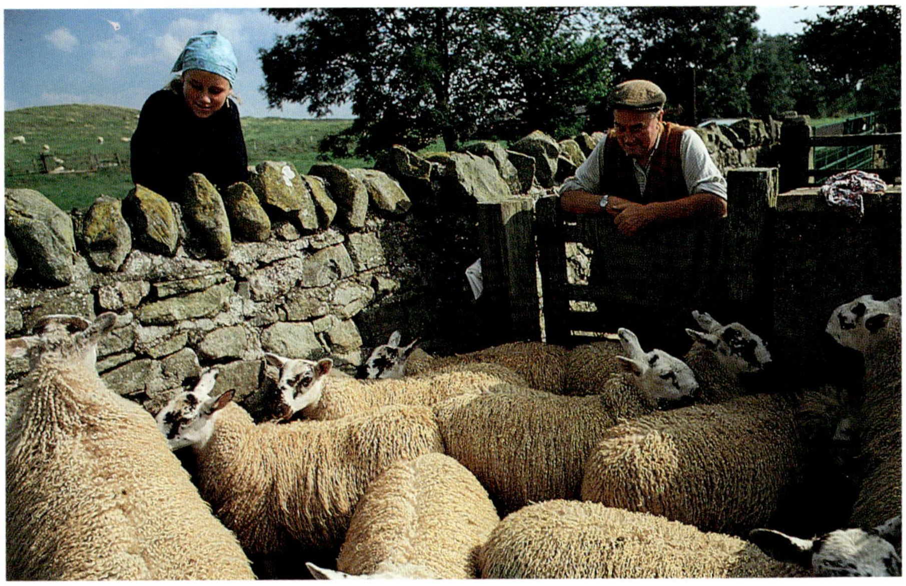

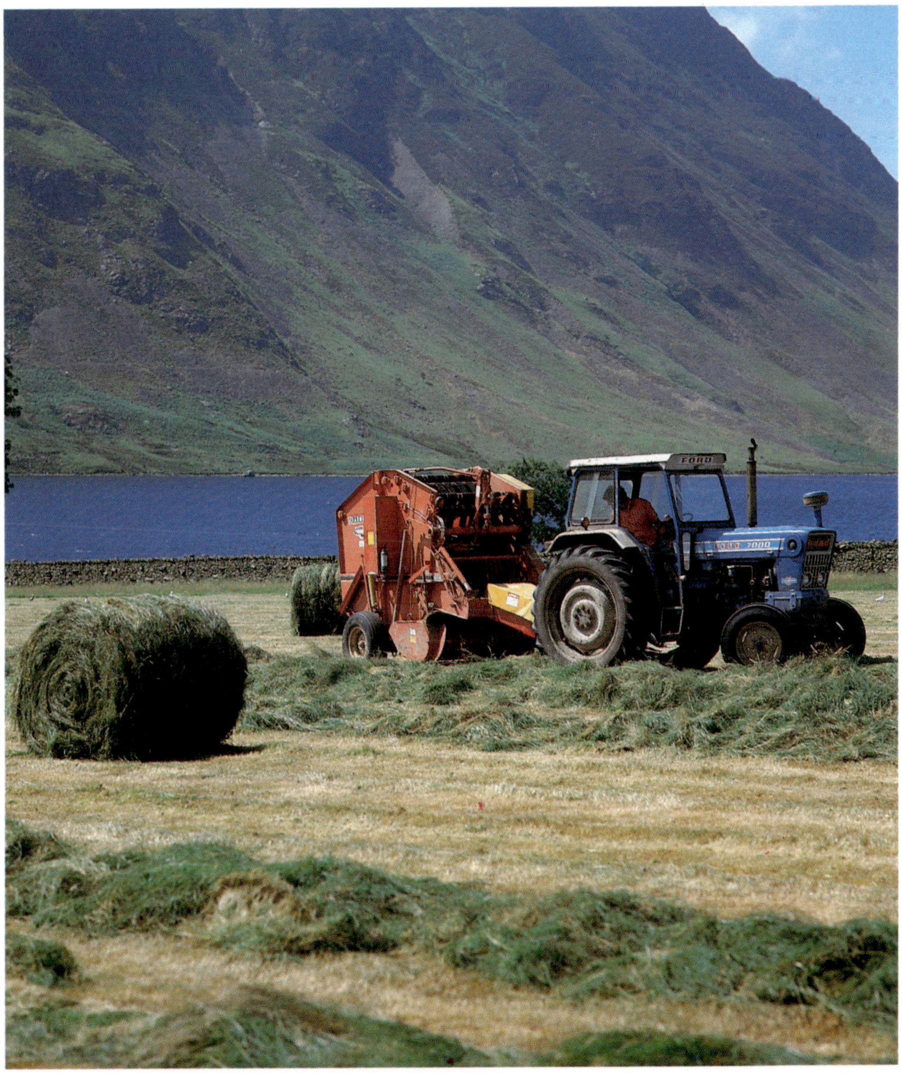

Most of us do not think of tractors as particularly attractive things, but in this case there would not really be any picture without the tractor; cover it up with your fingers, and you will see what we mean.

Landscapes

Landscapes look like the simplest thing in the world to photograph - but anyone who has tried will know how deceptive they can be. The most stunning scene can be reduced to absolutely nothing on an enprint, just a horizon against a sky.

Our Golden Rules are obviously important here, but the ones which are most important are the need for a clear *subject*, and the need for *composition* - indeed, most of the old Rules of Composition seem to have been designed especially for landscapes, and we have referred to them in the captions. The main subject need not be the *only* subject in the picture, but there must be something which your eye can pick up - a well-shaped tree, a thatched cottage, even the broad shape of a hill - or it will simply roam over the picture, find nothing, and dismiss it as 'boring'.

A particularly effective eye-catcher is a human figure, and although some landscape photographers go to great lengths to exclude people, they do lend scale and interest. On the other hand, if you are photographing a landscape, you do not want the people to dominate the picture with their sheer size: even a tiny figure can be very eye-catching, especially if it is dramatically contrasted against the background. Modern brightly-coloured rain-gear may be something of a cliché in these pictures, but it is still very effective when contrasted with a green hillside!

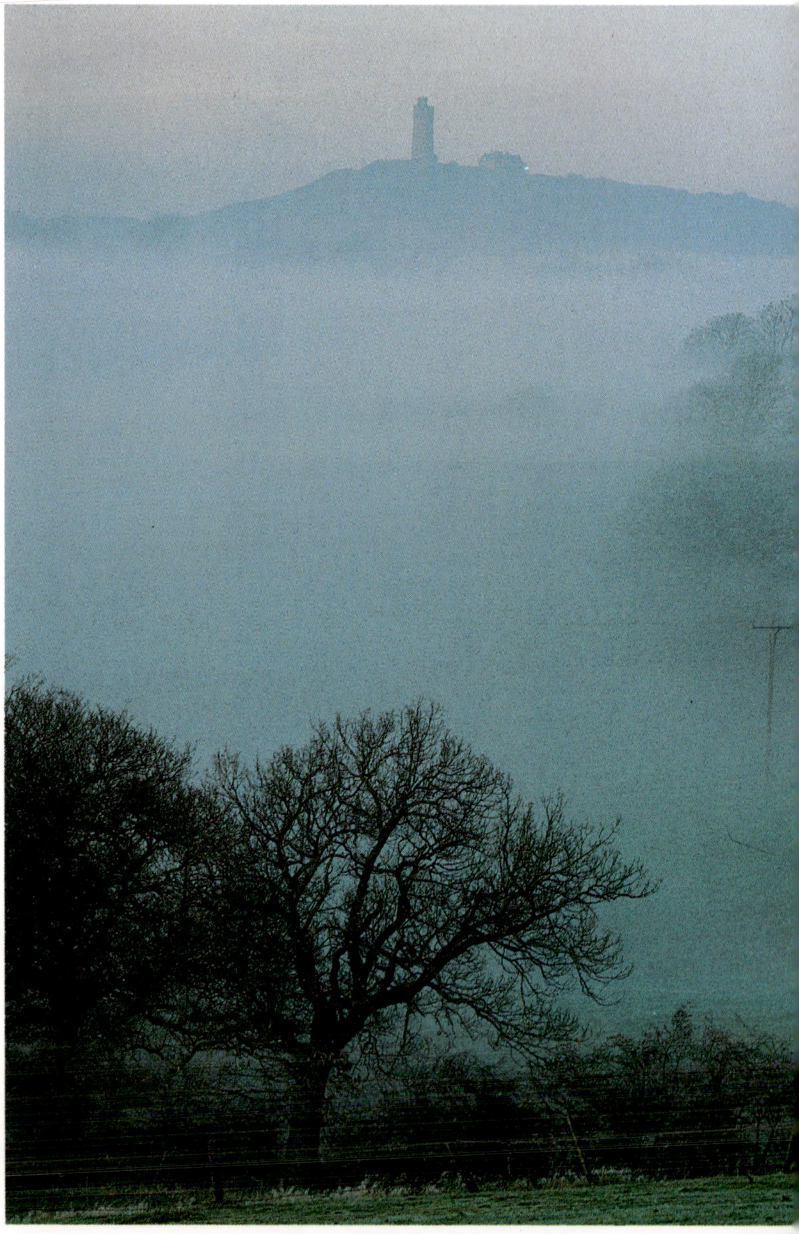

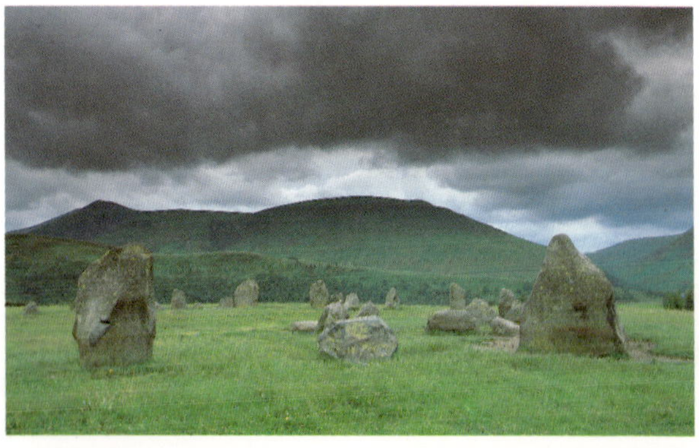

Some subjects are enhanced by introducing an element of drama. These mysterious-looking stones at Castlerigg in Cumbria have benefitted by darkening the sky using a graduated filter. The stones stand in relief to the background and convey a strong sense of depth.

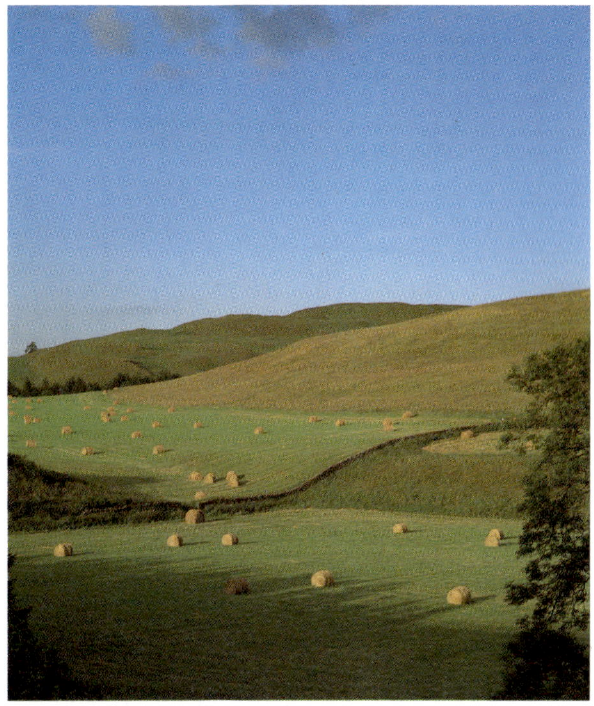

The neatly rolled bales of hay contrast with the rolling emptiness of the countryside; often, you can get good pictures by showing how the farmer must both co-operate with the countryside and seek to impose his will upon it.

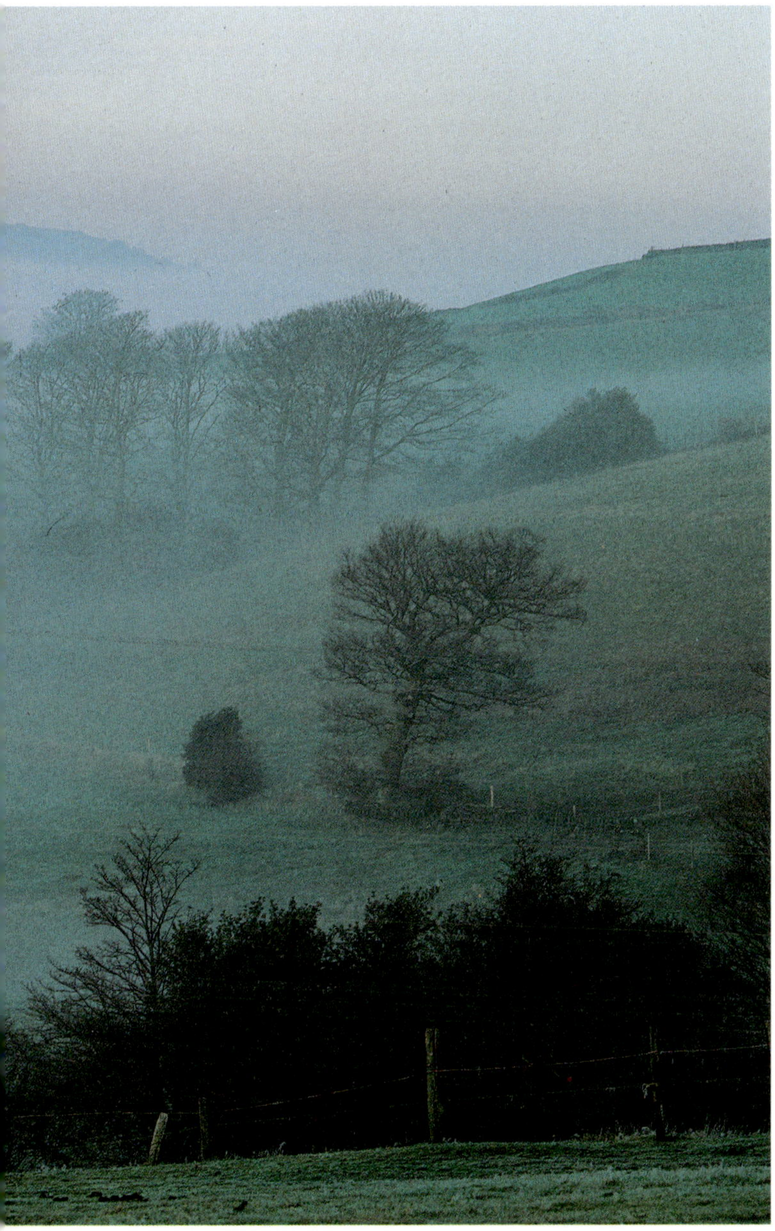

The sea of mist draws the eye towards the Jubilee Tower in this beautiful picture. The luring lines and areas of balance are strong enough to make the photograph successful, although it ignores the Rules of Thirds. Imagine how different the mood of the picture would be on a clear, sunny day or by using a vertical format.

Skies are important in landscapes, too, and some people use 'effects' filters to add interest if they are dull and flat, but the most effective skies are usually natural blue ones, preferably with fluffy white clouds. If the sky is white and overcast, your chances of obtaining a good picture are seriously curtailed. On a related point, though, you should always try to ensure that the horizon is *not* dead in the middle of the picture; by including (say) two-thirds sky and only one-third landscape, you can convey a feeling of openness, while by including two-thirds landscape and one-third sky you can minimise the effect of a dull day.

Finally, the *size* of a landscape photograph is often important, and perhaps more than any other kind of picture, landscapes benefit from being 'blown up' to 10 × 8″ (20 × 25cm) or larger. It is true that enlarging a small boring picture often does nothing more than give you a big boring picture, but with landscapes you may have some pleasant surprises, because the big picture is closer to what you remember. There is more about this on pages 78 and 79.

Rural Scenes

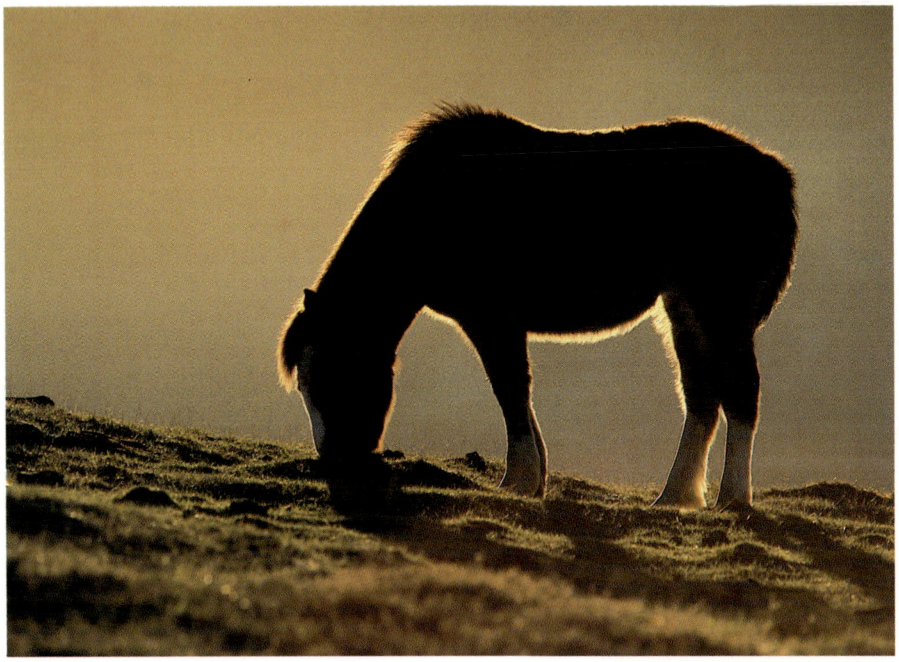

Ordinary subjects often benefit from backlighting, as seen here with this Welsh mountain pony captured in dawn light. Consider the application of this technique to other rural subjects, especially those that have well-defined silhouettes.

We all have in our minds a vision of the British countryside, and in that vision we include villages (which are covered on pages 68 and 69), farms (pages 72 and 73), and a whole collection of individual images: thatched or stone-roofed cottages, country inns, the hunt, or just walking with the dog. All of these images are actually surprisingly difficult to capture, because we have such a clear picture in our mind's eye that the reality never quite matches up to it.

With cottages, it is generally best to take the picture when the sun is shining on the front of the building, or it will look dull and cold and the sky will be washed out. Try to include the foreground if it is an attractive garden (as it so often is), but watch out for garden walls: a picture in which the bottom third is made up of roadway and blank garden wall is unlikely to look attractive. Walk up to the wall and shoot over it if you can, but remember that you are photographing somebody's house, and ask yourself how you would feel if someone were peering at you like a goldfish in a bowl.

Inns are more difficult, at least in England, because English licensing hours mean that when the light is best they are usually locked and deserted. Photographers in Scotland, where pub hours are more flexible, may be luckier! At lunchtime, the sun may be too high in the sky for a good picture, so the best bet may be on a summer's evening,when the lights are on but there is still enough light in the sky to get a good picture; if you are lucky, you may also have the low, slanting red rays of the evening sun.

Finally, if you want a good picture of someone walking his dog, you are almost certainly going to have to stage it. Either take your dog (and walker) with you, or wait in a likely place until someone comes along, and ask him if he would mind walking just *here*, so that you can get the picture you want. The promise of a print is only common courtesy! It may come as a disappointment to you, but many of the pictures you see in magazines and brochures are actually staged, with carefully chosen professional models. On the positive side, the very best pictures are normally the ones that happen by accident!

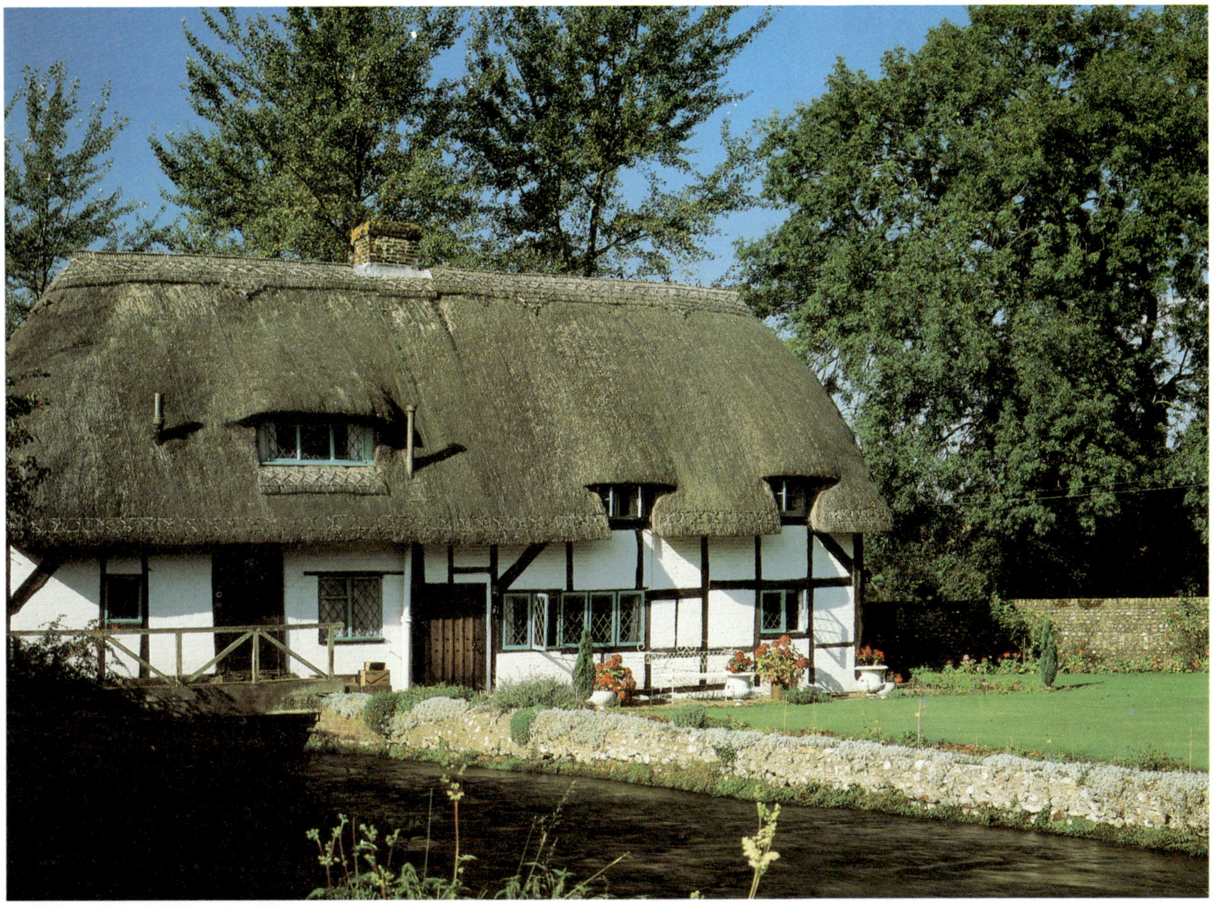

This picture of a scenic old mill is what most of us visualise when we think of 'rural scenes'. One of Britain's great charms is its intimacy: unlike (say) Arizona's Grand Canyon, or New York State's Niagara Falls, everything is on a very human scale - the result of centuries of peaceful rural living.

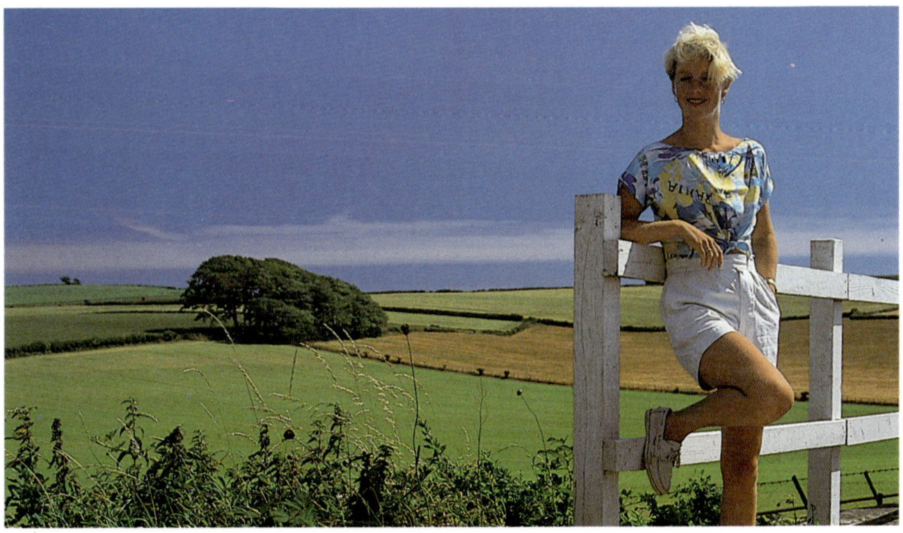

The countryside is a marvellous place for portraits — providing a limitless variety of settings. Combining 'portraiture' with 'landscape' can be a problem, usually because the photographer can't choose whether to give preference to the person or the scenery. However, with a little care and awareness of balance, there are great successes to be had.

Gardens

Like landscapes, gardens are deceptively difficult to photograph. The usual reason is that even in a garden which is a riot of colour, there is still a great deal of green grass and brown earth, and unless you are very careful, these are the two colours which will dominate the picture.

The easiest ways around this problem are either to concentrate on a single flower or bush, or to fill the foreground with a flower-bed that is absolutely packed with flowers: if you look at professionals' pictures, you will see that they often do the latter, but they normally use either a wide-angle lens to emphasise the foreground (which you can do if you have a focusing 35mm compact camera with a 35mm or 38mm lens), or a telephoto and a low viewpoint. This 'stacks' the perspective, and makes the blooms look closer together than they are. This 'stacking' or 'compressing' effect is characteristic of telephotos; the reason why the wickets seem to be only a few feet apart when we see televised cricket is because the TV camera is fitted with a long-focus lens.

A useful alternative to either method is to concentrate on an *architectural* feature rather than a horticultural one: a gate, a wishing-well, or a pond provides a principal subject on which to 'hang' the picture, after which the eye can roam around as if it were reading a book, drinking in the details.

For this sort of photography, you should not expect too much from disk or 110 cameras, as much of the attraction of a garden lies in the contrast of textures - the crew-cut lawn, the delicacy of the flowers, the roughness of bark, and so forth - and the very small negatives of these cameras simply cannot render this sort of fine detail with the sort of fidelity that is needed. Many professionals use rollfilm or even 5 × 4″ cameras in order to get the kind of detail that you really need.

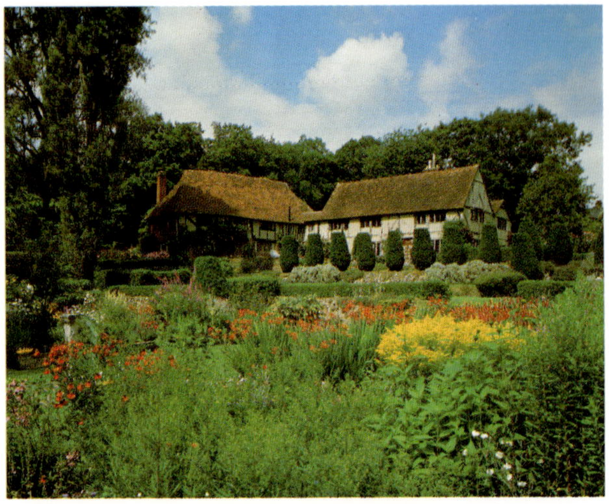

Two very different approaches to photographing a garden: one highly detailed (above), the other very impressionistic (below). Both are beautiful pictures, but different gardens and different photographers demand different treatments.

Experiment both with deep focus (stopping the lens down to f/16 - see page 118) and with selective focus, using the lens 'wide open' and letting everything in front of and behind the main subject go out of focus.

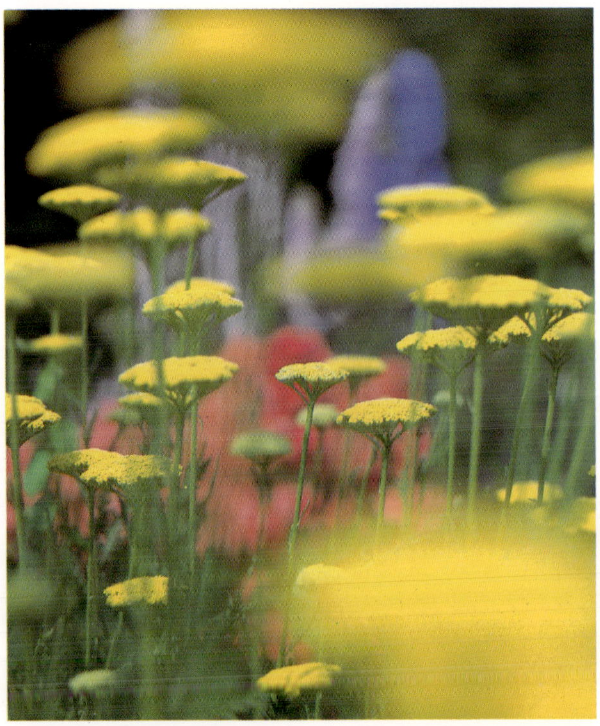

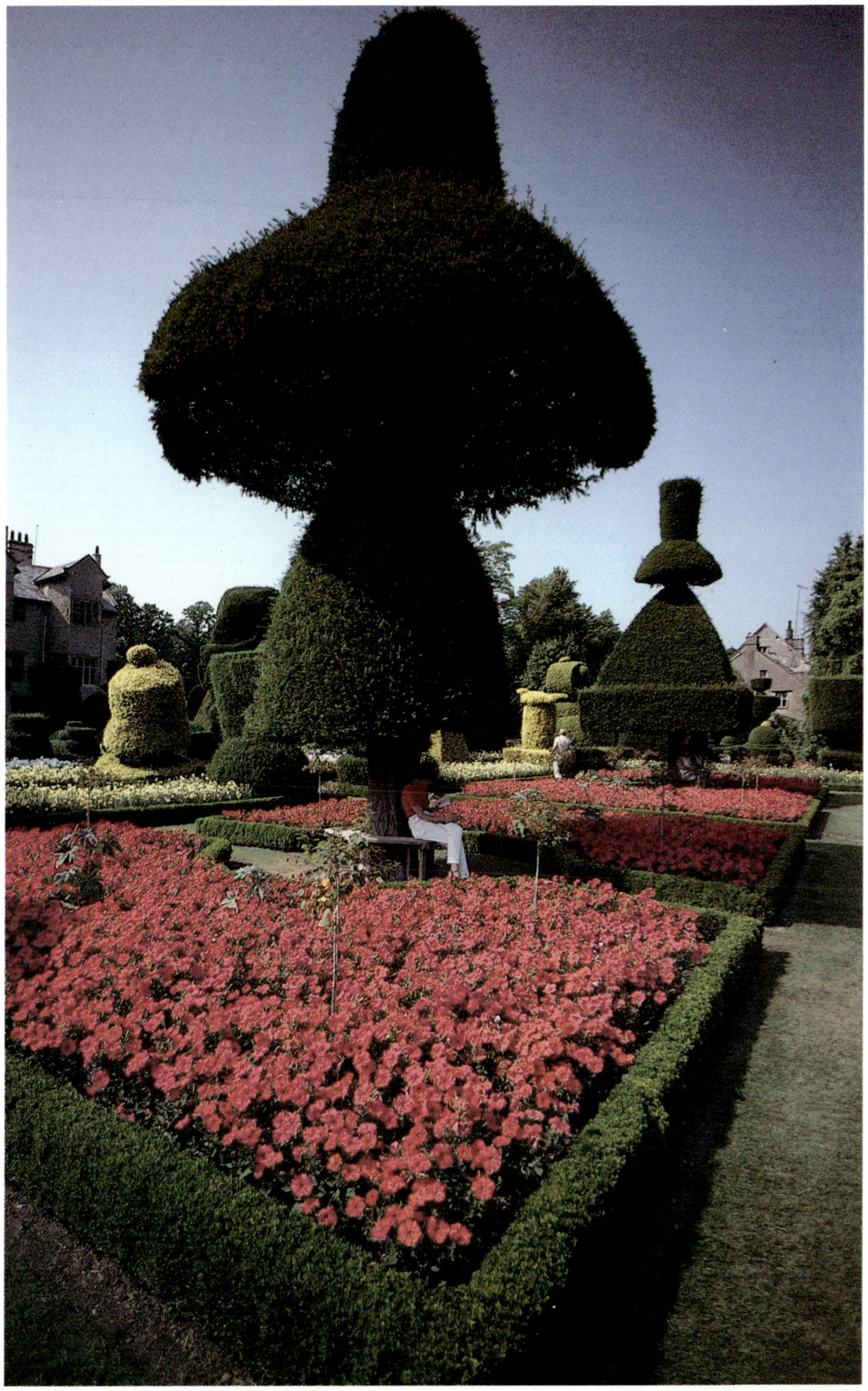

Unusual characteristics of a garden make an excellent focal point to a picture. Here the topiary at Levens Hall, Cumbria, captures the spirit of the garden and introduces strong perspective associated with a wide-angle lens. Where great detail is required and the keynote is sharpness, you will find that the simpler cameras such as disc and 110, cannot deliver this sort of quality.

Villages

Much of what was said about individual cottages also applies to villages, with the additional difficulty that the twentieth century is more and more obtrusive. Cars are likely to be parked in a way which obscures (or at least interferes with) many of the more attractive views, and the only easy way to get around this is to be up very early in the morning, before anyone else. Once again, this is one of the ways in which professionals work to make their pictures different from amateur views: being a professional holiday photographer is *not* like being on an extended holiday!

Often, you will need to frame your pictures carefully so that (for example) you can show the Tudor simplicity of one building without the glass-and-plastic frontage of the modernised newsagent next door. Similarly, moving a few feet up or down the road can enable you to lose the 'NO PARKING' sign which would otherwise be so prominent, while choosing a very oblique angle can help you to emphasise the foreground and diminish the importance of the background - and, if you are lucky, you can use the boughs of an overhanging tree to conceal the television aerials which grace so many thatched cottages. If there is traffic between you and your subject, always wait until it is clear before you take your picture.

Try to get a fair mixture of general shots and details. The village green with the church and pub, or a cobbled back-street full of historic houses may be the obvious subjects, but do not neglect Victorian shop-signs and store-fronts, Georgian milestones, old street signs, and village pumps: they are all becoming increasingly rare, and if you do not photograph them while you have the chance, the next time you see them may be in a museum.

Last of all, remember that a village *has* to come into the twentieth century if it is to survive. It is all very well to bemoan the TV aerials and the telephone lines, but these are living communities, not museums.

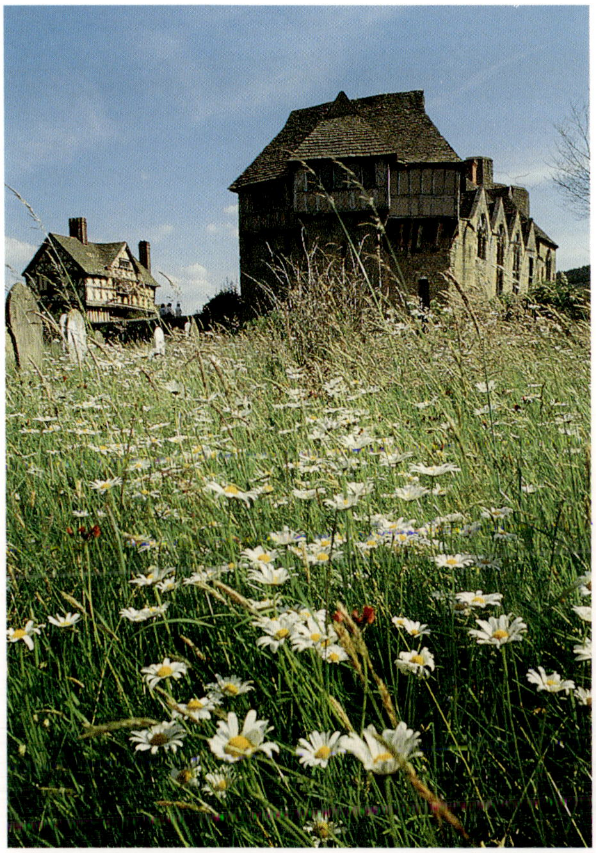

As with many other pictures in this book, we see here the principle that 'less is more'. By concentrating on the wildflowers in a village churchyard, and only hinting at the rest of the village, this photograph conveys the lazy buzz of bees on a summer's day.

Village stocks and a village character... The past and the present coexist in villages, from the days when the stocks were used to ensure conformity of behaviour to the days when unconventional dress and rugged individualism is not just the prerogative of the young. By visiting a village repeatedly, you can learn a little more about it each time, until you are accepted almost as one of the locals. Then you are in an even better position to take candid pictures.

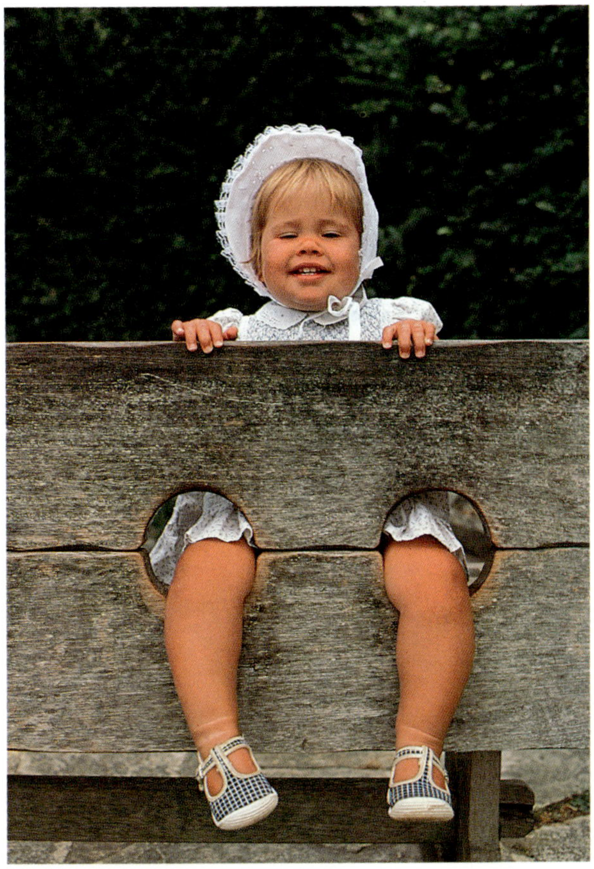

This is not strictly a village, but a farm. On the other hand, a traditional farm is almost a hamlet in its own right, and its collection of buildings, assembled over the years, can make it just as visually interesting as a village. This is at Clyst St. George, in Devon.

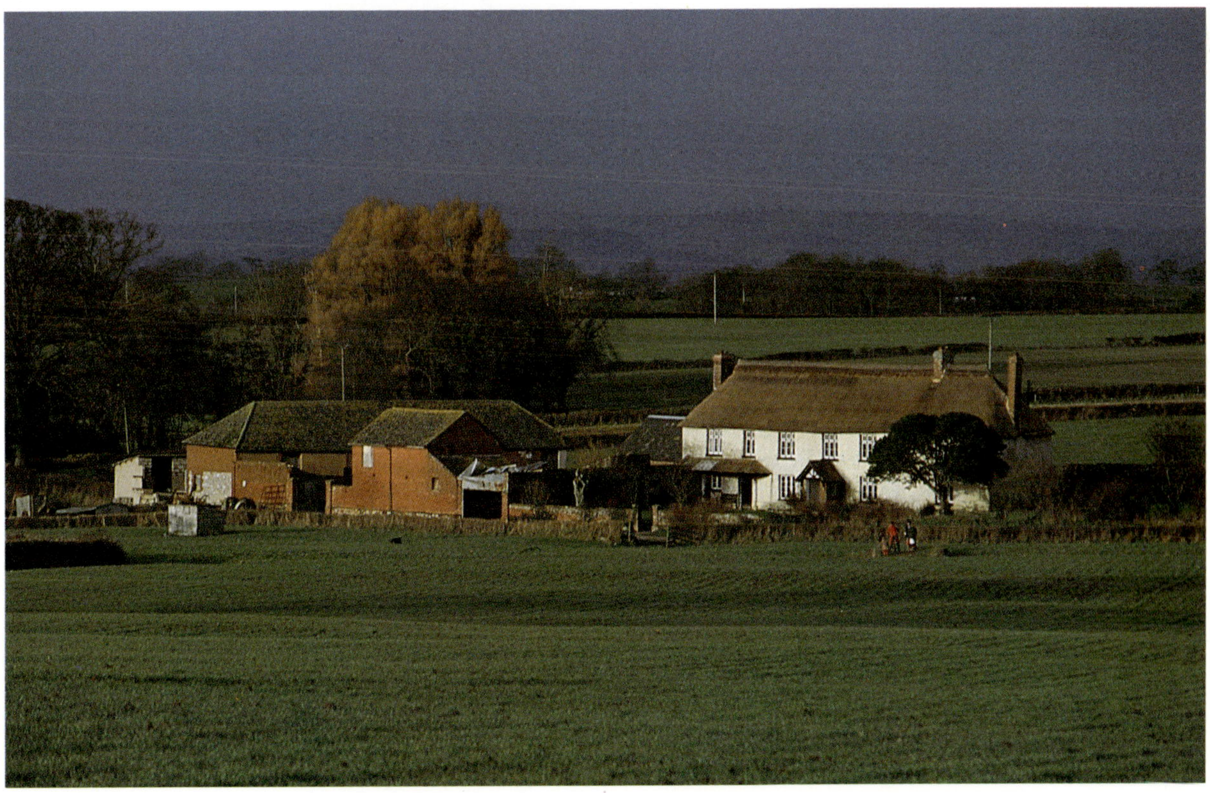

Crafts, Customs & Traditions

One of the attractions of the countryside is the way in which the past is preserved, not as if in a museum, but as a living tradition. The old crafts are often preserved because there is no modern alternative, or at least, no modern alternative which is as good, and the old customs are retained because the rhythm of life in the country is necessarily more seasonal and unchanging than it is in the city.

Among the old crafts, you should be able to find *thatching*, which (for obvious reasons) is normally done in the summer; *blacksmithing* and *farriery*, though much of a blacksmith's work is now concerned with ornamental rather than functional ironwork; *cider-making;* and even *coopering*, or barrel-making. With all of these, the golden rules are first, to *stay out of the way*, and secondly, to *try and show something significant.* The first is obvious: even on a guided tour, where the craftsman is aware of the camera, he still has to concentrate on what he is doing. Distracting him could result in spoiled work or even in injury to him or to you. For the same reason, use flash as little as possible, and always ask permission first. The second point, about showing something significant, is a bit more difficult, but what you need to aim for is a picture which is self-explanatory, and needs no caption.

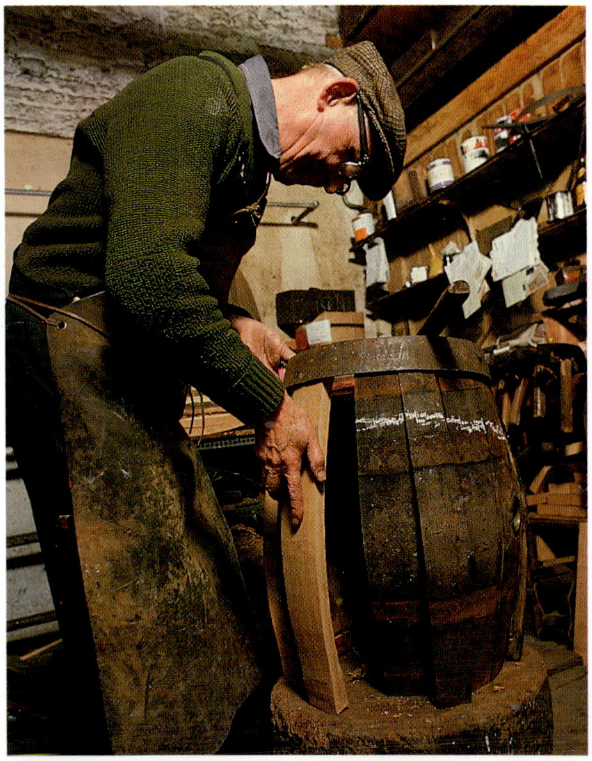

In some places they call it coopering, in others cooperage, but the craft of the cooper (barrel-maker) is still in demand. Here, a new stave is being fitted to an old barrel - an image of the continuity of rural life itself.

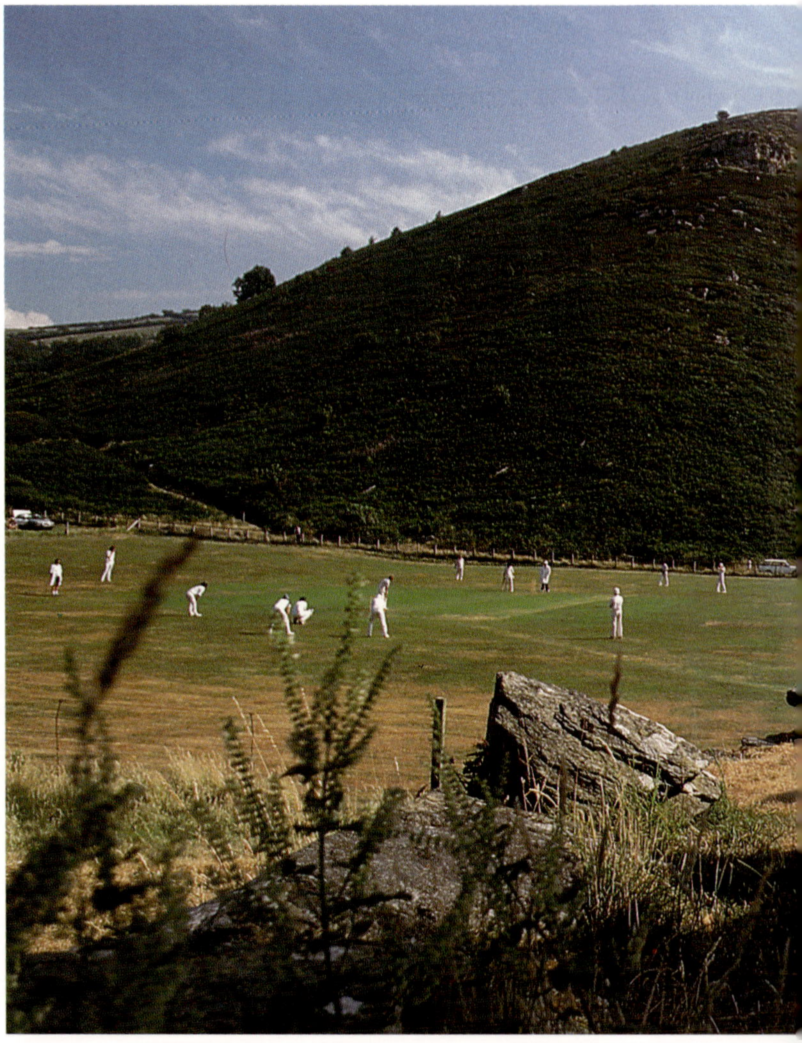

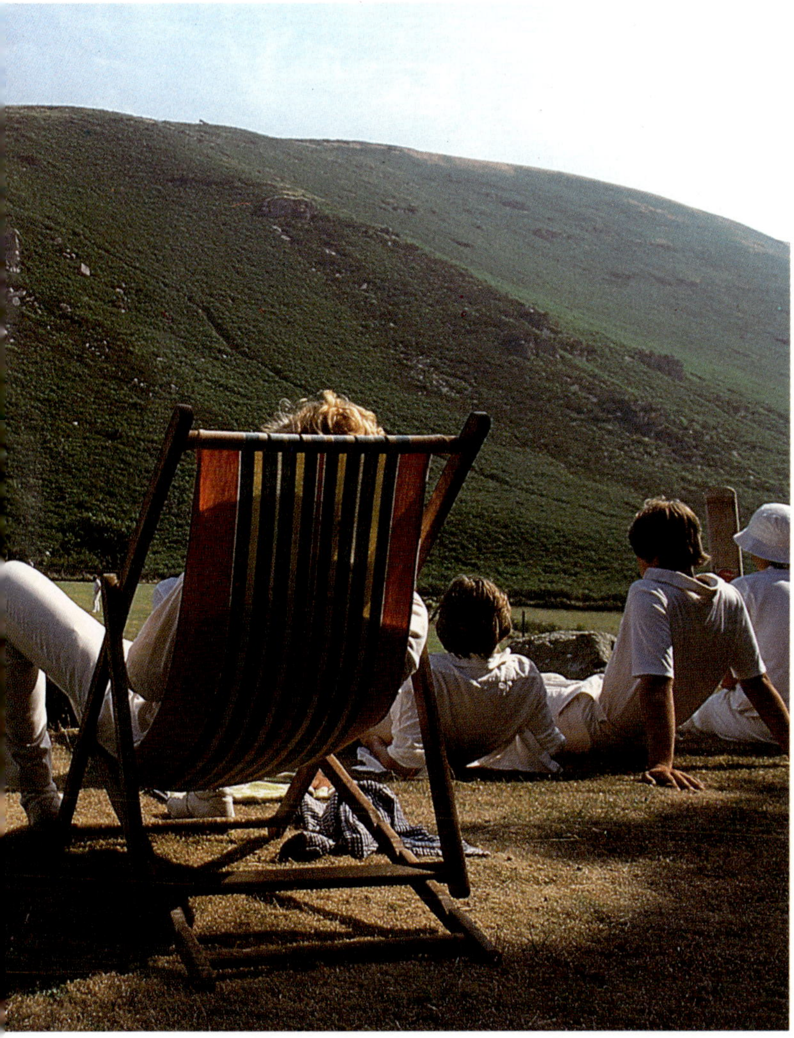

You don't have to be playing to enjoy a village cricket match! By filling the foreground with the spectator in his deck-chair and showing only enough of the game to make it clear what is going on, the photographer has again managed to use the 'less is more' technique to convey the spirit of a Sunday afternoon game.

For example, a cooper shaping a stave could be almost anyone doing almost anything to a piece of wood, but a cooper assembling a barrel and hammering the iron hoops into position is unmistakable. Likewise, a cider press should show the apples, or it may not be clear what is being pressed.

The old customs vary greatly from place to place, but morris dancing and other forms of folk dance are widespread, and there are many local customs such as well-dressing and swan-upping which blend the antique and picturesque with the modern (especially in the dress of the participants!) in an intriguing way. Regional tourist boards and tourist offices can often advise you of local customs and events, and you may well find that there are some surprisingly close to you, which you never knew about! Once again, the important thing is to show something clearly happening, preferably without intervening spectators, because it is all too easy to show a group of people standing around apparently doing nothing. You may have to worm your way to the front of the crowd, or to climb on a pillar-box or a wall, in order to get a better viewpoint. Ideally, of course, you should arrive early in order to get the best position.

Down on the Farm

Farming is a business like any other, but fortunately for the photographer (and perhaps unfortunately for the farmer) it can also be a very picturesque business. To get the best farm pictures, you must be aware of three things: first, the nature of farm routine, second, the need to keep out of the way, and third, the potential dangers of farm life.

The last is the easiest to appreciate. Modern farming machinery can pull an arm off as easily as it bales hay or harvests corn. You would not expect to walk around a factory with impunity: a farm can be just as dangerous.

The same applies to keeping out of the way. It is not just the risk which you could present to yourself, or to farm workers; it is the damage you can do to crops and livestock. Cornfields are wonderful places to walk, but if you trample the corn you are destroying what the farmer has worked hard to grow, and you cannot expect to be welcomed. Similarly, leave your dog at home: sheep can literally be scared to death by dogs, or chased over a drop where they can break a leg, even if the dog never touches them.

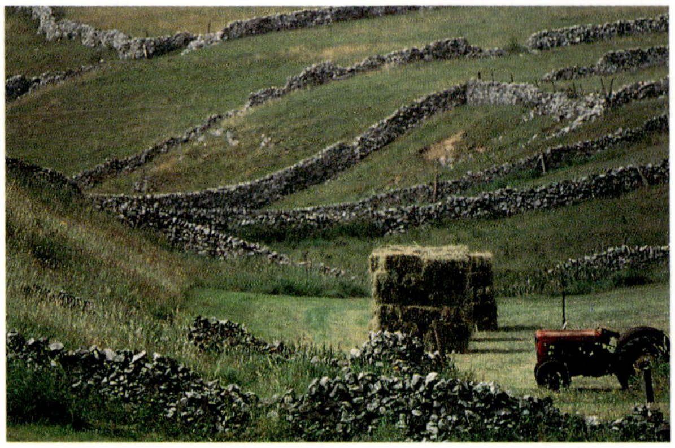

In this picture, the graphic element comes from the drystone walls. At first sight, the tractor is almost an intrusion, but it provides a focal point for the picture; without it, your eye tends to wander aimlessly.

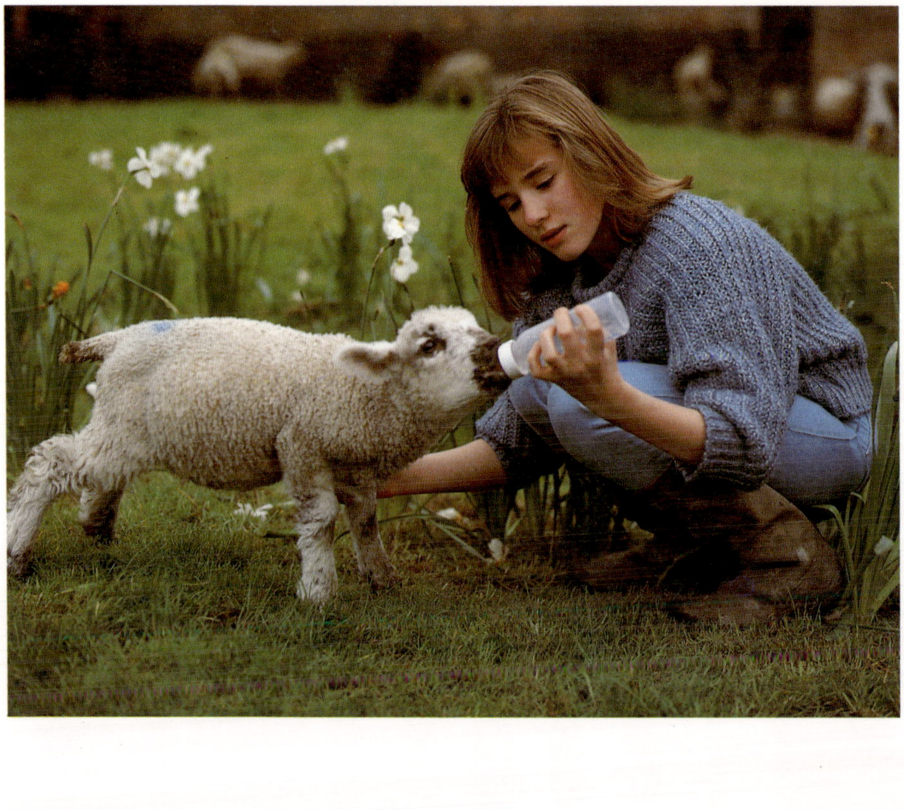

According to the old actors' adage, children and animals always steal the show. While this may be a disaster if you do not want to be upstaged, it is a delight for the photographer. A number of farms, particularly those offering farm holidays, have special areas where young children and young animals can get together.

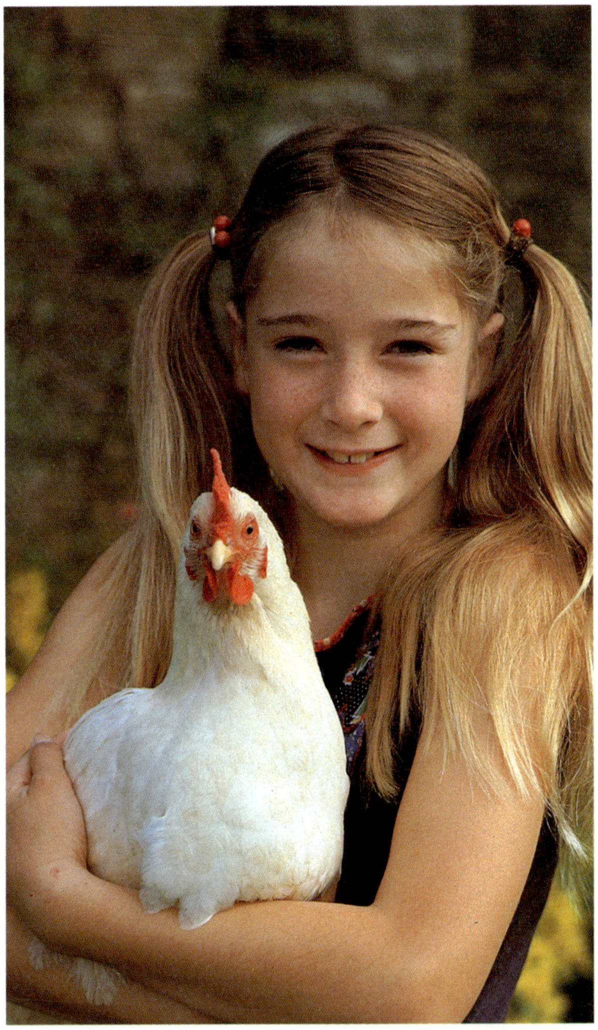

If you bear all this in mind, though, you should be able to get some first-class pictures. Stick to the paths - they are usually clearly marked - and stay on the far side of the wall from a field in which someone is working, and you can photograph the whole agricultural cycle from sowing to harvesting, often with the great machines looking very majestic as they roll across the fields. Wait until the machine fills just the right proportion of the frame (they often look particularly good as they are turning) and press the button. If you can find an 'organic' or 'traditional' farm, where ploughing is still done with horses and no chemicals are used, you can photograph farming from yet another perspective.

With farmyard animals, waiting until they are all in the right position can be very time-consuming, but it is worth it: cows are fairly curious creatures, and will come over to look at you sooner or later, but the highly intelligent pig will soon rush over to find out what is going on. With any animals, it is usually best to try to photograph several together, as photographing one animal close-up usually leads to an awkward distortion in which the head is disproportionately large. Professional livestock photographers often use lenses of slightly longer than normal focal length, just as portrait photographers do (see pages 120-121); a zoom can be very handy here.

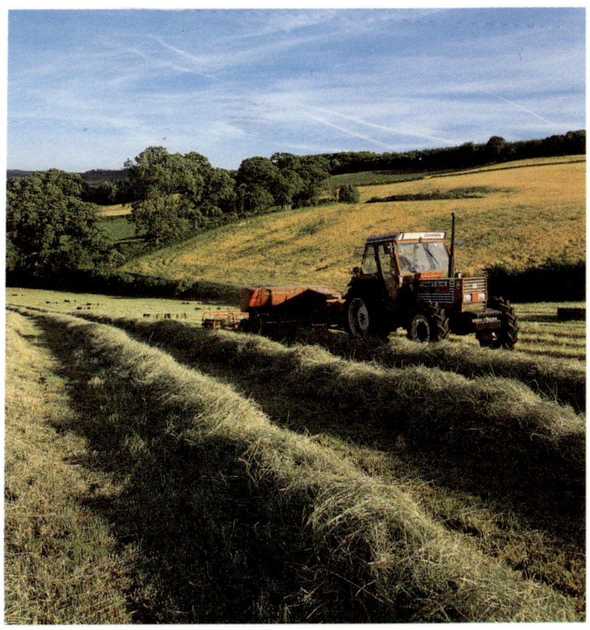

Mechanical balers are fascinating things to watch, and the graphic possibilities of the unbaled hay lying in rows are not to be ignored.

History all Around

The British Isles have been inhabited for many thousands of years, and almost all of the successive waves of immigrants and invaders have left their mark. Among prehistoric remains, Stonehenge is undoubtedly the best-known, but there are countless other standing stones, earth forts, grave-barrows and tumuli all over the country. The best guide to these (and a useful tool for any traveller in the British Isles) is the Ordnance Survey series of maps: the 'quarter-inch' (to the mile) series is adequate, but the 1:50,000 series (about an inch and a quarter to the mile, the successors to the old 'one inch' maps) is wonderful. Each map provides as much reading material as a short novel, and shows the half-forgotten paths which lead to the places where no-one goes any more.

Moving up through history, there are Roman ruins all over the place; Celtic crosses, especially on Dartmoor; Norman castles, cathedrals, and churches; mediaeval houses and buildings of all kinds; a scattering of Renaissance architecture; plenty of Elizabethan and Tudor buildings; a great deal from the Age of Reason, with Palladian mansions, and Georgian Bath, acknowledged as one of the finest eighteenth-century cities in the world; relics of the Industrial Revolution, including canals, factories and industrial buildings of all kinds; a great deal from the supremely self-confident Victorian age; and much from more recent history, such as Art Deco or eccentricities like a World War I tank preserved as a war memorial at Ashford in Kent.

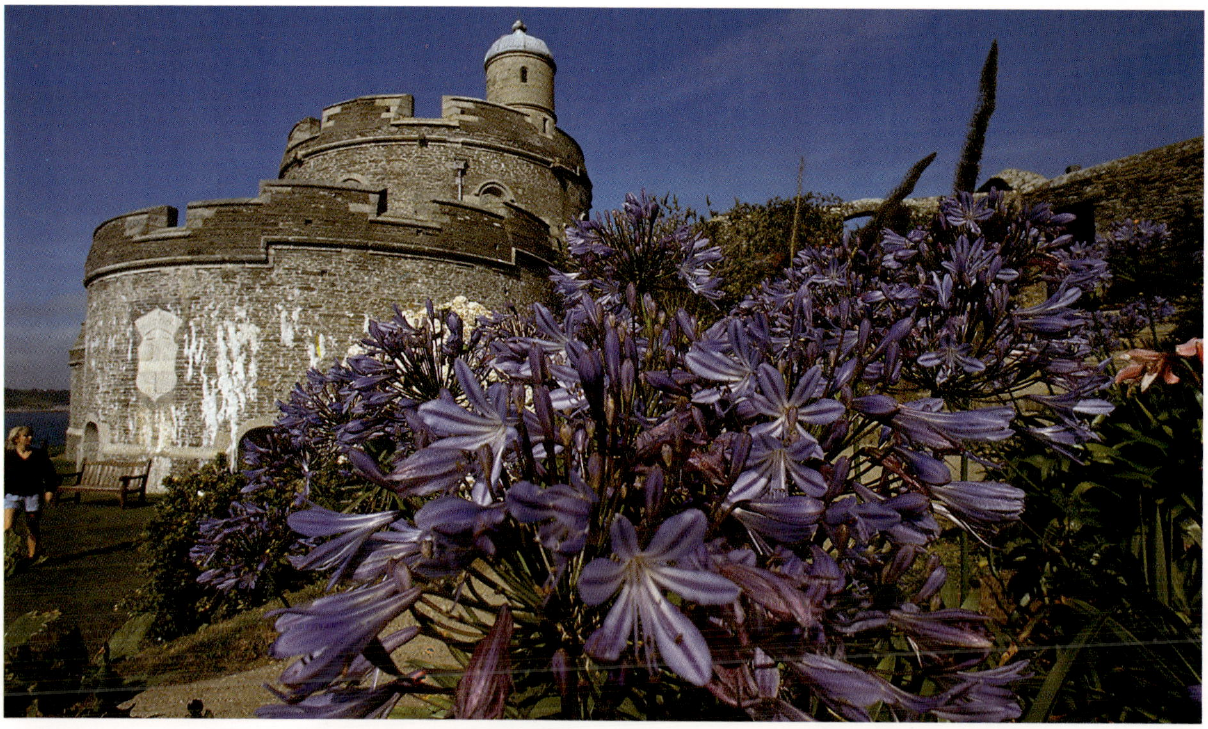

One of the most delightful things about Britain is the casual attitude towards history. Much that would be roped off, or festooned with 'DO NOT TOUCH' signs in other countries, is freely accessible to the wanderer. Castles like this at St Mawes, Cornwall - some of which date back to Norman times while others are comparative newcomers from the Napoleonic wars - abound in the British Isles.

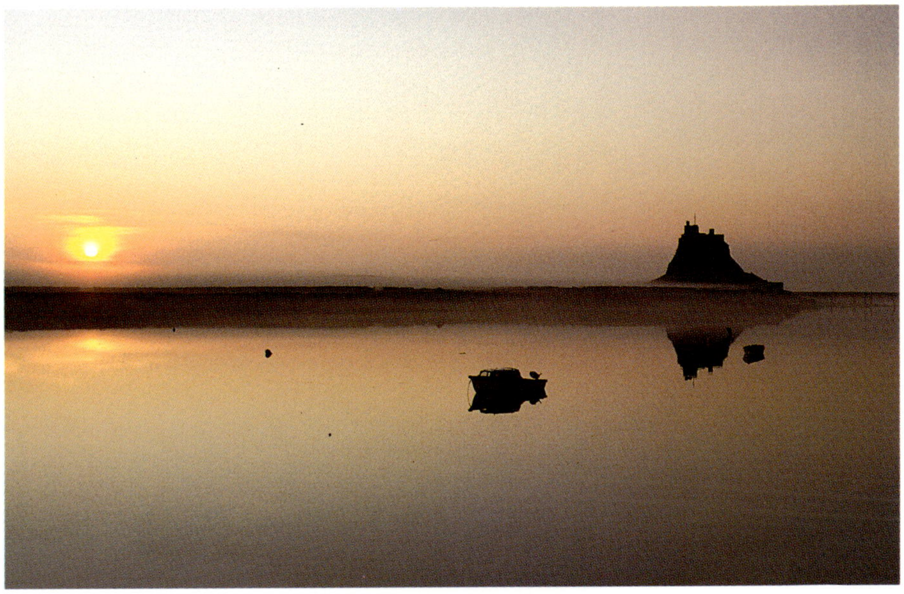

When you see Holy Island, you can see why the monks chose it. Physically remote, it has an aura of spirituality. The best pictures, like this one, capture the remoteness while still showing enough of the shape to make it clear where it is.

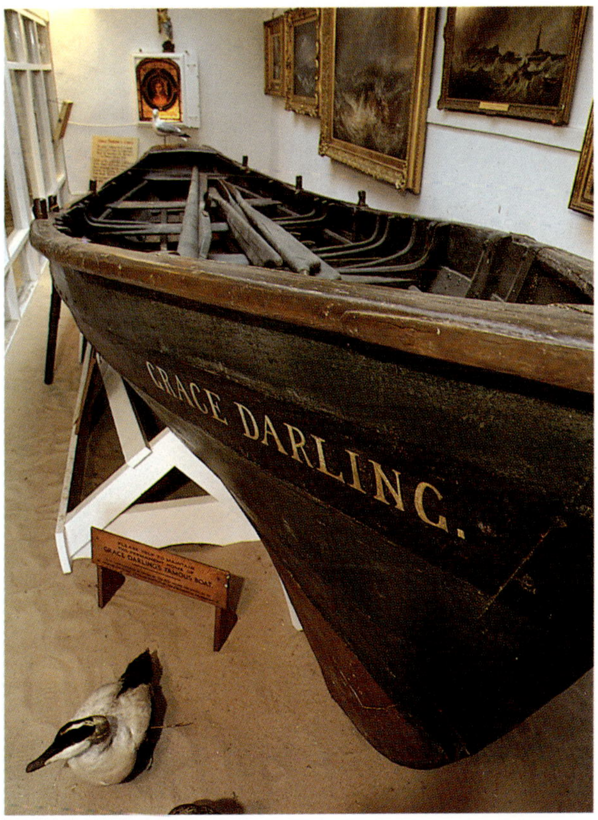

Add to this a tremendous range of memorabilia about famous people - their birthplaces, the houses where they lived and worked, and so forth - and you have an overwhelmingly rich field to explore. It is well worth considering joining the National Trust, and English Heritage, as membership gives you free access to all the properties run by these two organisations that are open to the public.

The general rules for photography are much the same as those described earlier, with two additional reminders. First, always try to get the sun shining on the subject, rather than from behind it, as this will give better modelling and a much cheerier appearance. Second, do not neglect details; a well-chosen detail can tell you as much as a considerably broader shot, and often conveys the past with more immediacy than a general view.

A good eye for the 'graphic image' shows here. The photographer leads the viewer into the frame by taking advantage of the sweeping lines of the boat. The success of this type of picture lies with the ability of the photographer to be selective and to concentrate on shape and form. Uncluttered simplicity has made this a very pleasing picture.

Castles & Palaces

The British countryside is fairly awash with castles and palaces, from sumptuous mansions still lived in by those whose ancestors built them, through magnificent properties owned by the National Trust, to majestic ruins from the days of the Normans, the Marcher Lords, the feuding Scottish clans, and everyone else who fought and built their homes in Britain.

The techniques for photographing exteriors and interiors are very different. The exteriors are usually easier, but the way to get a really good picture is to make sure that the sun is striking the side you want, preferably at a slanting angle, so that it throws into relief the shapes of the building and the textures of the stones; as an additional bonus, the sky is at its deepest blue behind the building when the light is at this angle.

Another way to photograph exteriors is in silhouette, especially if you can include a sunset or even the sun itself behind the building. You can do this by *underexposing* the film severely; the building will become a black outline, but the sky will be afire with colour. If you are not sure how to underexpose with your camera, you can do it by *increasing* the film speed on the film speed setting dial by a factor of two or three times: set 200 or 300, or even 400 if you are using 100-speed film, but do not forget to set it back again afterwards!

Inside pictures are more of a problem. In some buildings flash is banned, but this rarely matters in any case: in huge baronial halls, or even medium-sized ones, the flash that is built into your camera is unlikely to be powerful enough to penetrate the gloom. If flash is banned, and if your camera allows long automatic exposures, your best bet is to try to find somewhere you can lean against and support your camera, and try a long exposure without flash. Often, two or three seconds will be enough, and it is surprising how steadily you can hold a camera if your elbows are resting on a table, or if you are leaning against a door frame. Even so, it is best to take two or three exposures, just in case one of them is spoiled by camera shake.

Where flash is permitted, you will usually do best to concentrate on a detail - a particular piece of furniture, a corner of a room, or whatever - and let the rest of the picture fade off into a romantic gloom. If a professional needed to light a big room, he would use several flashguns (or floodlights), mounted off the camera, to create as even a light as possible; he might also take the picture in the early evening, when the fading blue light outside the windows would not cause them to 'burn in' as they would in a daylight shot. And of course, he would use a tripod, probably with a very wide-angle lens - and this is one of the places when you realise that there is a limit to what you can do with a simple camera!

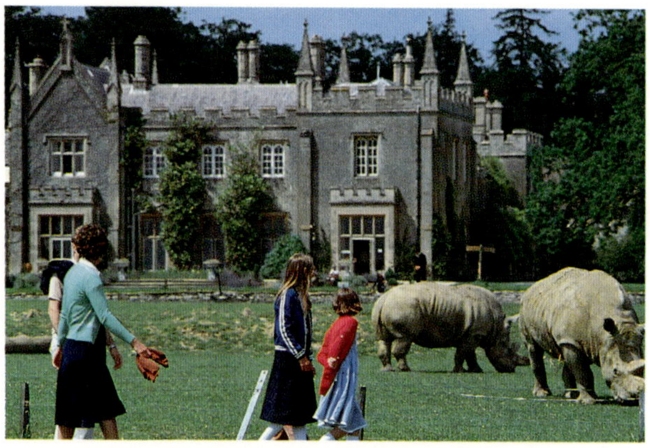

In Italy, Longleat would qualify as a palace, but in England, it is just a 'house'. What makes it particularly fascinating, of course, is the surrounding 'safari park' where rhinoceros, elephants, lions and many other exotic animals roam freely.

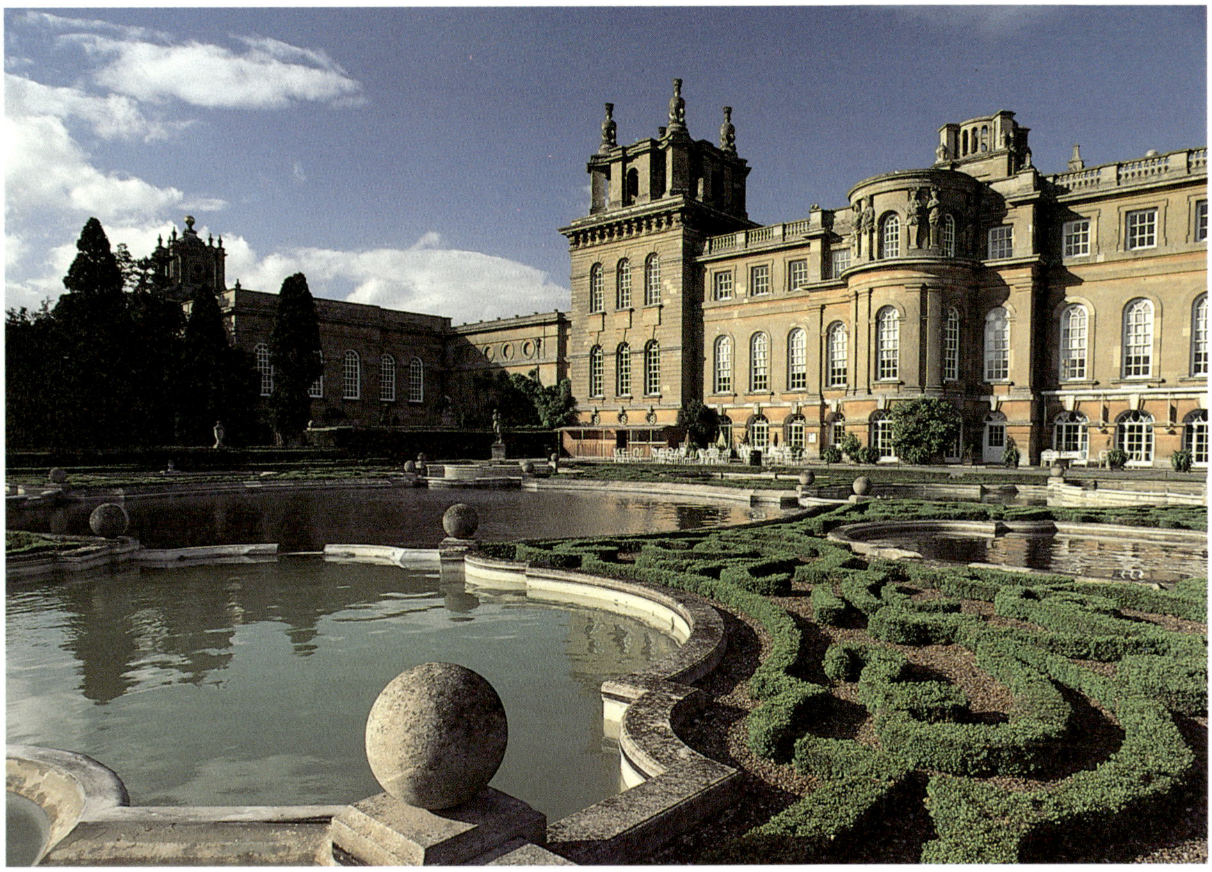

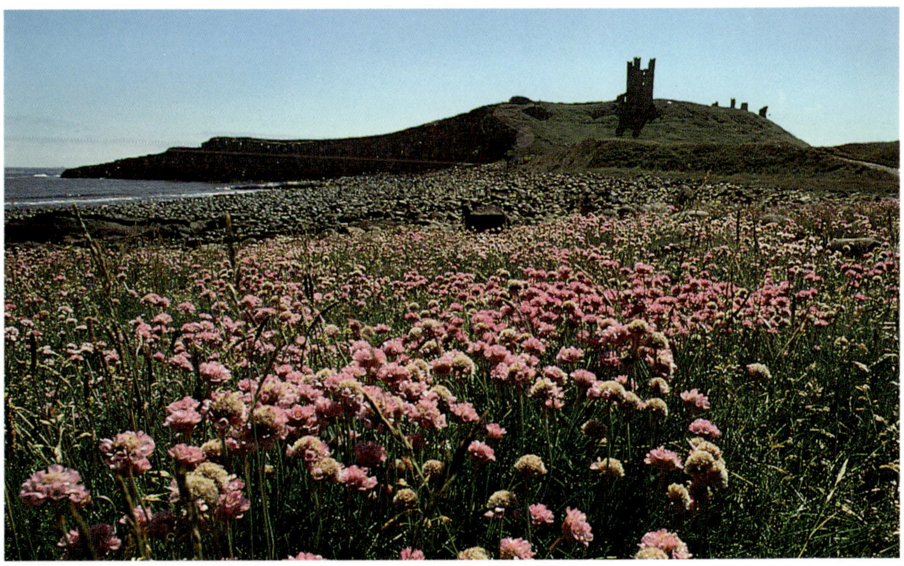

Britain offers a unique selection of historic buildings. Blenheim Palace (above) is one of the most picturesque, providing a multitude of interior and exterior photographic possibilities. Although wide-angle lenses are often the most suitable for this sort of photography, it is important to be aware that they can also create distortion.

Some castles are ruins, and some are lived in; but with the exception of the newer castles, built when there was no longer any need to fortify your home against your neighbours' attacks, most of them have magnificent settings on easily-defended land. Contrasting the warlike castle with the peaceful wildflowers that surround it has here resulted in a very attractive picture.

Getting Away from it All

Although we have looked mainly at 'attractions' in this chapter, there are many people whose idea of a holiday is getting away from everything and everybody, and being alone with nature.

The British Isles may be relatively small when compared with, say, the United States or even France, but there is still plenty of wild land - and because the vast majority of people live in the cities and towns, even cultivated rural land can be surprisingly free of people. Once again, Ordnance Survey maps are invaluable for finding those little-used paths, and for walking on the trackless parts of Dartmoor or the like. A word of warning here, though: a place like Dartmoor may not be very big when you are driving across it in a motor-car, but on a human scale it is more than big enough to get lost in. If you are going well off the beaten track, it is as well to go with a companion, and at the very least you should tell someone where you are going and when you intend to be back, so that they can raise the alarm if you do not return.

Most of the pictures which you will want to take will be landscapes, and the advice on pages 62 and 63 is relevant here. There may also be old cottages, farms, and ruins, in which case the other sections of this chapter are also relevant. For wildlife photography, you really need specialised equipment, including long-focus lenses, as well as a knowledge of the animals you want to photograph: most are very wary of man. Generally, though, it is important not to overburden yourself with equipment - you see some photographers staggering like pack-horses under the weight of their gadget bags - and to carry at least a bar of chocolate, and preferably something to drink as well. Even experienced walkers need supplies, and for the majority of us who are not accustomed to walking, rest and fuel are vital.

As with any landscape, the scale of the final picture may be critical. A part of the attraction of 'getting away from it all' is the sense of scale and openness which the wild places bring, and this simply cannot be conveyed in a tiny enprint. Consider a 10×8" (20×25cm) enlargement of your better shots, or even a poster-type blow-up: several companies offer something like a 20×30" (50×75cm) blow-up at a very reasonable price, and a picture this size can be a source of peace and inspiration long after the holiday itself is over.

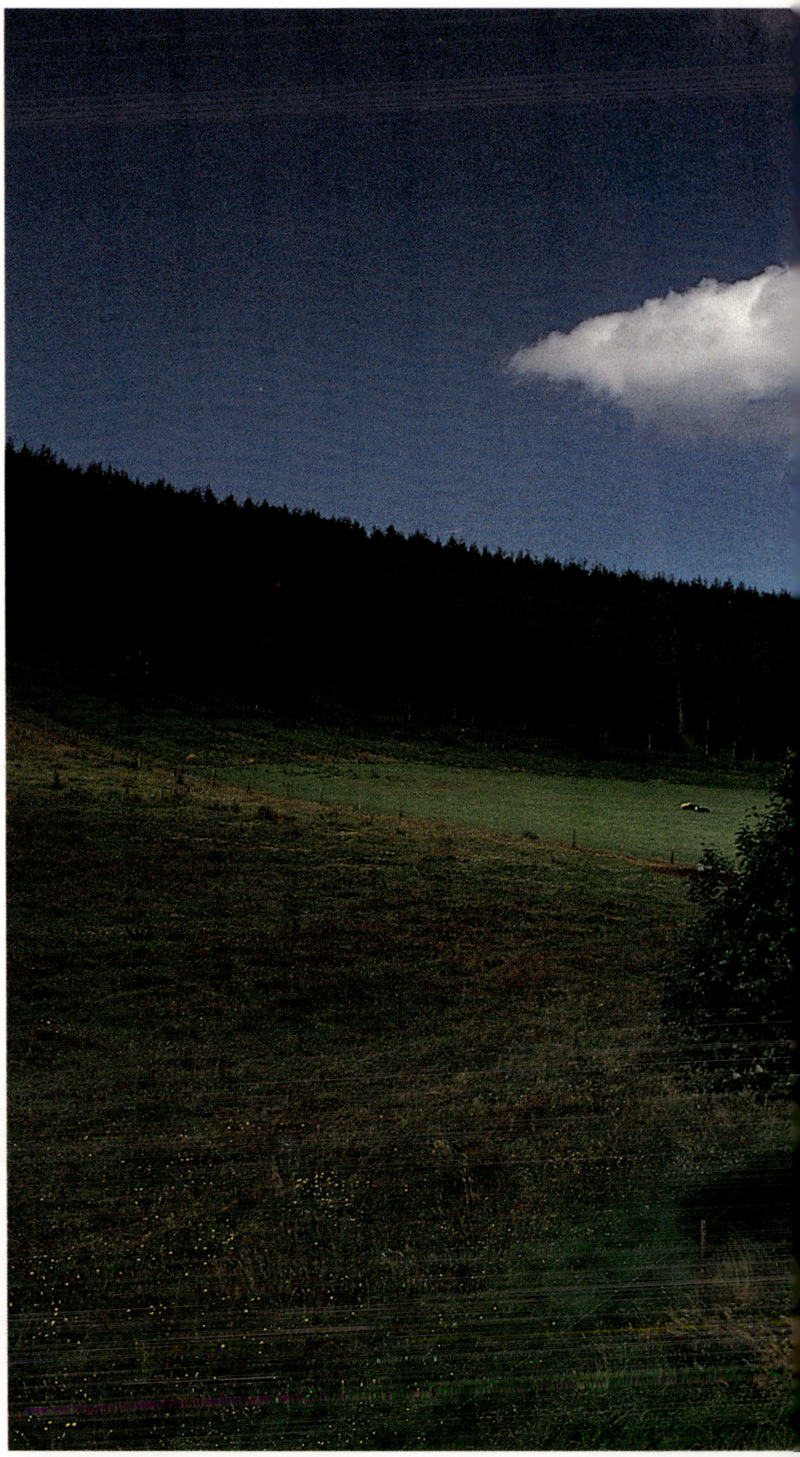

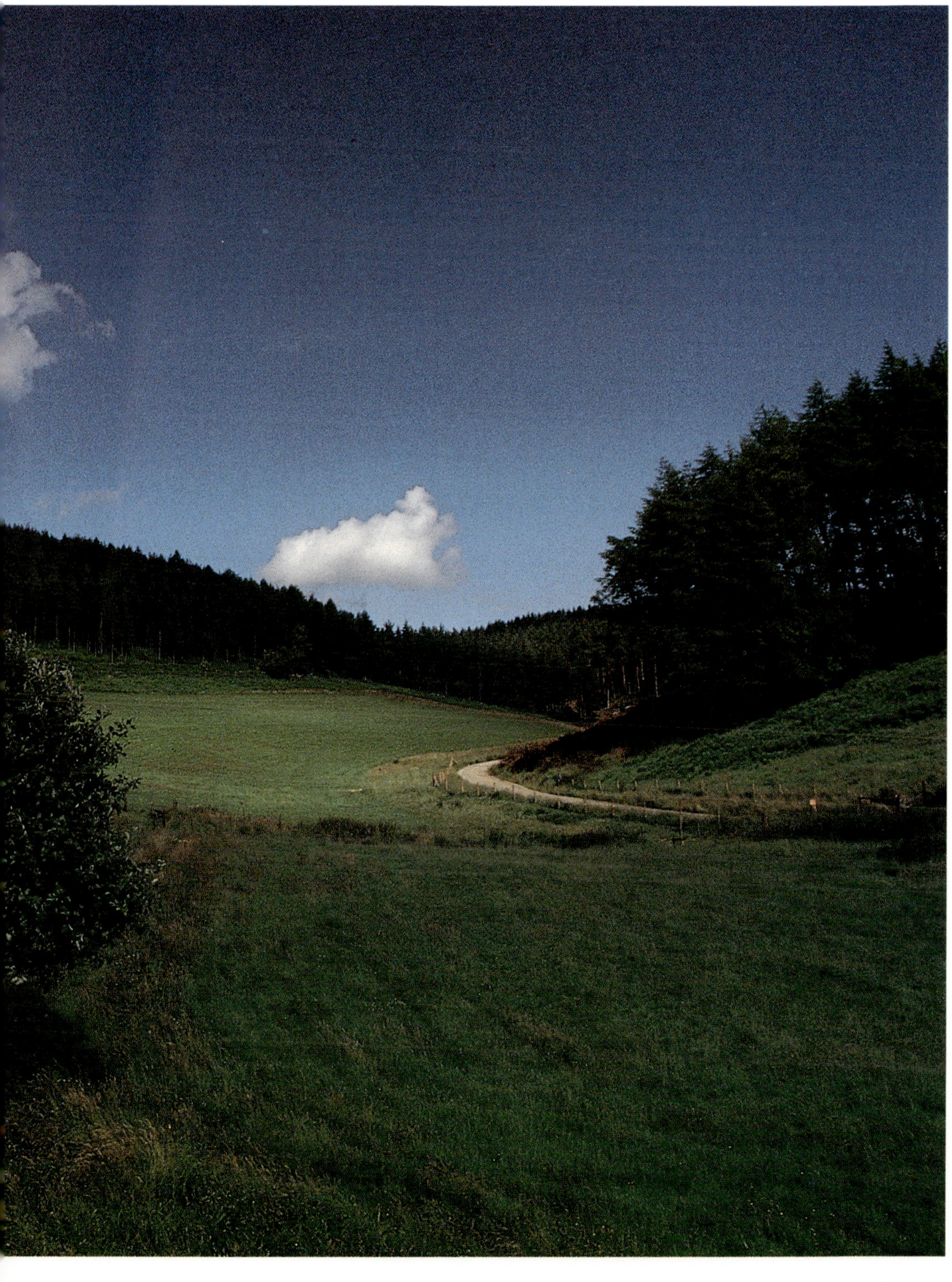

Away from it all: Dalby Forest in Yorkshire, with no-one in sight and beautiful countryside. Opinions are divided about how best to convey that 'away-from-it-all' feeling in pictures. Some maintain that it is best to leave people out of the scene, and this picture certainly argues that case very well.

CHAPTER SEVEN

Action Holidays

Get in on the action with the best angle and your pictures can rival those taken by top professionals.

'Action' photographs fall into two categories. You can be a participant, or you can be a spectator. If you are participating, though subject to the constraints of what you are doing, you can shoot from in among the action. As a spectator, practical or safety considerations (or the sheer number of people present) may limit your access.

As a participant, you can use almost any sort of camera, provided you can keep it away from the risk of damage: water (in the form of rain or spray) and actual physical impact are the main risks. As a spectator, the unpalatable truth is that you really do need a single-lens reflex, with interchangeable lenses, so that you can use long telephoto lenses or at least a zoom (see pages 118-121). If you do not have this sort of camera, you can still get some perfectly good pictures, but they will not usually be able to compete with the sort of heart-stopping peak-of-action photographs which you see in magazines and newspapers.

With any spectator sport, it is best to practise on the smaller events first, rather than to try to move straight into Cowes, Brands Hatch or Wembley. With amateur events in particular, you can usually persuade the organisers to let you enjoy the privileged positions which would be reserved for professionals at more important meetings. Then, it is quite surprising what you can do with even a simple camera!

In most kinds of action photography, there are three main techniques. One is the *dead point;* one is *panning;* and the third is *blur.*

The *dead point* is the point at which action is momentarily halted: examples include a pole-vaulter at the top of his jump, or a footballer in the act of heading the ball. At this 'dead point' between rising and falling, the athlete is likely to be moving quite slowly, so you can 'freeze' them in a very dramatic way.

Panning just means following action through, and pressing the shutter *while the camera is still moving:* this gives an impressively blurred background, but still shows your subject perfectly clearly. Panning can be used for running, jumping, or anything where the action is in a reasonably straight line.

Blur is normally something you try to avoid, but it can also be used to convey movement in a very powerful way. If you can control your shutter speed, remember that a longer exposure will increase blur, but it will also increase the risk of camera shake.

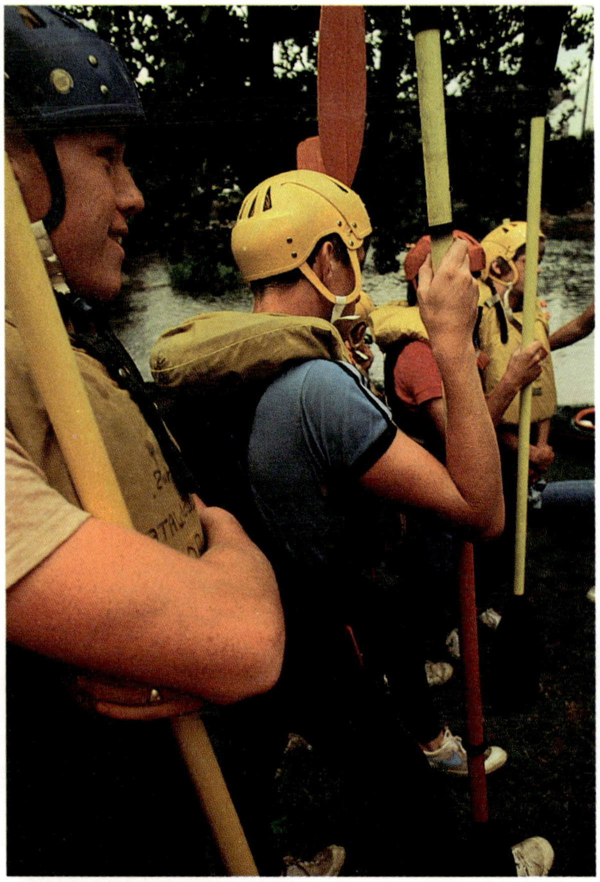

Although action pictures of canoeing are the most dramatic, you can also get interesting photographs of the canoeists preparing for action, or recovering afterwards. As with many activities, the way to get the very best pictures is to learn all you can about the sport - by trying it yourself!

Cycling is a sport which can be enjoyed at many levels, from out-and-out racing to a gentle ride in the country. For a race, tight, dramatic shots are best; for a gentle ride, like this, it is better to show plenty of context.

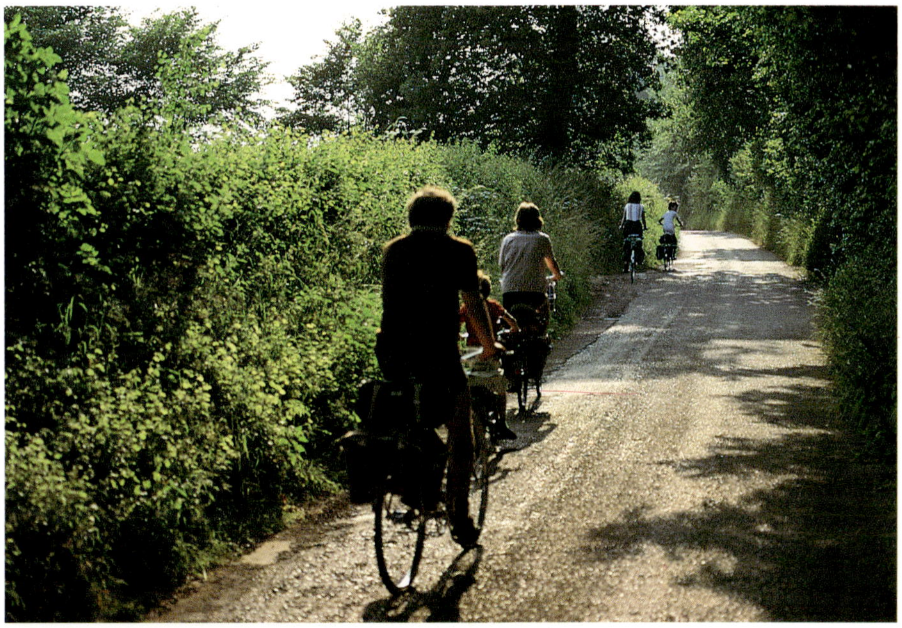

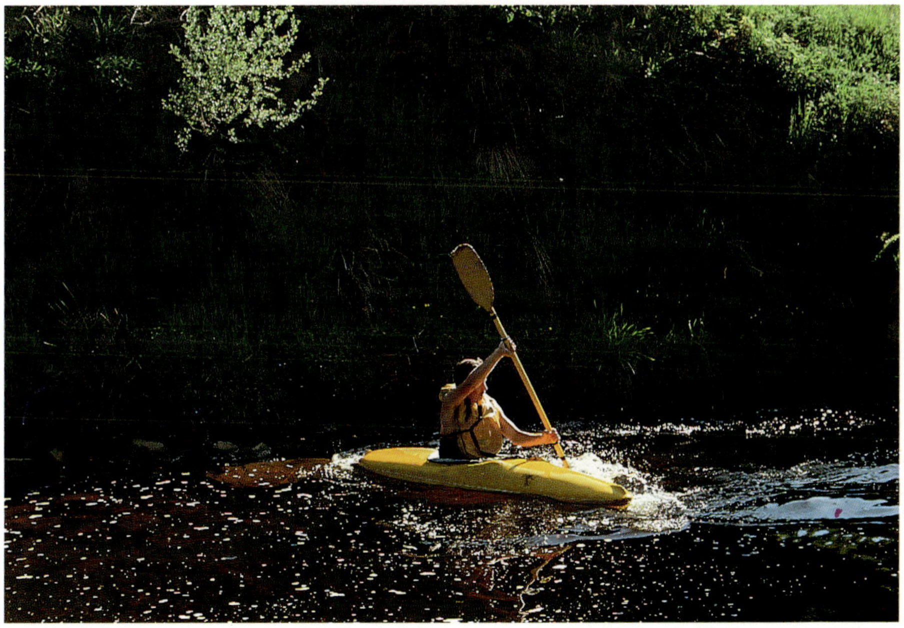

The movement of the subject usually demands that you use a fast shutter speed, thus freezing all movement. The photographer must therefore pick his moment with care, using good anticipation in order to freeze the action at the point that will best convey the excitement of the time. This moment, when the button is pushed, is often referred to as the 'decisive moment'.

A Day at the Races

'Racing' means many different things to different people. Traditionally, it means horse-racing, but it can equally well mean dog-racing, and plenty of people will take it to refer to some sort of motor racing (though this is covered in the next section). 'A day at the races', though, does not just mean racing: it means a day out, and you will get better pictures if you treat it as such, rather than concentrating on trying to photograph the horses. Indeed, those dramatic pictures of the races which you so often see can usually only be obtained by professional sports photographers, standing in privileged positions and using highly specialised equipment.

Instead, you should concentrate on the other aspects of the day which convey the spirit every bit as well as half a ton of horseflesh thundering down the straight. Photograph the horses as they are led in and out (not forgetting the expressions of their jockeys, which will be very different before and after the race) and their owners' reactions; photograph the other people at the race, especially if they are dressed for the occasion; photograph the bookmakers and (if you can still find one) their tic-tac men. Look for details which are not immediately obvious, too: a little child bored to distraction, or a picnic with everyone tucking in.

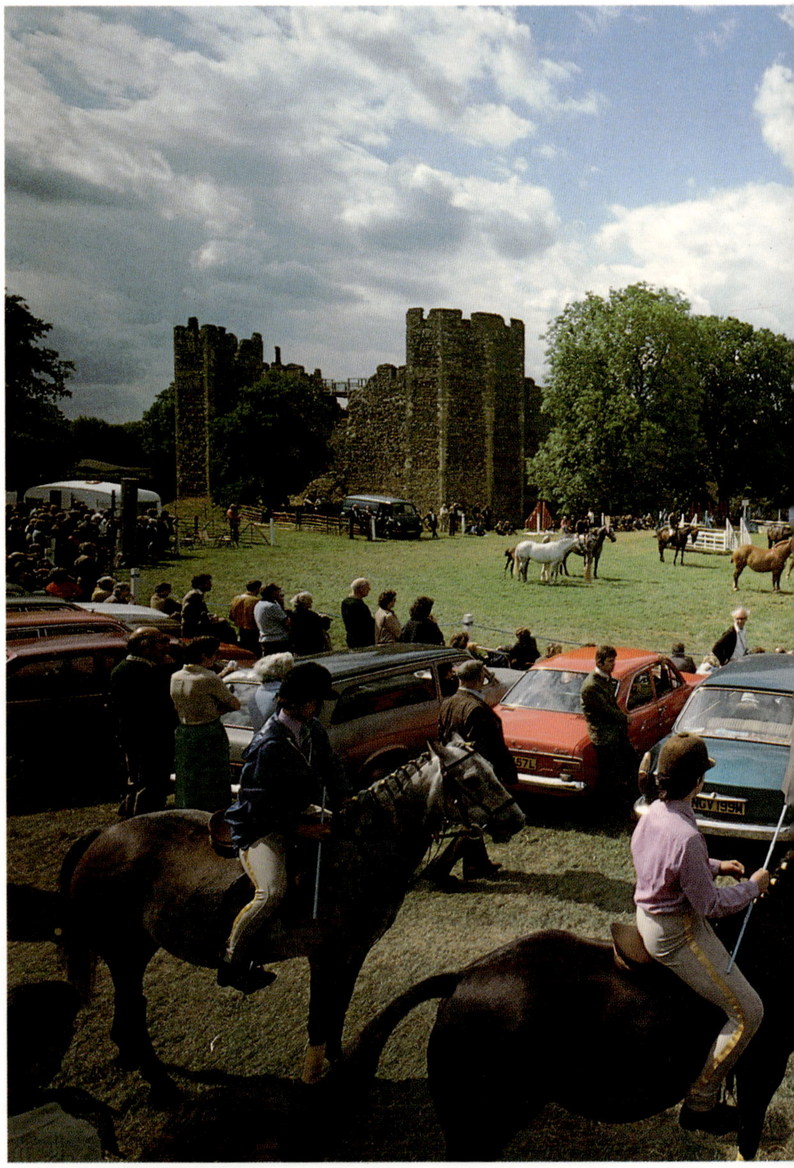

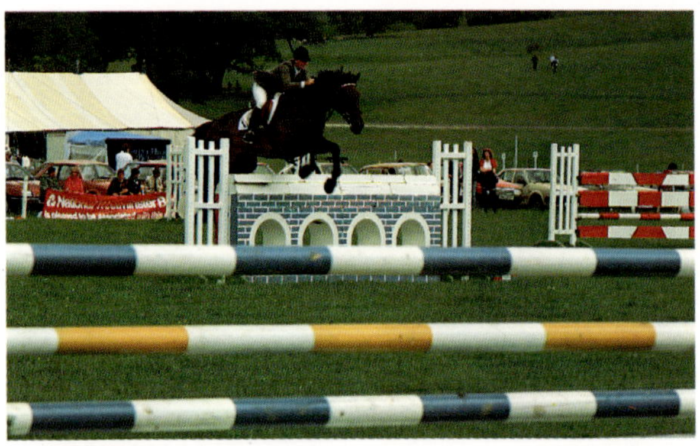

As these two pictures (above and centre) illustrate, smaller, local shows often furnish better opportunities for photography than big events; because you can get closer to the action, you do not need the sort of super-telephoto lens that press photographers use.

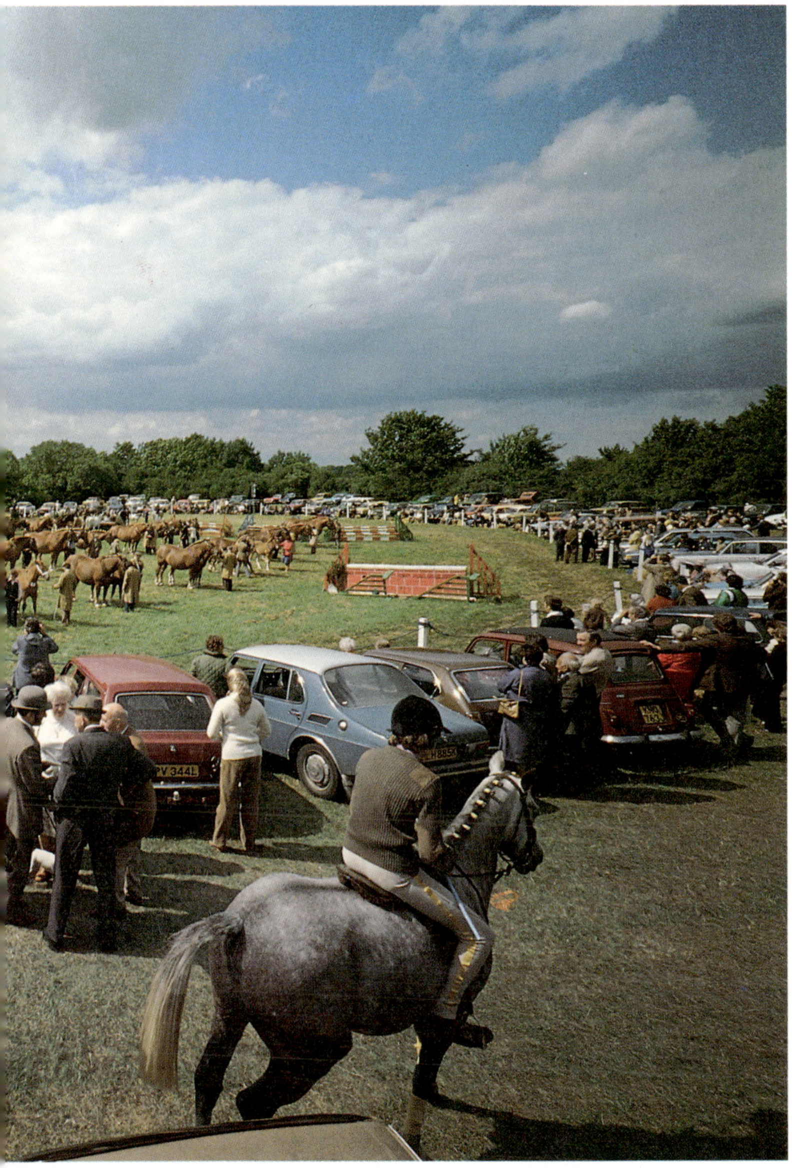

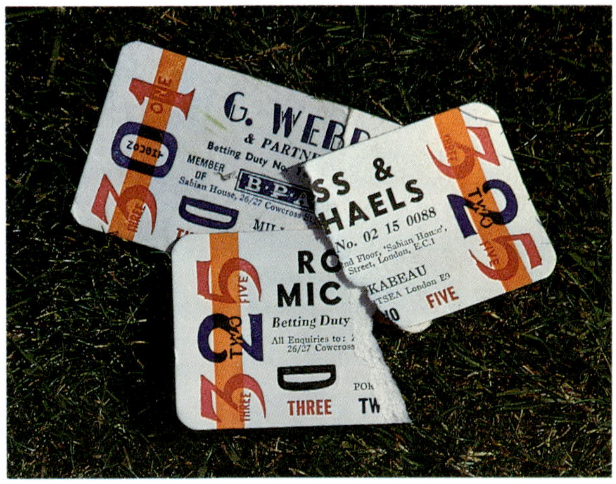

You can learn a lot about still photography by watching movies and television programmes. Notice how they use 'cutaways' - short sequences aside from the main action - and details, as a means of conveying a message. A betting slip, torn in half, says a great deal about horse racing and the luck of the average punter. Once again, this is an example of 'less is more'.

Alternatively, consider going to a smaller and more intimate sort of race meeting, such as a point-to-point, or even show jumping. The big events will be fenced off, but smaller local ones are likely to be much more free and easy, and if you ask permission, you will usually be allowed to take up a 'privileged' position; as usual, going back with some pictures will greatly enhance your chances of a better position next time. You might even wish to volunteer your services as a marshal at a small event: your duties will usually be no more onerous than replacing posts which are knocked over at the jumps, and you can get some very impressive pictures indeed. *Do not* use flash close-up, though, as it can blind both horse and rider, which can obviously be very dangerous.

At dog races, you will need very fast film indeed; tracks vary in their opposition to flash, but most ban it, and you are unlikely to get close enough to the track for the flash to have any effect anyway. As with horse racing, the very beginning of the race is one of the best shots, as you can get the whole field bunched together; once the race is under way, it is all too easy to get a lot of track, and very little animal.

Motor & Motorcycle Racing

Of all the sports in this chapter, it is perhaps most important to 'think small' at first with motor racing. The Grands Prix are very difficult indeed to photograph without special equipment and without access to the best spots (which will be closed to the public, because they are too dangerous), but smaller local events and club races can be very much easier.

If you look at your ticket, you will see that it carries the warning, MOTOR RACING IS DANGEROUS - and they aren't kidding, so don't take any chances which could endanger any competitor, particularly by straying onto the track or by firing a flash directly in the face of a driver or rider.

With this warning out of the way, there is no doubt that the speed and danger of all forms of motor racing is exhilarating, which is why people do it. Capturing that speed and exhilaration on film is not, however, easy.

To begin with, *choose your location.* Corners are generally a good place for action; the vehicles tend to bunch together, motorcycles will be well banked over, and a three-quarters view is almost always more interesting than the sort of side-on view you can get on the straight. For off-road events, such as motorcycle scrambles or four-wheel-drive events, a 'yump' where the vehicle leaves the ground is likely to be dramatic - but be careful where you stand, as a quarter of a ton of motorcycle and rider landing on you will not do either of you any good.

Secondly, *use panning and blur* (pages 80 and 81); all too often, 'frozen' movement makes a car look stationary.

Thirdly, if you can, *use the most powerful telephoto available*, or at least set your zoom at its longest focal length (see pages 120 and 121): this is how professionals achieve that dramatic 'stacking' of perspective, where the vehicles appear to be on top of one another.

Fourthly, *try to get into the pits;* pictures of the mechanics rapidly servicing the machine, and of the drawn face of the driver, can be very dramatic. Obviously, permission to enter the pits will be easier to obtain at a smaller event.

Finally, do not neglect the *lap of honour*, where you can (usually) get closer to the track, and speeds are much lower.

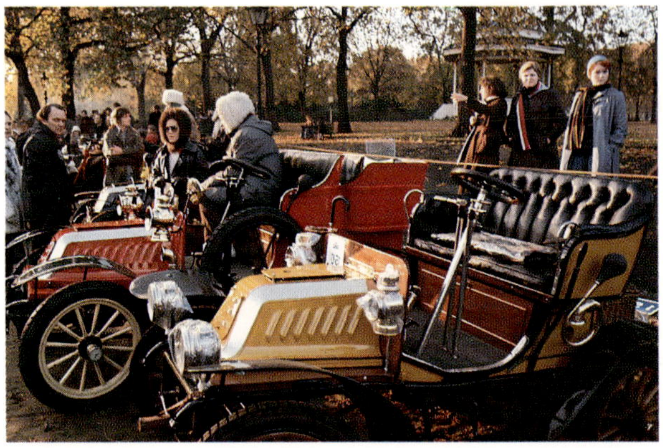

The interest and excitement that cars generate provides the photographer with fine subject matter. If you can't avoid getting people in the picture, always try to use them to your advantage by moving in close and studying the variety of facial expressions. Most people, however, will be drawn towards the sheer speed and glamour of the racing car. To capture this glamour successfully you must be aware of the problems of photographing objects which are moving at high speed. Remember the importance of pre-focusing, panning and good anticipation.

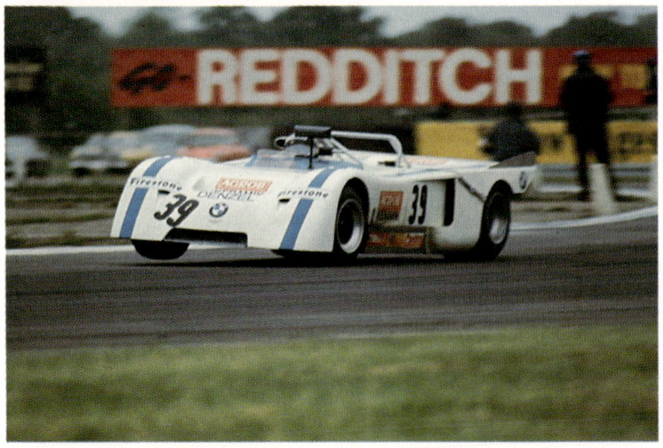

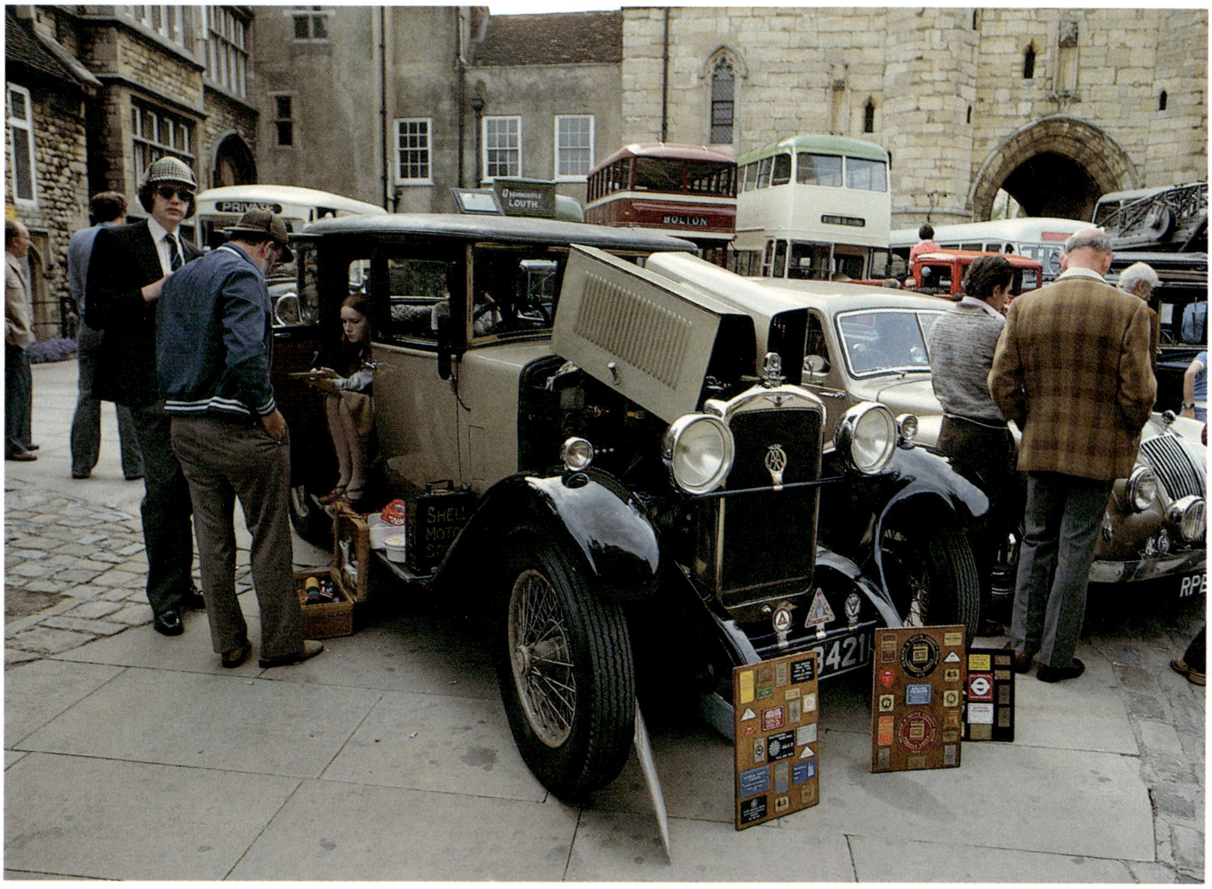

Not all motor sports are track races, of course: rallies are also worth considering. Professional rallies, with their highly modified cars and 'special stages', can furnish good pictures, but there is also a place for the more modest rally, including veteran and vintage events.

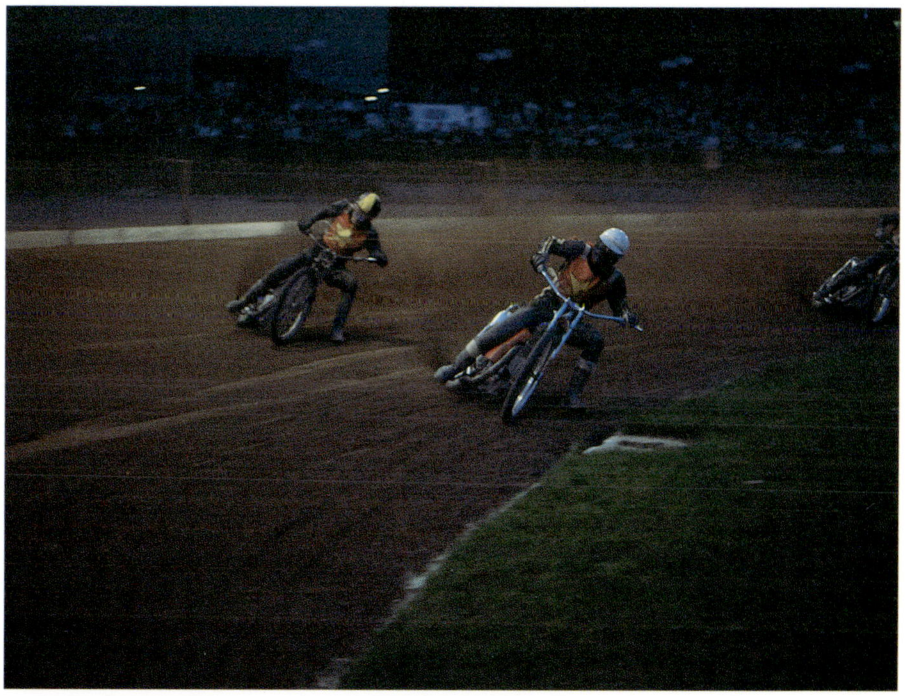

Corners are always a good place for pictures in any form of sport, as they allow you to photograph the competitors coming towards you at an angle (instead of the usual head-on or side-on view). Also, controlling a powerful vehicle so as to make it go around a corner fast is not easy, so dramatic slides and cornering angles are likely.

Power Boats

A surprising phenomenon in the last few years has been the growth of powerboat racing in old dockland areas. Although this is a very dangerous sport for participants, because of the combination of high speeds and the high walls of unyielding Victorian masonry which surround the course, it is also extremely dramatic. Among the most spectacular races are the ones held every year in Bristol Docks, where boats travelling at speeds in excess of a hundred miles an hour pass within ten or twenty yards of the spectators for much of the course.

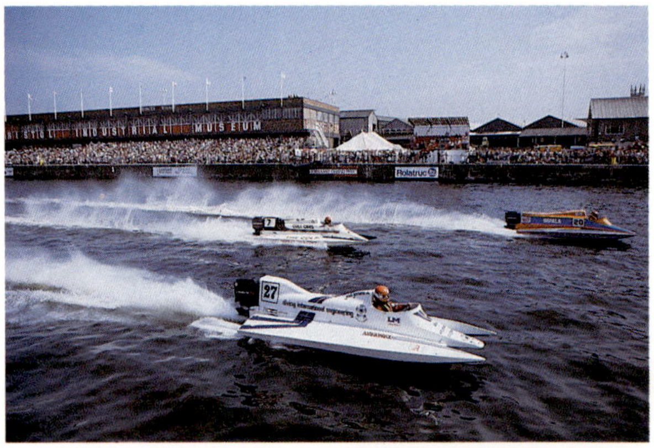

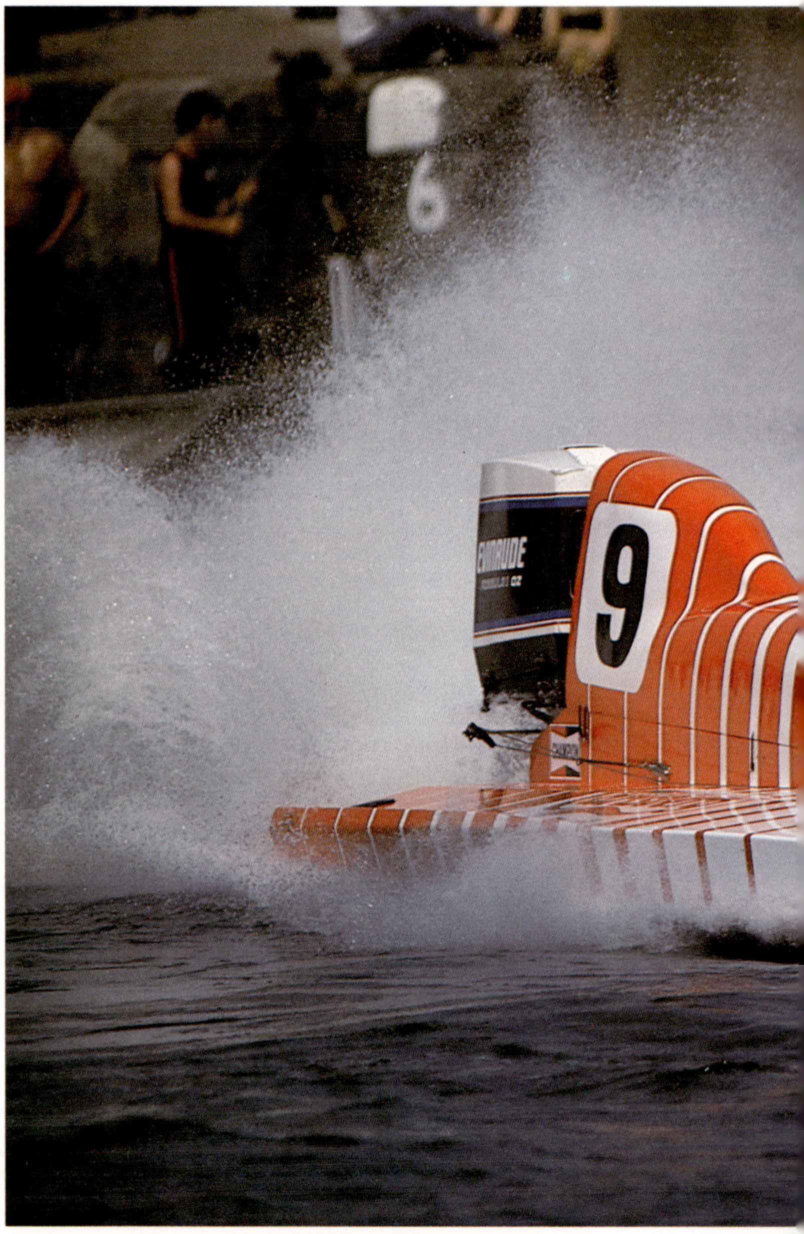

Neck-and-neck powerboat racing, here in Bristol docks, makes for very dramatic pictures. As in all high-speed action photography, anticipation is crucial. An advantage which powerboats have over racing cars is that the plumes of spray always make them appear to be moving fast. Watch the spray though, as one drop of salt water on the wrong place on your camera can ruin it.

Many of the observations about motor racing apply to powerboat racing, especially about photography at corners (or, to be more accurate, around buoys); the spray kicked up by these fast-moving projectiles can be very dramatic indeed. The start is another dramatic moment, as the boats jockey for position among clouds of spray and exhaust. From the photographer's point of view, there is little danger of being hit by a fast-moving boat, though there is, of course, the danger of falling in the water. Apart from being uncomfortable and potentially risky, this is also an excellent way of writing off your camera! As with any event of this kind, you will need to get there early if you want a choice of the best positions.

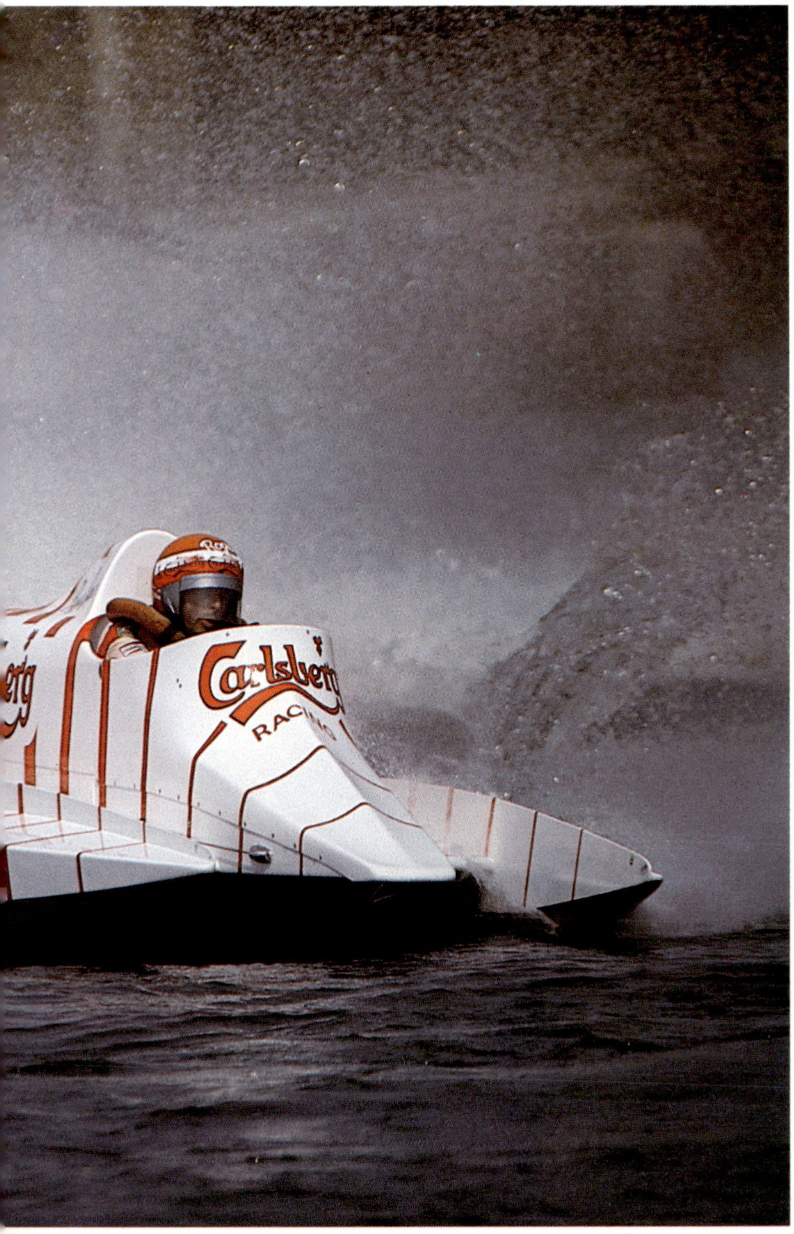

If you have a zoom lens, you may be surprised at what moderate focal lengths you require; the typical 70-210mm zoom (see pages 120-121) is ideal, and at the start or even at some of the turns, you may find that a standard lens is more appropriate. Obviously, you should protect the lens itself with a skylight or UV filter and a lens hood (see pages 122-123), but otherwise, there should not be enough spray to do any serious harm. If you can get a clear line of sight down a long straight, then 'stacking' the perspective with a longer lens (as described in the last section) may be a better idea.

The above remarks apply only to dockland powerboat racing, though, as offshore powerboat racing is a completely different game. Even a powerful telephoto is likely to be insufficient for land-based shots, and press pictures are normally taken from boats carefully positioned in safe areas - inside buoys, for example - and great care must be taken to protect the cameras from flying salt spray: if the race is important enough, a newspaper may decide to treat some of its older cameras as disposable, not worrying if they are written off or not, which gives some idea of the difference in priorities between professional and amateur photography!

The use of a fairly long telephoto lens has lifted this one boat out of the throng and framed it alone in all its splendour. Telephoto lenses (see pages 120-121) can be used to 'compress' an advancing field of boats into a mass of colour and spray. Remember to pre-focus on a point ahead of the boats and to press the button the moment the boats reach that point.

Water-Skiing, Surfing & Windsurfing

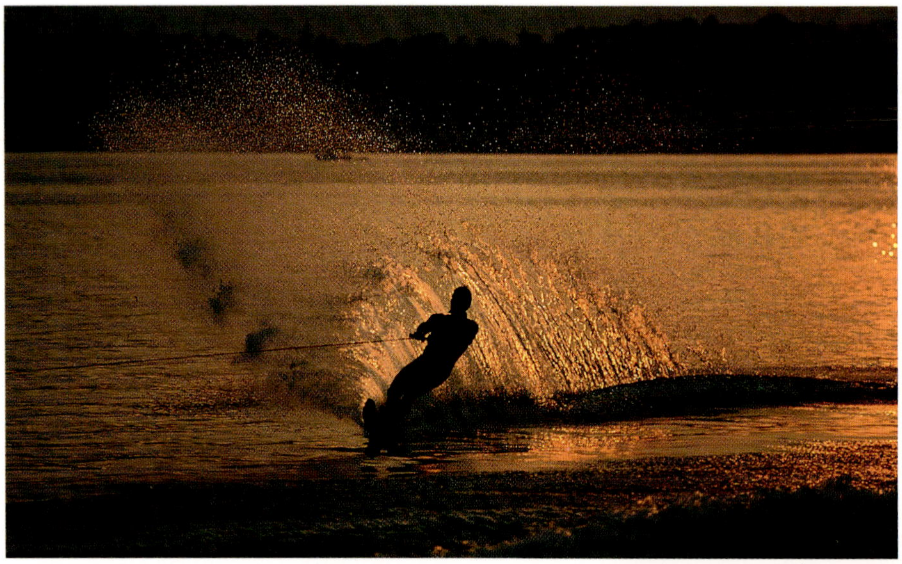

The best shots from the boat are the ones where the skier is swinging out, or where the boat has turned; the skier is then in comparatively flat water (instead of being in the boat's wake) but is kicking up spray on his own account. You also have a three-quarter view, which is much more interesting than a head-on shot. Notice how the skier is silhouetted against the sunlit water; it would be almost impossible to get a picture which was this dramatic and showed the skier's face. This was actually taken from another boat travelling alongside the ski-boat, but the same general principles hold.

There are a few hardy souls who take pictures while they are actually water-skiing, surfing and windsurfing, but they mostly use special waterproofed remote-control cameras bolted to the skis or boards. This is beyond the reach of most people, though it is worth mentioning that there are a few (relatively) low-cost waterproof cameras and that if you are involved in a lot of water-sport, it may be worth getting one.

Otherwise, it will be a question of taking pictures from the shore, or from a boat. The points made earlier about flying spray are relevant again here, though there are significant differences between the three sports.

For water-skiing, the best pictures are often taken from the boat towing the skier, in which case the spray will (usually) be predictable in both direction and quantity, and one of the 'plastic mac' protectors described on pages 122-123 will be quite adequate; you can even make up a protector with a plastic shopping bag, a filter, some adhesive tape and (preferably) a couple of bits of clear plastic to protect the viewfinder. Rather than shooting while the skier is directly behind you, you are likely to get better pictures on curves where he (or she) is swinging wide, or performing some sort of acrobatic manoeuvre. If you are shooting from the shore, you are (once again) going to need at least a zoom lens, though for skiing in reservoirs and disused gravel pits, a 70-210mm will be plenty.

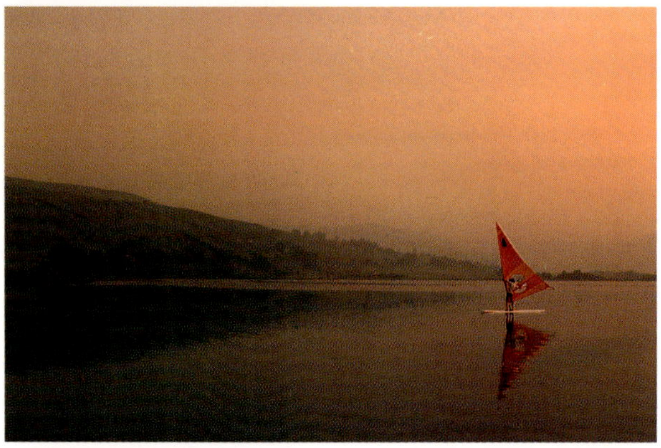

With windsurfing you can aim either for a tight, graphic composition (right) in which the board fills or even spills over the frame, or for a picture which shows much more context (above).

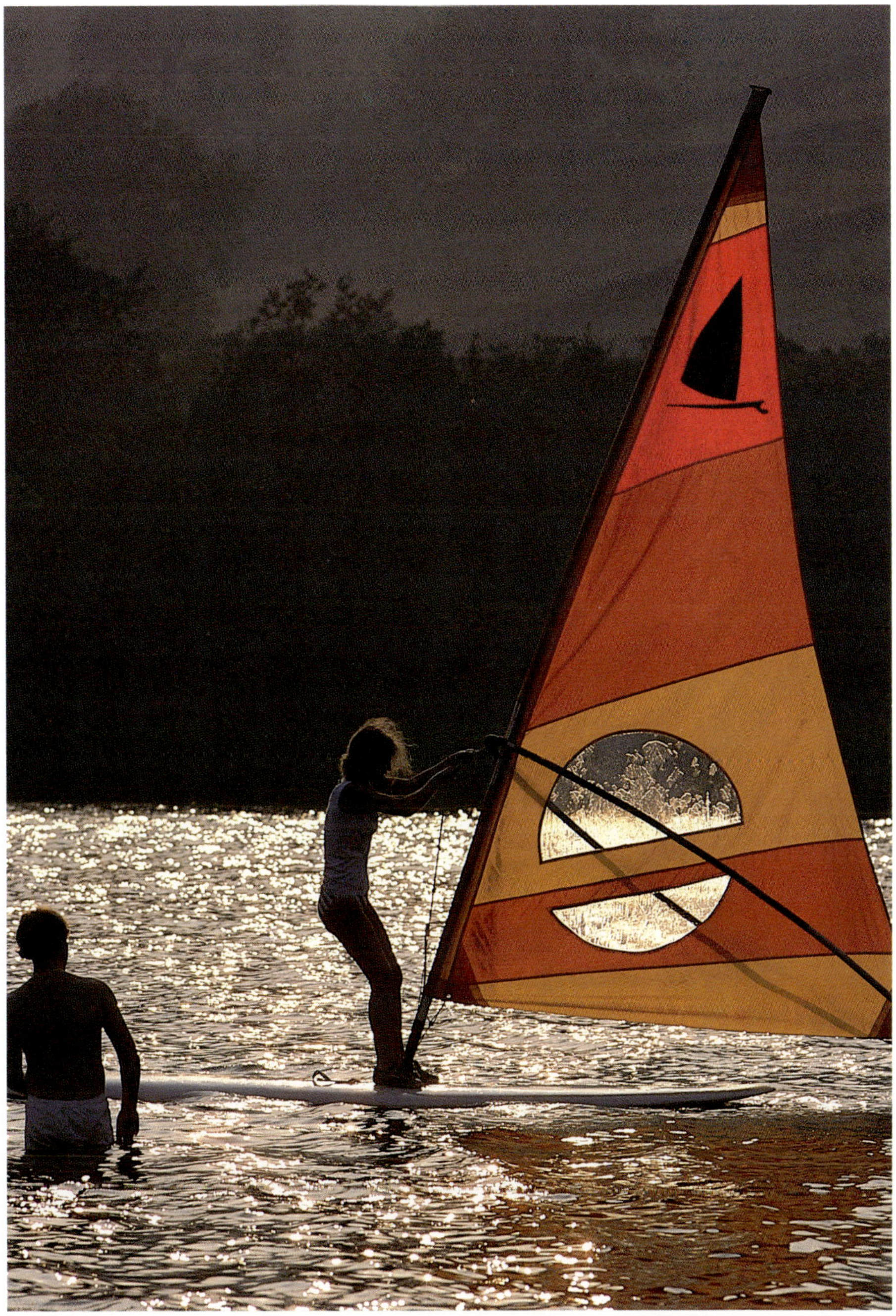

Although you will probably need to use a zoom or telephoto lens, a close-in approach to your subject enables you to stress the excitement of the sport, occasionally even capturing the expressions of determination on the faces of the surfers.

Surfing is another matter again. Most professionals use both powerful telephotos and waterproof cameras, the former for shore shots and the latter for 'getting in among it' on the breaking surf. Here, a proper waterproof casing which will survive total immersion is essential, as you can easily be knocked down by a big wave when you are taking pictures. A zoom will give you fair surfing pictures from the shore, but it will not have the real 'pulling power' of a longer lens.

Finally, windsurfing is comparatively free from the risks of spray, but you will still need a zoom if you are to get anything like a close-up of the surfer. If you are shooting into the sun, you can also have exposure problems, though a silhouette (which is what the meter will automatically give you) can actually be more effective than a detailed shot. If you have manual exposure control, consider *bracketing*, giving one shot at the recommended exposure, one at two stops (two shutter-speeds *or* two aperture settings) more, and one at two stops less; this is how professionals deal with these problems, though they have to be more precise because they are normally using colour slide film.

Sailing & Boating

Messing about in boats is a fine old British tradition - hardly surprisingly in an island race - and there is a tremendous spectrum of pictures to be had.

At its most intense, competitive sailing is surprisingly similar to offshore power-boat racing (see page 86): speeds are very high, there is spray everywhere, and the only practicable way to shoot is from another boat.

In their less dramatic forms, sailing and boating are very much easier to photograph, though some form of camera protection is advisable if there is any spray about. Photography on board a boat is rarely successful, unless you have a very wide-angle lens, because you cannot get far enough from your subject to show enough context. Photographing one boat from another can however be very effective, especially if both are moving fairly slowly; this is equally true whether you are on board a yacht costing a quarter of a million or in a sailing dinghy (or even rowing boat) which cost a few hundred.

Narrow boats, or canal boats, are particularly rewarding subjects to photograph because they are normally brightly painted and (if you choose your position carefully) you can show them passing through attractive countryside or emerging dramatically from a tunnel. If you can, try to find a reasonably high viewpoint (so that you show the boat sitting in the water, not blocked off by the canal wall) and shoot from a three-quarter angle, which usually shows the shape of the boat better than either a head-on shot or a side-on shot. Nevertheless, head-on from a fairly low viewpoint, can also be very dramatic.

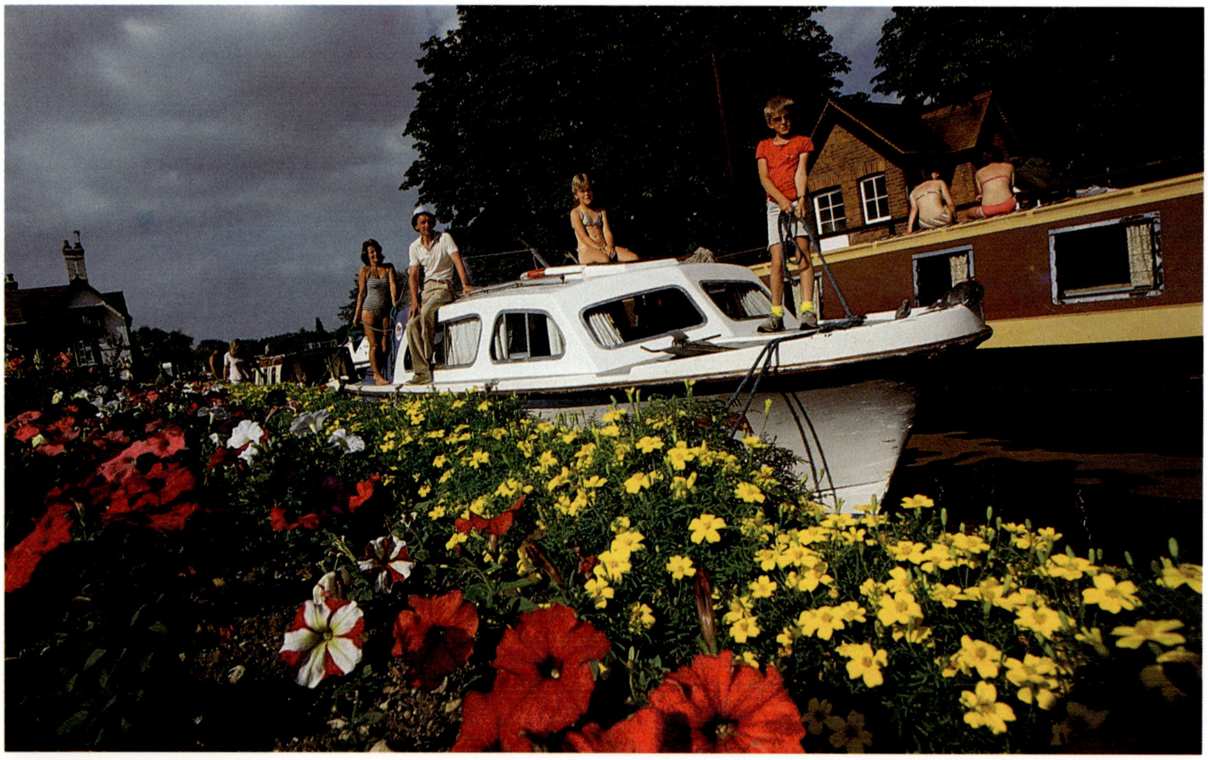

More leisurely boating, whether on a narrow boat or a river cruiser, is better suited to a more leisurely kind of photography. The flowers in the foreground of the picture of the river cruiser create a very peaceful image.

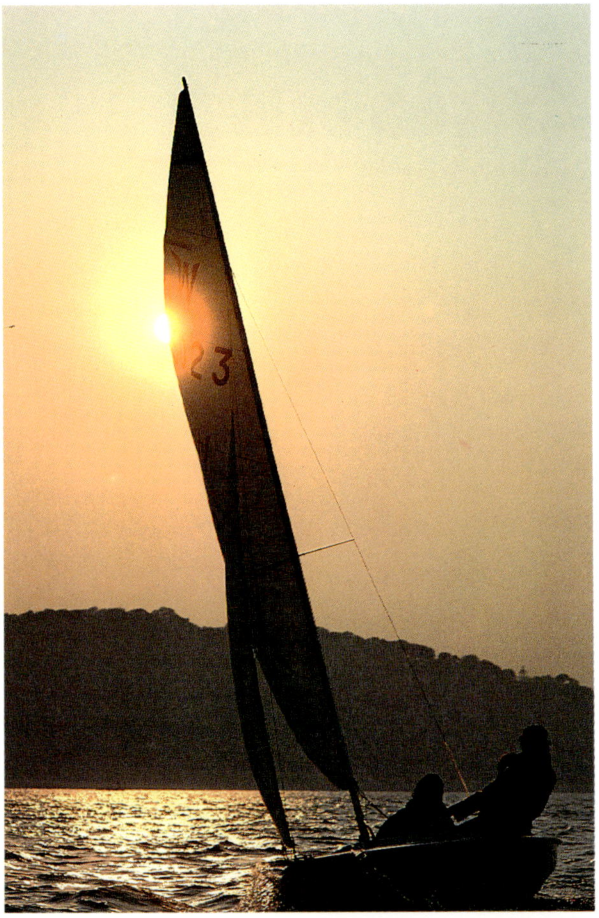

For this kind of picture, you need either a waterproof camera in a nearby boat - even a small sailing dinghy can kick up a surprising amount of spray - or a powerful telephoto lens (see page 120) and a safe base on dry land. The latter approach was used here.

Whatever sort of boats you photograph, do not neglect the details, both of the boats and their occupants. The carving and painting of narrows boats is an obvious example, but many of the fitments of a modern yacht have a sculptural quality which can be very appealing, while pictures of someone painstakingly scraping the barnacles from the bottom of his boat, or lovingly painting it, can tell you every bit as much about him and his boat as photographs of the boat in the water. Waterside (or canalside) pubs which are frequented by boat owners can also prove a happy hunting ground for pictures, especially just as dusk is falling: the yellow lights of the pub and the boats contrast beautifully with the blue twilight. You might also care to photograph the ships' chandlers and marine clothing stores which cluster around every boating centre: their cluttered windows and arcane wares can make for very interesting pictures, though you really need decent-sized enlargements if you are to do justice to them.

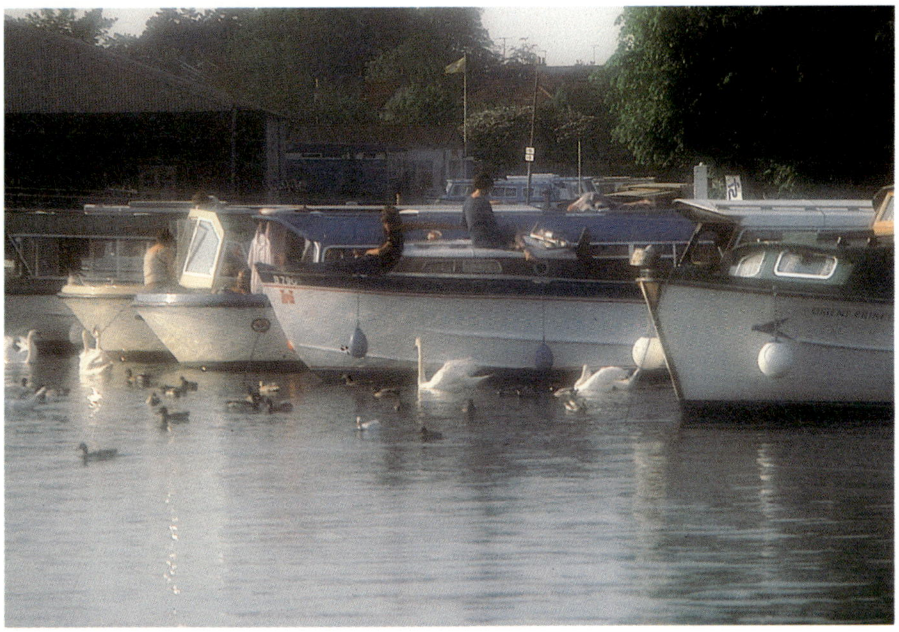

Most people think of soft-focus as something to be used mainly for portraits, but as this picture shows, you can create a dreamy, romantic effect in a comparatively prosaic marina shot, simply by screwing a soft-focus attachment onto the front of your camera.

Rowing & Canoeing

As with water-skiing, surfing and windsurfing, taking pictures of rowing or canoeing as a participant is not easy, but taking pictures from the sidelines is not particularly difficult and can be rewarding.

If you can, you should choose a position which is well above the water-line and which allows a three-quarter view of the boats. The most successful shots are usually those which show the sheer muscular effort (in the case of oarsmen) or the concentration (in the case of canoeists) in the faces and bodies of the participants. On the other hand, one of the most striking pictures ever made of a rowing eight was taken from almost directly above and in front, on a bridge, with a long shutter speed which blurred both the oars and the rowers - which all goes to show that there is no substitute for personal vision when it comes to photography!

With eights and fours, a standard or wide-angle lens will normally be ideal for showing the whole boat from a bank or a bridge, though a zoom will be needed to pick out individuals. With doubles, sculls, and canoes, you have the choice of using the standard lens and concentrating on the pattern of the boats in the water, or using a zoom for more detail.

With a standard or wide-angle lens you can also show rather more context: with racing in particular, you may be able to catch the coach cycling along beside the river, and yelling instructions to the crew through a megaphone - which looks a lot more difficult than rowing! You should also remember the standard rule of action photography: do not neglect the faces of the competitors both before and after the race or event.

White-water canoeing is a particularly exciting aspect of the sport, but it is very difficult to photograph. If you are not familiar with the term, 'white water' refers to fast-flowing water across rocks and rapids. Photographing this very demanding sport requires lightning reflexes and (usually) a zoom or telephoto lens, and you have to be careful to protect the camera and lens from splashes and spray - though because the water is fresh rather than salt, it is nothing like as dangerous as sea water. Because these events are usually organised by and for enthusiasts, it is not always easy to find out where they are being held, but if you do manage to find one, you can be sure of some very exciting pictures, with very little in the way of restrictions on where you can photograph from - though you must be careful not to fall in! As usual, a few prints as a present will normally result in your being invited back for the next event.

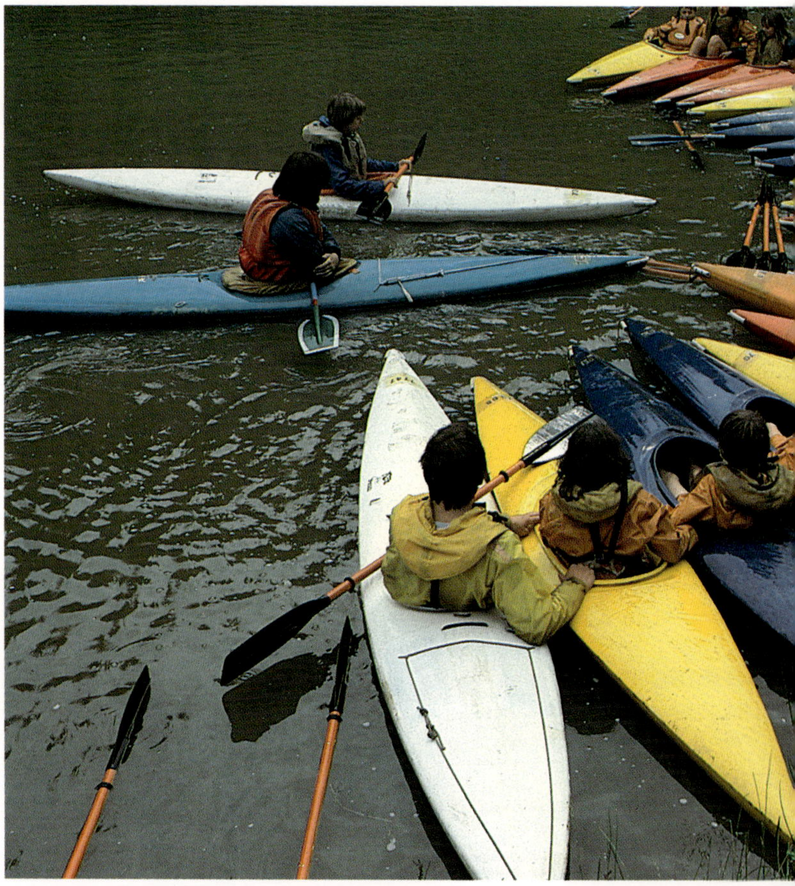

Modern canoes are usually brightly coloured, and if you can shoot several together you can get a very dramatic graphic composition.

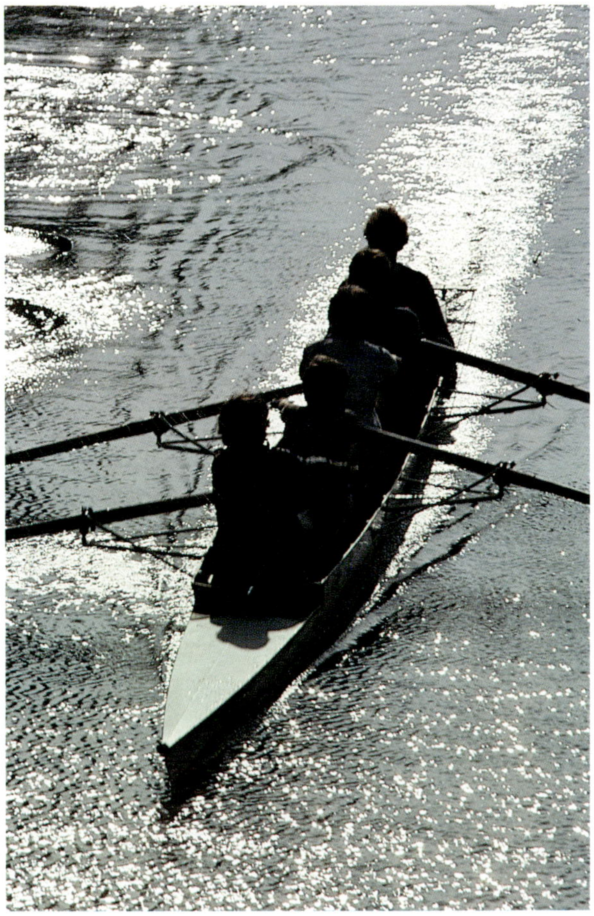

Sometimes, pictures taken against the light are underexposed and uninteresting; at other times, as here, the silhouette effect is extremely effective.

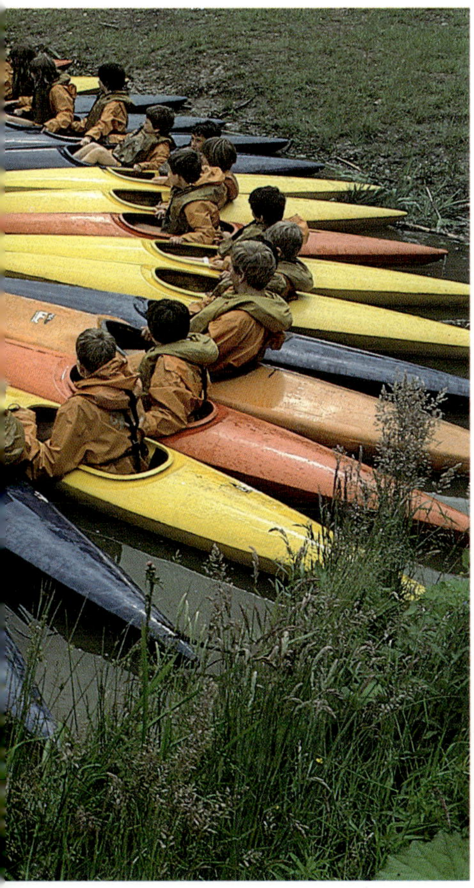

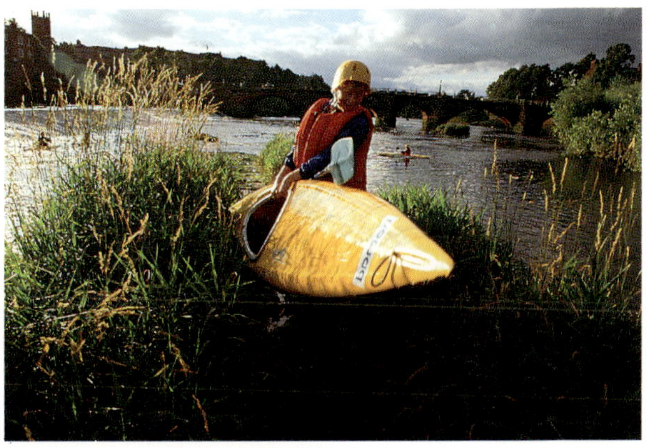

If you are a canoeist yourself, you can reach some remote and often very beautiful places, or (as here) little islands in mid-river which are not otherwise accessible. This illustrates the difference between photography as a participant in a sport, and photography as a spectator.

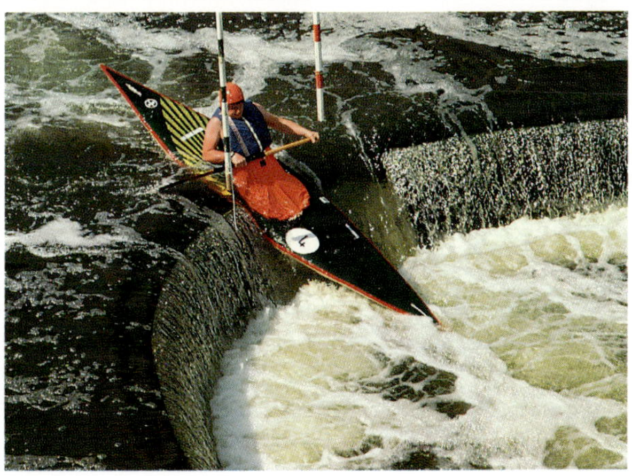

Competition canoeing can be very exciting, as the canoeists attempt (and succeed at) the apparently impossible, such as going through this narrow 'gate' by a fast-flowing weir just downstream from Bath's Pulteney Bridge. A high viewpoint - easily available in Bath, though less readily so in some other locations - makes it easy to show the canoe and canoeist in full.

Rock Climbing

Rock climbing is one of those sports where it is virtually impossible to get a good picture unless you participate yourself - and it is a sport which scares most people witless! On the other hand, a really dramatic rock-climbing shot can pack tremendous impact, and if you are even a modest Sunday climber, you really ought to consider taking your camera with you.

One of your first considerations must be to protect your camera from damage; another must be ease of use, because you do not want to waste any time or to have to fumble when you are hanging on by the fingernails of one hand. Even professionals often use autofocus compacts for this sort of photography, so you need not worry too much about your equipment.

The main difficulties lie in conveying just how hard the climb really was, and in making the scenery look sufficiently dramatic, and there are some fairly simple techniques for doing this.

First, show plenty of context. For once, you do not want to go in too close: conveying the sheer scale of the mountain is what is important.

Secondly, show the climber hanging on. It usually looks far more dramatic to see someone perching on a tiny ledge, body pressed close to the rock, than it does to show them standing confidently on a crag. Of course, you have to find somewhere to shoot from!

Thirdly, do not be afraid to tilt the camera, if by doing so you can get a more dramatic picture. You can overdo it of course, but making a slope look steeper than it really was will usually convey a much better impression of what the climb actually felt like.

Fourthly, when it comes to scenery, try to include some foreground. Without this, there is no sense of scale, and the aerial perspective or haze which contributes so much to the impression of sheer vastness looks instead like the murk of a badly processed picture.

Finally, be ruthless when it comes to sorting out your pictures. If a picture needs a lot of explanation, it has probably failed as a picture. It does not matter how difficult it was to make the climb, or how dangerous it was to take the photograph: the picture stands alone.

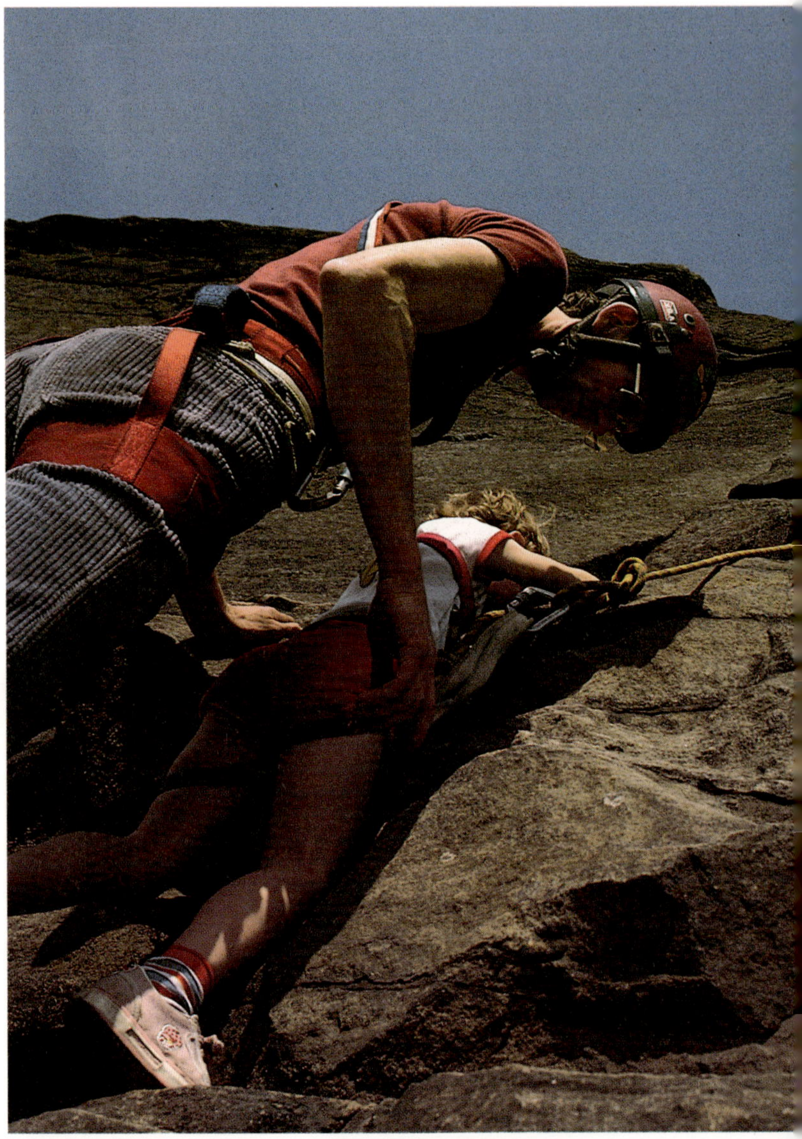

Surprisingly, rock climbing is one of the most difficult activities to photograph successfully. The problem lies in trying to balance the massiveness of the mountain with the skills and efforts of the climber. Invariably the photograph fails to show either. A way around this is to go in close, concentrating on the expression of exertion on the climber's face, but to do this you must also be able to climb, usually as well as, if not better than your subject!

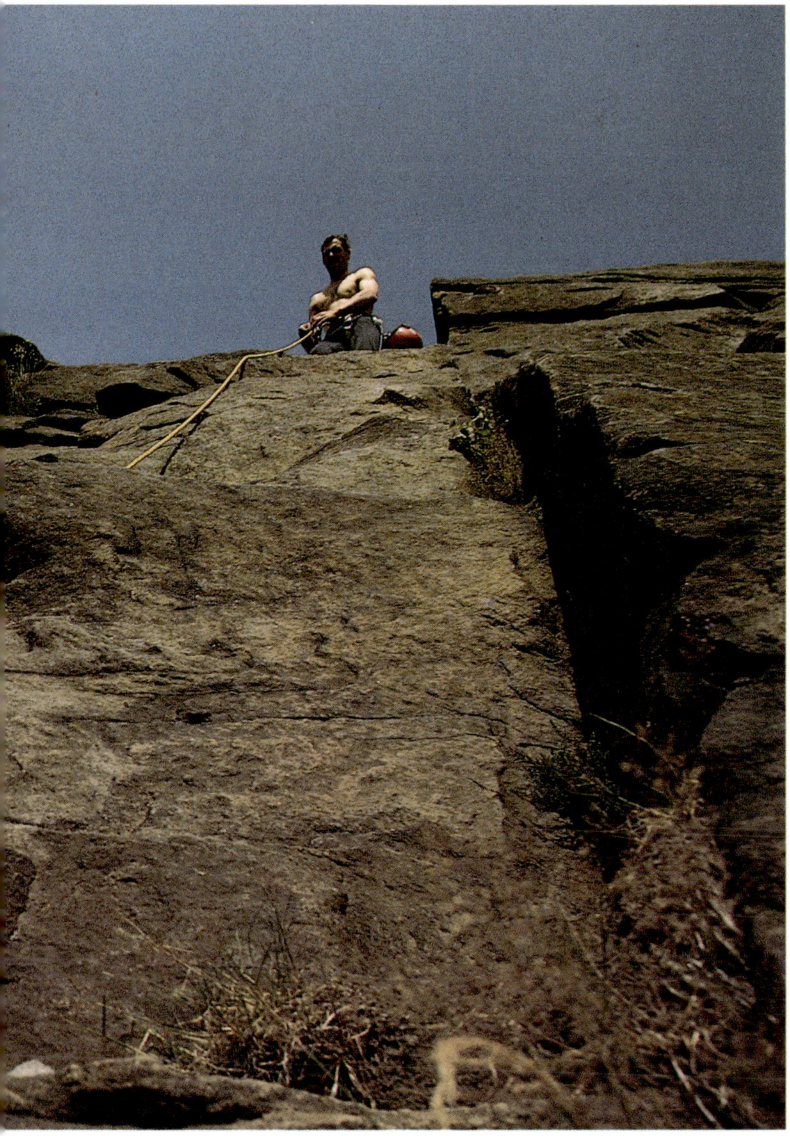

Although this is hardly a classic rock-climbing picture, it leaves you in no doubt that the gentleman in the picture is very serious about his climbing. This is another example of the 'cutaway' or 'less is more' technique, and would make an excellent picture in a slide-show about rock climbing.

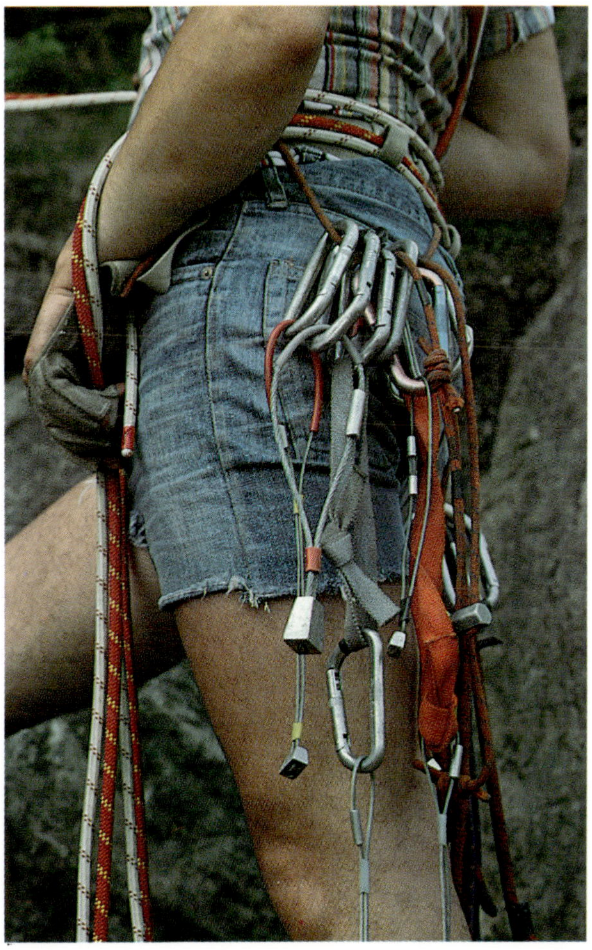

Air Sports & Air Days

More and more people are realising the age-old dream of mankind, to fly. In addition to traditional gliders and light aircraft, there are hang-gliders, microlights and hot-air balloons, and if you stretch the definition of 'flying' a bit, there is also parachuting and sky-diving. Even if you don't fly yourself, there are air days with static displays, aerial stunts and parachutists.

As a participant, you should not consider adding photography to the already formidable list of things which you have to remember, unless you are confident that you will endanger neither other people's lives nor your own. One professional photographer was nearly killed when the heavy motor-driven camera bolted to an outrigger of his hang-glider upset the balance of the craft and made it crash on takeoff. A motor-driven camera is of course virtually essential if the camera is to be fixed in position and remotely operated.

Because of the large areas of sky that there will be in some types of picture (notably sky-diving), you may well find that you will need to reset the film speed on your camera (see pages 124-125) to something like two or even four times the manufacturer's recommendation. Also, be sure to explain to the processing lab that there are sky-diving pictures on the roll, and that you want to be able to see some detail in the figures and faces; otherwise, you may get only silhouettes. Sometimes, the exposure will be such that the lab cannot help, but if you give them advance warning, at least they can try: if you can see the detail on the negative, using a strong magnifying glass, they should be able to print it. The sky may, however, look rather 'washed out', without the rich deep blue that you want, but unfortunately you cannot have both.

For air displays, you can pretty much forget about individual aircraft in flight, unless you have a powerful telephoto lens. The same is true of trying to photograph parachutists from the ground. Airborne display teams are very much easier, though, especially when they are trailing smoke for a 'burst'; even if the aircraft themselves are barely visible, the smoke trails can make intriguing patterns. Static displays, on the ground, require wide-angle lenses: the looming nose of an aircraft, or the instrument-crammed interior of a cockpit, can make very dramatic pictures.

Finally, ballooning is rather different from all the other types of air sport in that there is no vibration (at least when the burner is not roaring) and because you can afford to take your time over everything; you do not even need a motor drive. Aerial views are always fascinating, and they will look even better if you can get another balloon in shot!

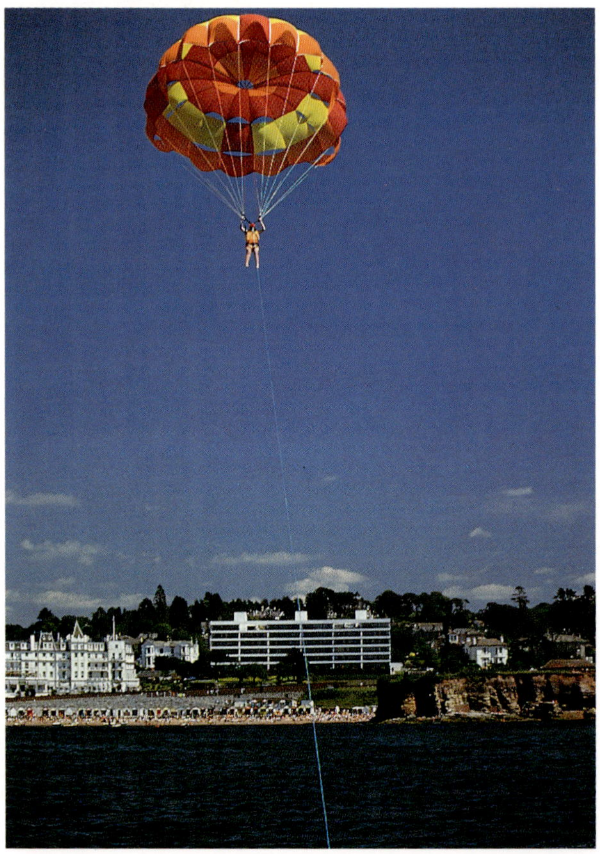

One of the latest ways of getting airborne is 'parascending', which is a bit like water-skiing in the air. It is a surprisingly difficult sport to photograph, because if you are in the boat, you can normally only get a featureless silhouette, while if you are on land, you need a zoom or telephoto lens in order to be able to see anything.

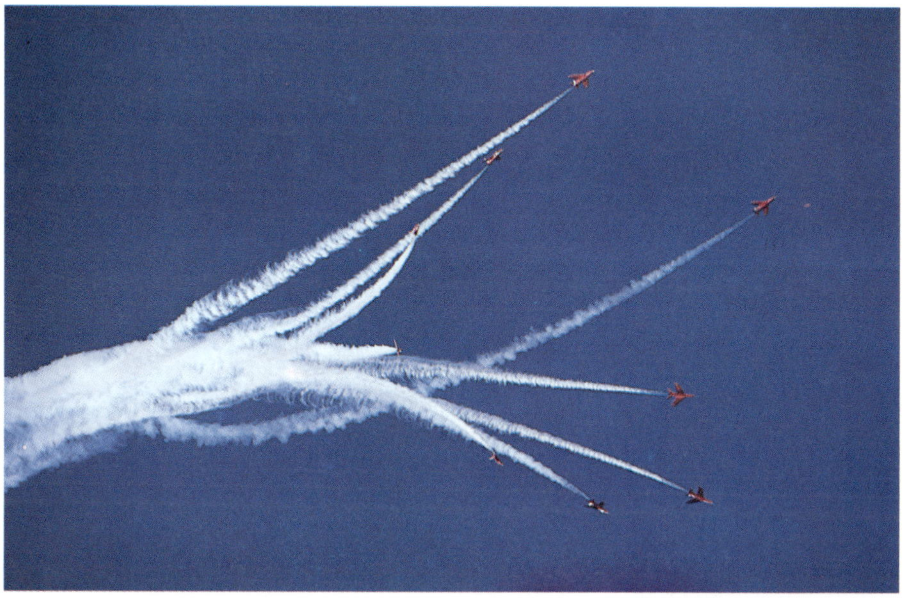

The Red Arrows sign off with a 'Bomb Burst', captured here at its most spectacular point. Anticipation is all-important here; you have to press the shutter a fraction of a second before the aircraft are in the position you want to photograph.

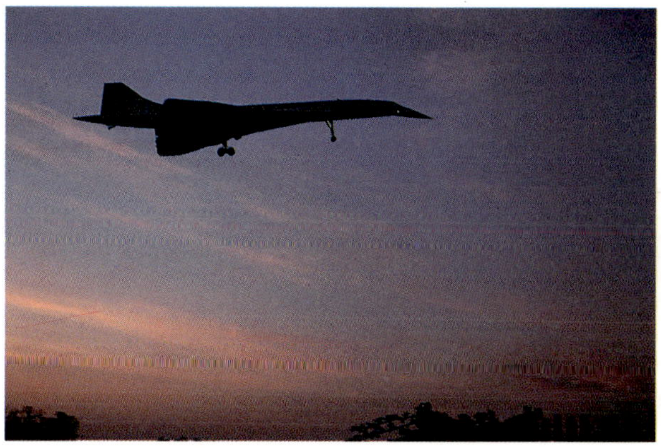

This dramatic picture of Concorde was taken in the late evening; the unmistakable silhouette contrasts beautifully with the tree-line horizon. It appears as some sort of futuristic bird, with an all-seeing eye!

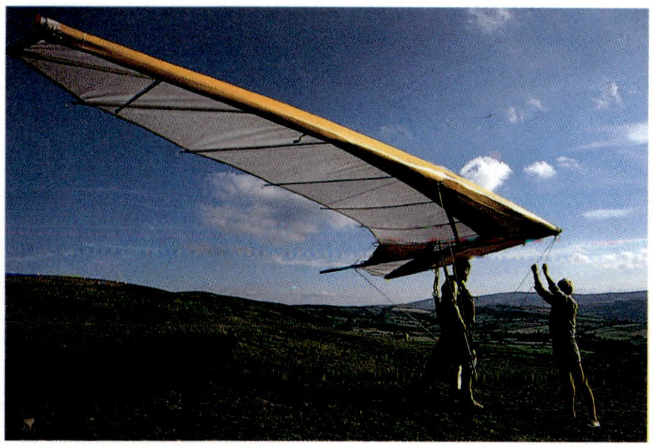

The best time to photograph a hang-glider is shortly after take-off, for the simple reason that it is good and close to the ground. It is also worth considering a shot just before take-off, because the graphic shape of the glider can make an excellent composition.

CHAPTER EIGHT

Special Events

From spectacular airshows to quaint and quirky customs, take a tip from the professionals if you want the best pictures.

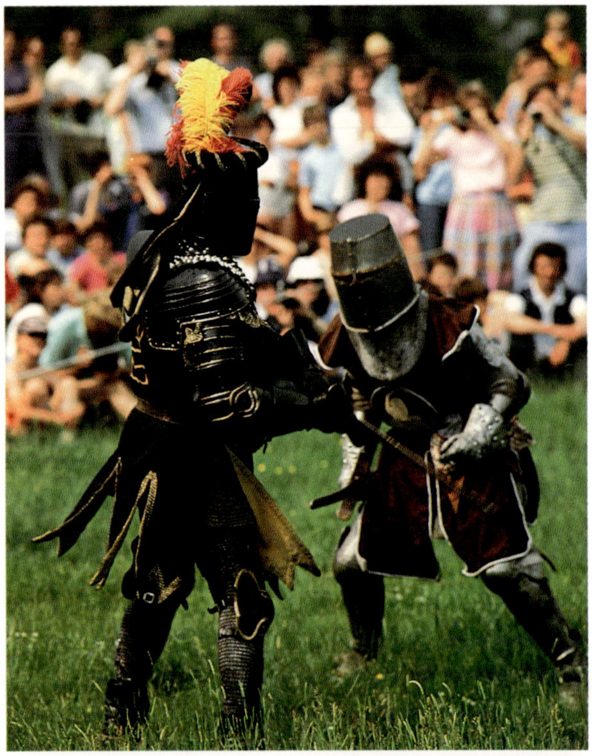

Mediaeval-style tournaments and jousts are becoming increasingly popular. They certainly constitute a 'special' event in that you do not see them every day, but it is essential to get in as close as possible in order to show what is going on.

There are innumerable displays, exhibitions, and special events all over the British Isles every year. Mostly, they take place at a weekend or in the evening, so they are not strictly 'holidays' in the sense of an extended vacation, but they are still subjects well worth photographing.

In this chapter, we have dealt mainly with outdoor events, but it is also worth remembering that there are all sorts of indoor events from circuses to flower shows to model engineering exhibitions to such spectacles as the Royal Tournament at Earls Court. For these indoor events, a fast film (see pages 124-125) is usually much more use than flash; this is especially true where you are photographing action, as flash is likely to be either dangerous or useless, or sometimes both. It can be dangerous if you are close enough to blind the performers - imagine what could happen to a trapeze artist who could not see to grasp her partner's hands! - and it will be useless in any case if you are more than about fifteen or twenty feet (five or six metres) from your subject, as the light simply will not carry that far.

For those indoor events such as circuses and the Royal Tournament, where the action is mostly brilliantly spotlit against comparative darkness, it is usually a good idea to set the film speed dial on your camera (see pages 116-117)

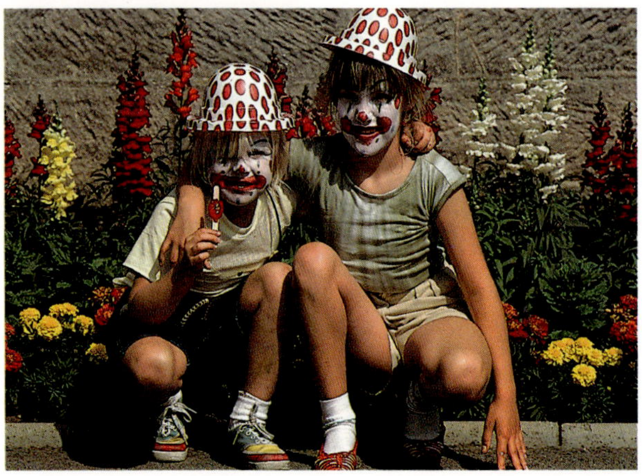

Many fairs nowadays operate face-painting stalls for children - and most children love it! Most pictures of this kind are strictly snapshots for the family album, but because they are so humorous, they can also be used for decoration, and grandparents usually love to have copies.

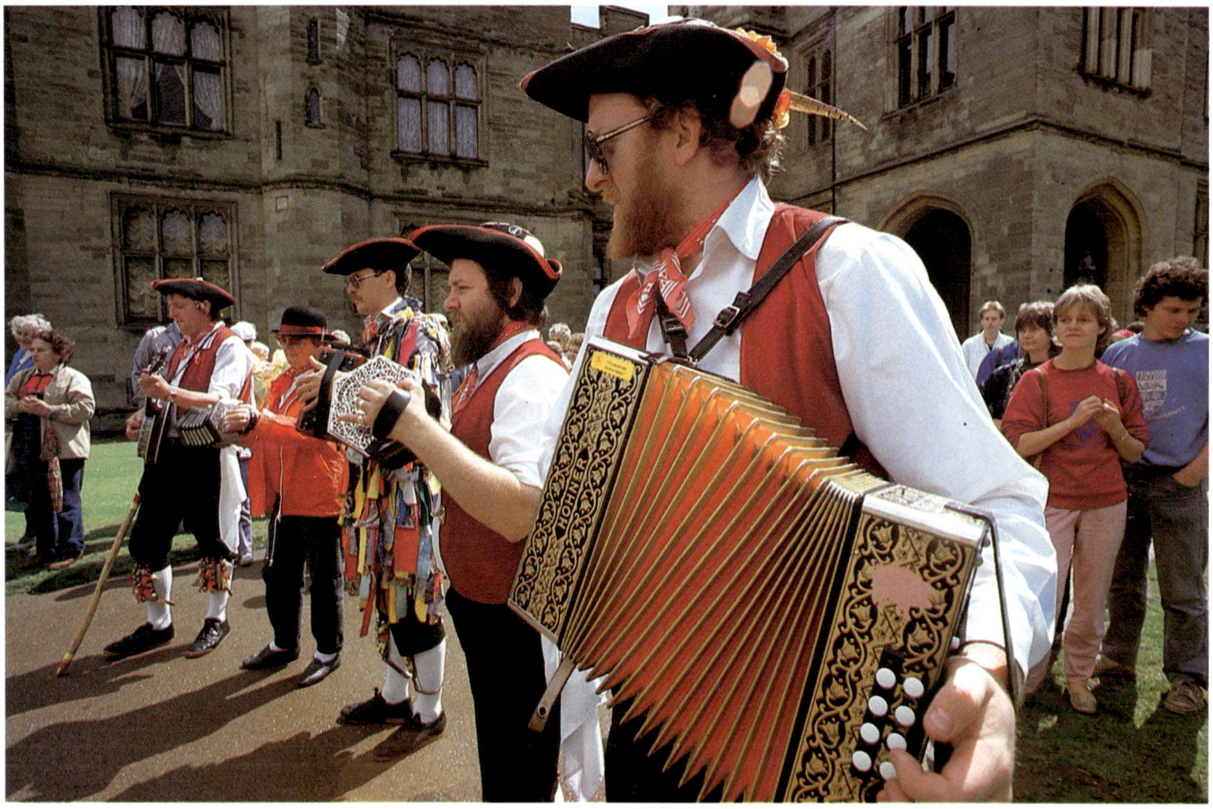

Rather than shooting this picturesque trio 'head-on', the photographer looked for a different angle. By leading the viewer into the frame in this manner, the result is far more visually pleasing than the more obvious formal portrait.

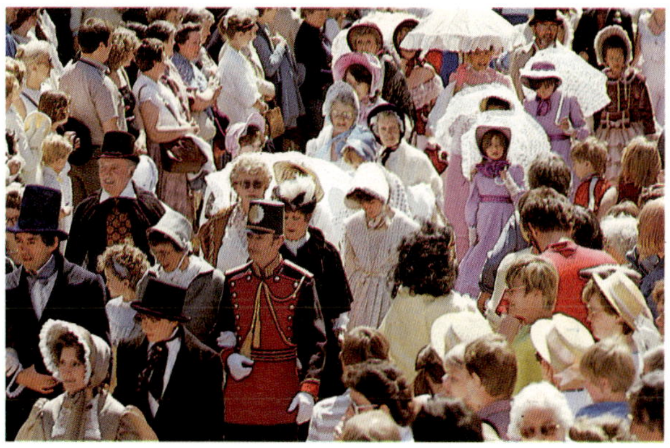

Parades and carnivals are always worth shooting, but get there early so that you can secure a good position.

to two or three times the manufacturer's recommended speed, as the large areas of darkness will otherwise fool the meter and your pictures will consist of nothing more than brilliant white blobs against a murky background. If you are using ISO 1000 film (pages 124-125 again), this means setting the dial to 2000 or even 3000: if the camera will not accept this, just set it as high as it will go.

At any event, indoors or outdoors, your main concern is going to be to get an unobstructed view of the subject, without other people in the way. Generally, this means arriving early, so that you can have your pick of the seats or camera positions; this has the additional bonus that you may be able to get pictures of people or vehicles arriving, especially at the various kinds of rallies, before the crowds arrive. There is more about this overleaf.

For news of displays, exhibitions, or local events, you can watch your local newspaper or (once again) contact your Regional Tourist Board or local Tourist Information Centre.

Vintage Car Rallies

This picture of a 1932 Sunbeam New 20 shows the two typical problems of shooting at vintage car rallies: a messy background, and an awkward horizon line which more or less coincides with the driver's head. Ideally, you should use a significantly higher viewpoint (so that the background is mostly grass) or a significantly lower one (so that it is mostly sky) - and in this case, it would have been a good idea to photograph the car a few yards further down the road, so as to lose the telephone wire.

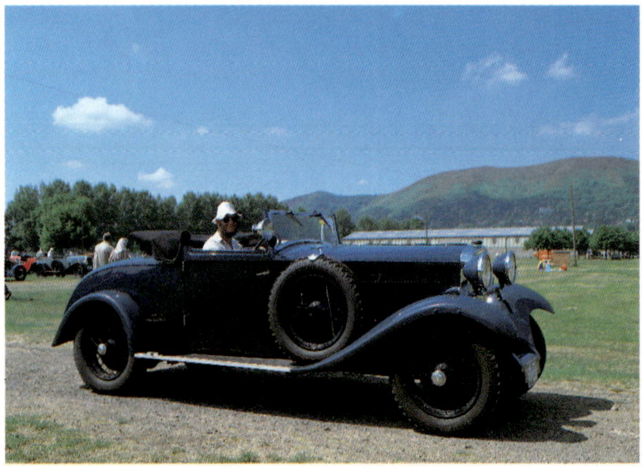

Even at a crowded rally (right), you can take close-ups, and they are often more effective than the 'long shots' because they do not suffer from distracting backgrounds.

Although vintage car rallies (and vintage motorcycle rallies too, for that matter) are fascinating events, the best opportunities for pictures are *not* to be found when the cars are parked in neat rows for inspection, awaiting the judging. There are untidy crowds of people, judges wandering to and fro, and unsightly signs giving the history of the car and warning you not to touch it.

Ideally, you want to be there *as the cars are arriving*, preferably in a carefully chosen position so that you can photograph them as they roll past an attractive backdrop; a country house is particularly good, as the odd knot of people standing around outside does not look out of place. Because the cars will normally arrive fairly early in the day, before the crowds turn up, you can often get a good, clear view of them - and because you are there early, the drivers will assume that you are a fellow driver, or at least an enthusiast, rather than just another hanger-on. This makes it very much easier to talk to them, and you can sometimes persuade them to move their vehicles to a more attractive place for photography.

Alternatively (or as well), you could wait until the meeting breaks up, when you can photograph the cars as they leave. Sometimes this will not be terribly satisfactory, because there will still be groups of spectators leaving, but at other times you may be able to photograph the owners picnicking around their cars, which they may well have moved away from the judging arena.

The third choice is to photograph the cars as they roll around the judging enclosure: usually, at least the winners will do this, and sometimes the others will too. The background may be a little messy, but at least there should not be any people between you and the car!

Whatever you do, try not to ask stupid questions: think of the hundreds of times that the owners must be asked the same thing, and bite your tongue. If you know something about the *marque*, and can ask something intelligent, the situation is very different: you may be welcomed as a fellow-*aficionado*.

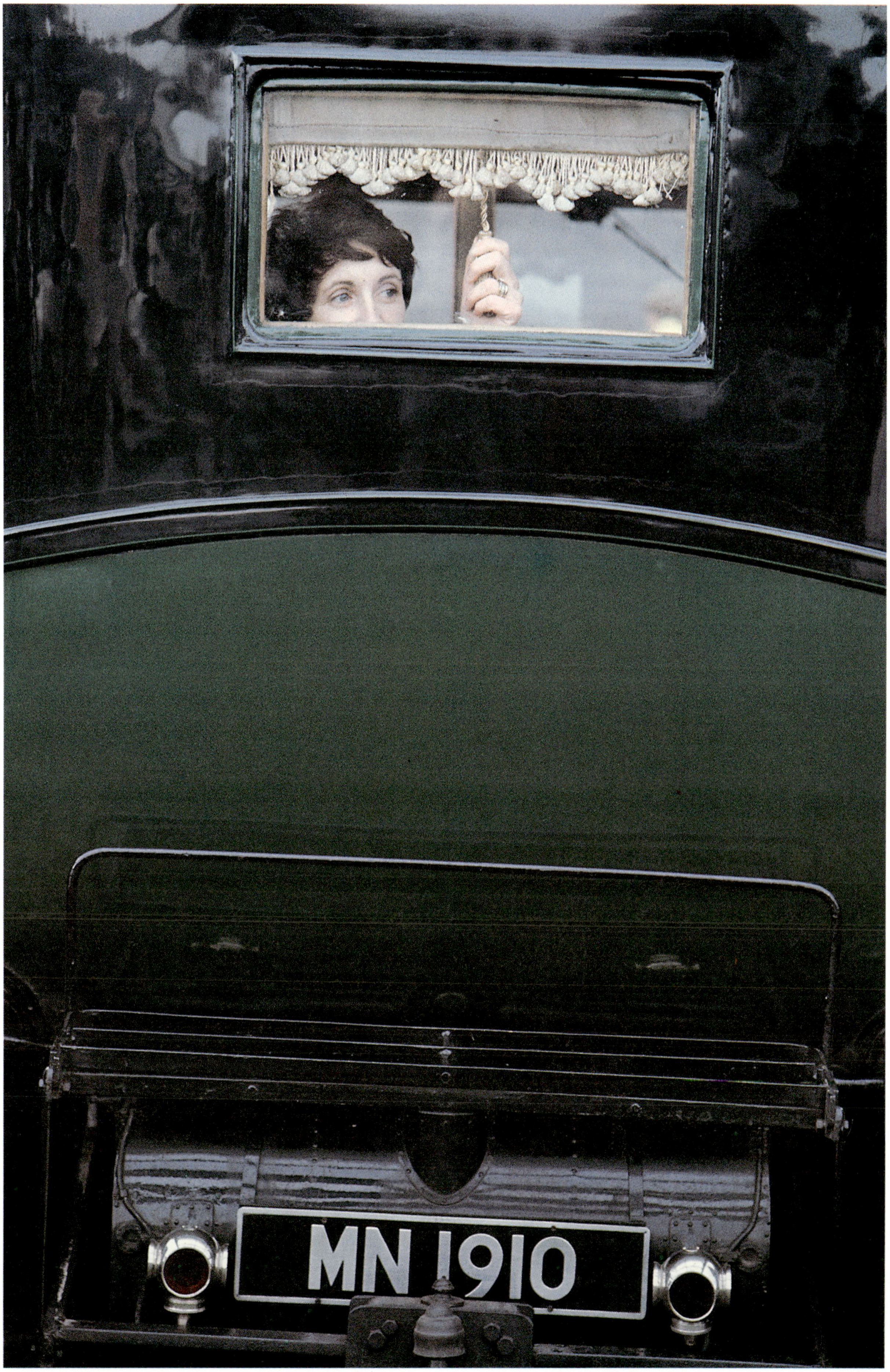
MN 1910

Steam Rallies

All through the summer, there are traction engine displays and steam fairs at locations throughout the country. A day trip to see these mighty road engines is usually welcomed by all the family, but you can increase your enjoyment (photographic and otherwise) by finding out a little about the subject first.

To begin with, there are likely to be three types of vehicles present, plus stationary engines. Traction engines are the best known, and there are two main subdivisions: agricultural engines, and showmen's engines. Agricultural engines were the forerunner of the tractor, and were used for pulling and powering agricultural machinery, while showmen's engines are much more gaudy and ornamented and were used both to tow carnival rides from one town to another and to drive them when they were set up. Sometimes, there will be 'tug-of-war'

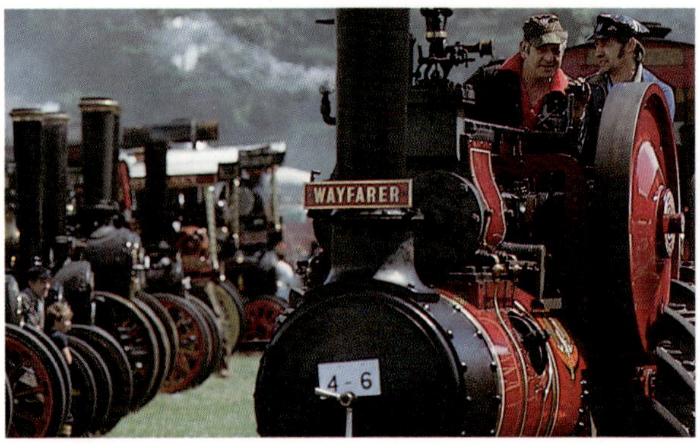

The drivèr and fireman of the Wayfarer provide another lesson in composition; they are very nearly on the intersection of thirds, and they are looking into the picture. The only discordant note is the modern judging number on the front of the boiler.

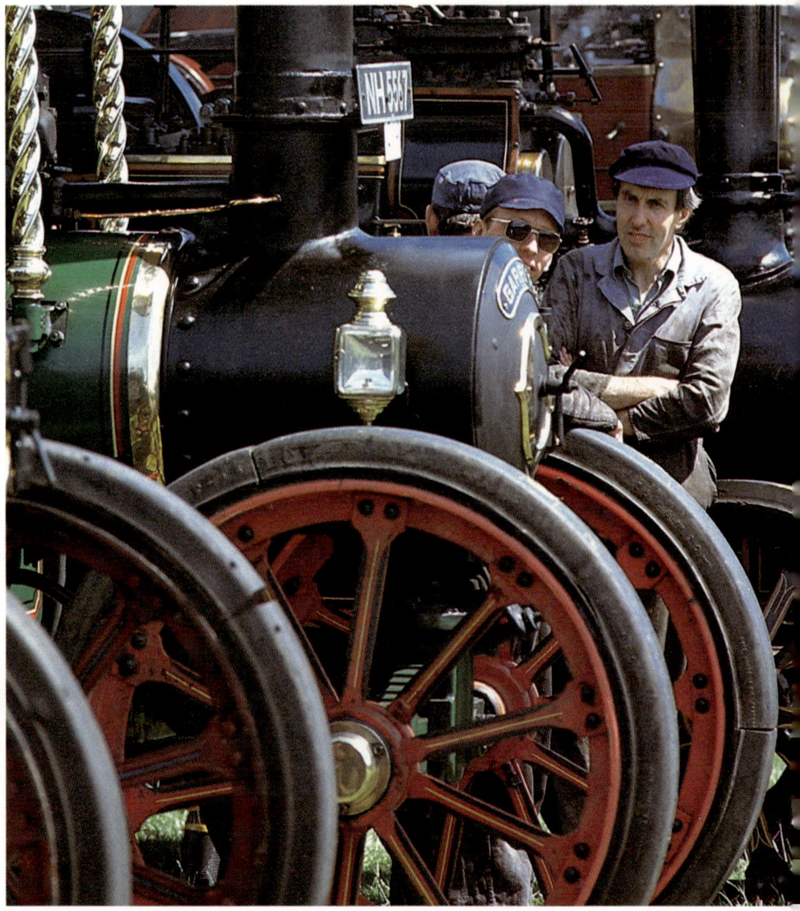

competitions between traction engines, which are an impressive sight as the great engines strain to pull each other in opposite directions. Interestingly, a steam engine delivers maximum torque at zero r.p.m.; this, together with its great weight, means that if you get a chance to bet on a tractor/traction engine tug-o-war, bet on the traction engine.

Secondly, there are likely to be steam lorries. These are all the more intriguing when you consider both how recently they were in use (even into the 1930s) and how incredibly slow they were: London to Bristol, now a couple of hours on the motorway, could take two days with a steam lorry.

Thirdly, there will be steamrollers - real steam-driven steamrollers, not diesel steamrollers. The sheer size and weight of these monsters is impressive, and their

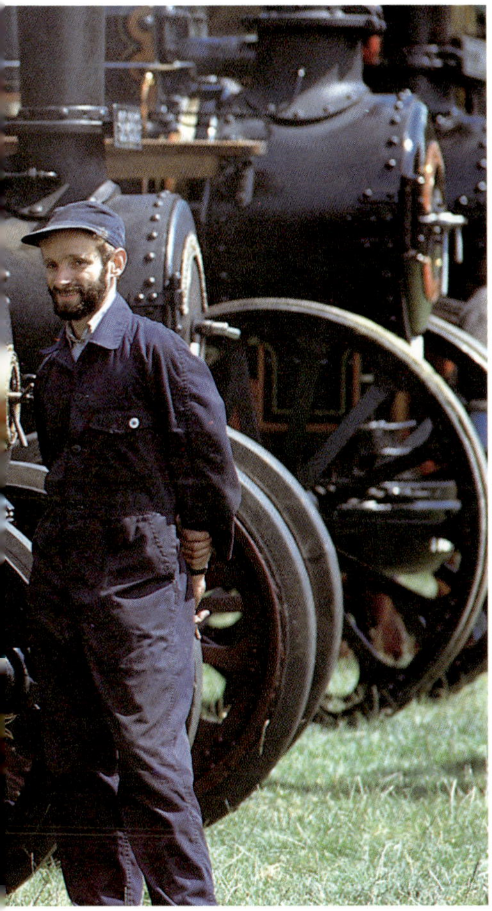

Only rarely can you get a clear shot like this: there are normally just too many people around. The best way to do it is to get permission to go inside the judging enclosure, or simply to arrive early, before the crowds. Note how our 'golden rule' about details applies here: the pose and expression of the driver at the end of the row of engines is delightful.

maximum speed of two or three miles an hour makes them look all the more ponderous.

Finally, stationary engines are like traction engines, but cannot move themselves: they have to be towed.

All these engines make fascinating pictures both 'all in' and as details: the beautiful brasswork, machining and so forth all repay close-ups. As with car rallies, you will do best to arrive early and leave late, so that you can see the vehicles in motion. The only warnings are not about photographic technique, but about the engines themselves. Steam engines often vent steam, which can flay you and wreck your camera, so be careful. They are also very heavy and ponderous, and frequently have no safety guards at all, so stay clear both of moving vehicles and of moving parts, and make sure that the driver is aware of your presence.

A close crop, using a vertical format, allowed the photographer to fill the frame with this Fowler showman's engine; only one sightseer is in the picture, but it might have been better to swing the camera slightly to the right and 'lose' her too.

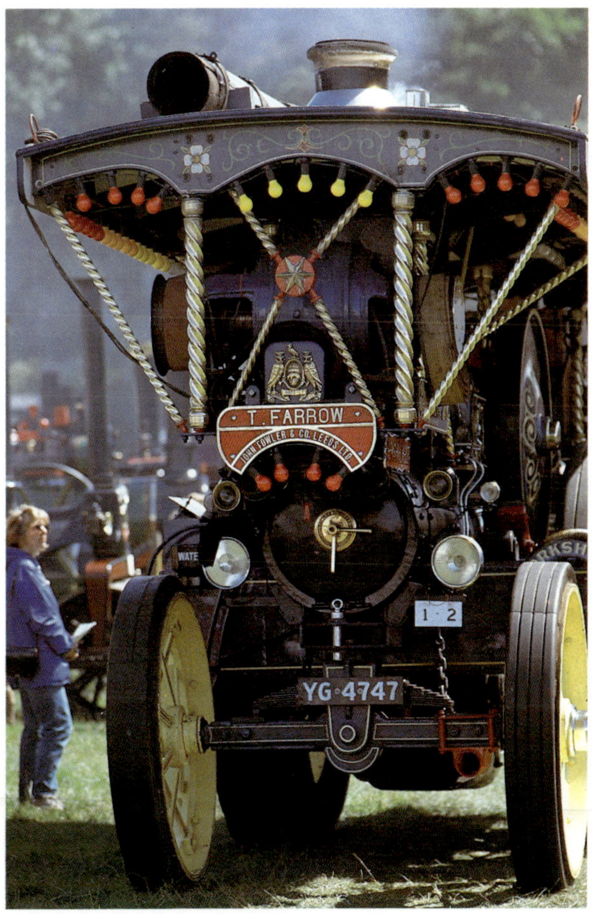

Railways

Although modern diesel locomotives are far quicker and more efficient than the old steam locomotives, there is no doubt that they do not have one-tenth of the romantic appeal. Several clubs throughout the British Isles are dedicated to 'playing trains' on the grand scale, and for children in particular, a ride on a steam train is an unforgettable experience.

The general safety observations given in the last section about steam-driven machinery are equally applicable here, with the additional warning that trains are very difficult to stop quickly and precisely. If you want to get down onto the track, then ask a member of the steam club, follow his instructions, and do not overstay your welcome. Remember again that giving people prints when you go back is an almost certain way of getting better access, and that you may even be able to get in to private sessions, when the public at large is not admitted.

With trains, the attractions lie not only in the engines themselves - though there is plenty to photograph here, and the interior of the engine cab, from the footplate, could make a splendid shot - but also in the carriages, the station furniture and fittings, and even the station canteen: some clubs carry realism to extremes! The contrast of luxury and austerity which the old railways embodied still lives on in these clubs, and you will (if you are lucky) be able to show both first-class luxury and the threadbare mass-transport aspect of Third Class.

If you possibly can, you should also try to get a reasonably 'long shot' of the whole train, with the locomotive in action; on a sunny day, the sparkle of the white steam from the pistons and whistle can be very dramatic.

While you can also get a lot of what the newsmen call 'reaction shots' - people's expressions, especially children's - you may also care to try some deliberately vintage effects. We can all remember those railway-station parting scenes in old movies, and you might wish to try re-creating a vintage *photographic* atmosphere, just as the railway club creates a vintage transport atmosphere. If you have never used it before, this might be the place to try a black and white film.

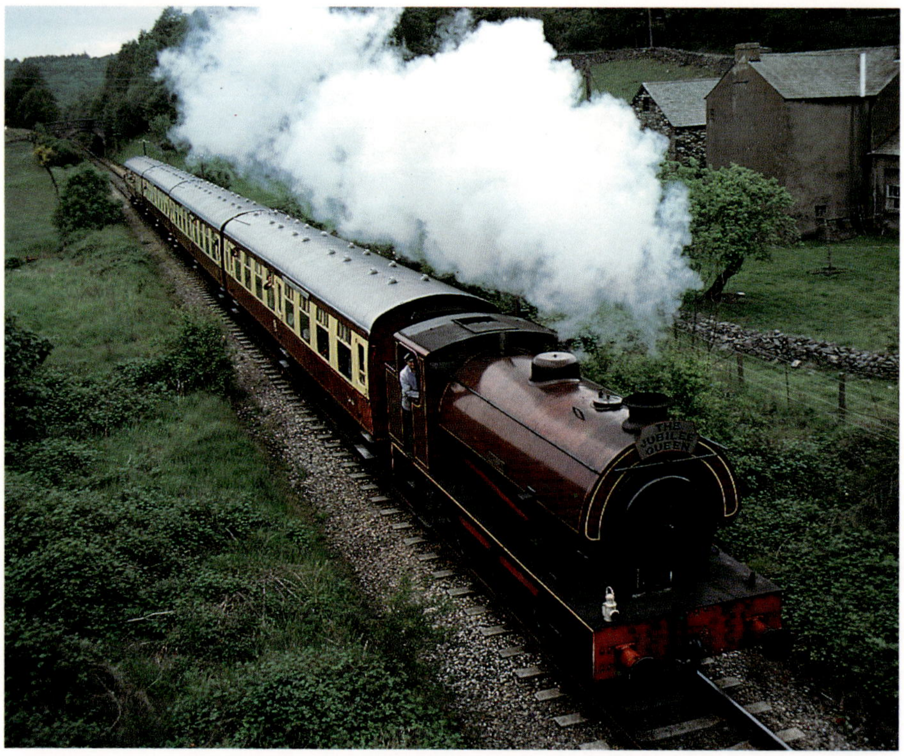

Although details can make wonderful shots, do not neglect the whole train. This steam engine, puffing and steaming self-importantly, is very different from the romantic GER shot opposite, but it is still a charming picture in its own right.

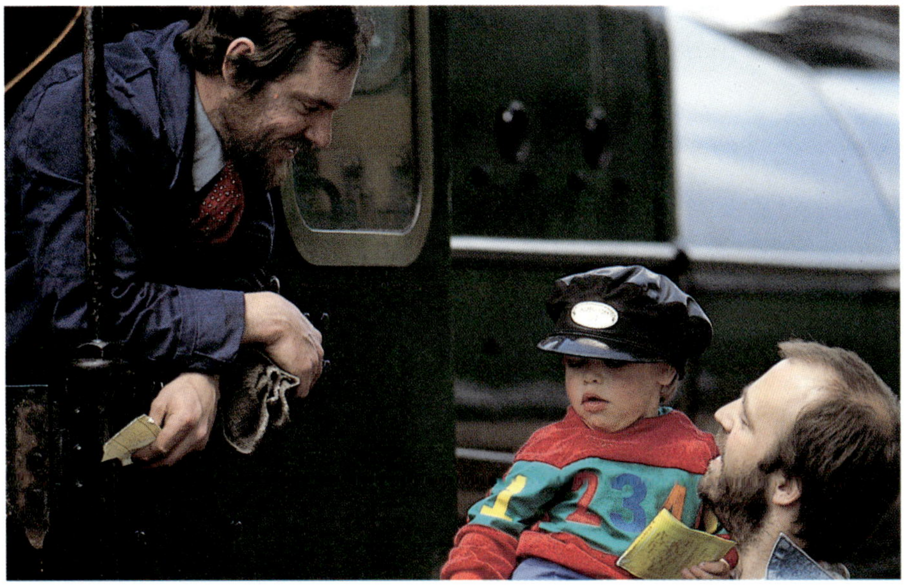

Concentrating on detail can often be just as informative as trying to record the whole picture. Here, the photographer uses the 'less is more' technique to convey the image of railways. It is useful to remember that rather than taking a step backwards in order to include the whole scene, more impact can be made by taking a step closer and concentrating on a small but representative element.

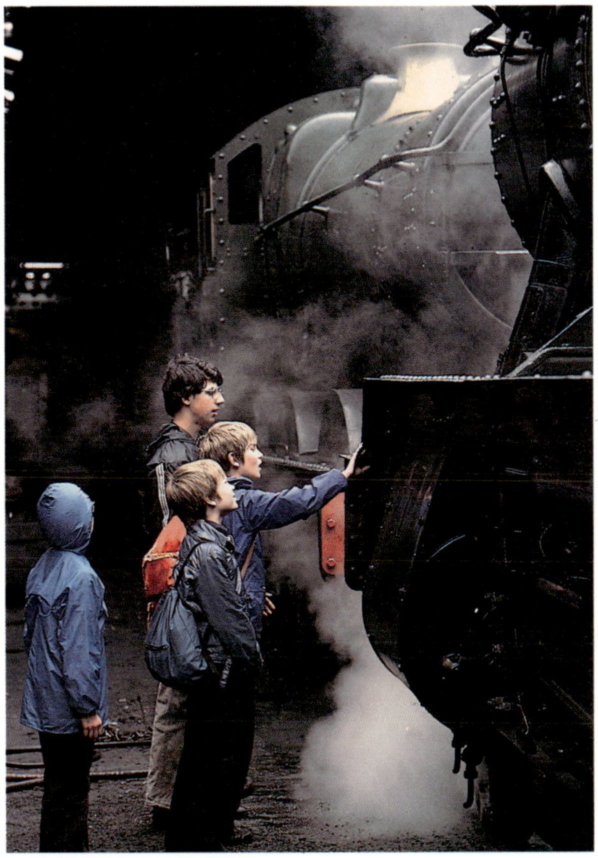

Children are often entranced by steam engines, though it is usually the older child who is really interested; very small children are often frightened by them. The picture of the children silhouetted brightly against the dark engine shed beautifully conveys the sense of wonder that steam locomotives can instill.

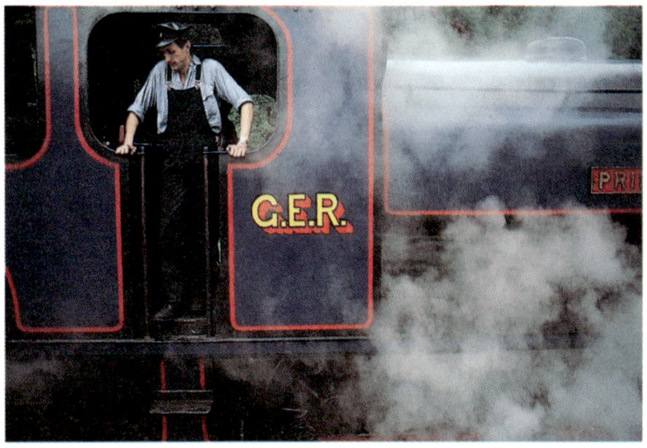

It is the billowing steam that makes this picture really memorable; that, and the curious pose of the driver. It is a most impressive picture and (once again) it is of the 'less is more' school of composition.

Fairs & Shows

There are two kinds of fairs: funfairs, and rural fairs which are more like markets. Both can provide some excellent pictures.

For funfairs, the best time of day is usually early evening, when there is still enough light for comfortable hand-held exposures but the lights of the fair themselves are not swamped by daylight. You may wish to use a fast film (even ISO 1000 - see pages 124-125), because the loss of image quality will be more than offset by the originality of the pictures you can get; indeed, the grain may actually enhance the effect of darkness and hurdy-gurdy which a fair projects.

If you can control shutter speeds, try some long exposures, where the whirling patterns of light can provide dramatic and unusual effects: steady the camera against a tent-pole or a fence-post, but beware of vibration from generators and from the rides themselves.

Photograph the expressions of the people on the rides, and at the stalls: there can be some fascinating mixtures of exhilaration, fear, surprise and concentration. Photograph the barkers and showmen too, but if you can, always avoid flash: not only does it change the atmosphere, but it can also be dangerous if the operator of a ride is temporarily blinded.

At agricultural fairs, watch out for 'characters', the old farmers who have been coming to the fair since before you were born (no matter how old you are, there's always one who will swear he is older than you), with their weatherbeaten faces and tweed suits. You can also photograph the prize fatstock and all the side-shows and stalls, which are much the same as at a funfair, except that you are likely to find the local Women's Institute selling jam and home-made cakes, rather than itinerant stallholders selling candy-floss and hot dogs.

North of the Border, Scottish fairs are as likely as not to incorporate Highland sports such as caber-tossing, and there may well be sword-dancers as well. If you can get to one, a Gathering of the Clans such as the Braemar Gathering or the Cowal Gathering is well worth photographing.

For the best pictures at any country fair, go along as soon as it opens (which is usually at some alarmingly early hour such as six or seven in the morning) and, if you can stand the pace, try to document the progress of the whole day. At most country fairs, the pubs are granted a special extension to stay open all day, though whether this will be a help or a hindrance to your photography is for you to decide!

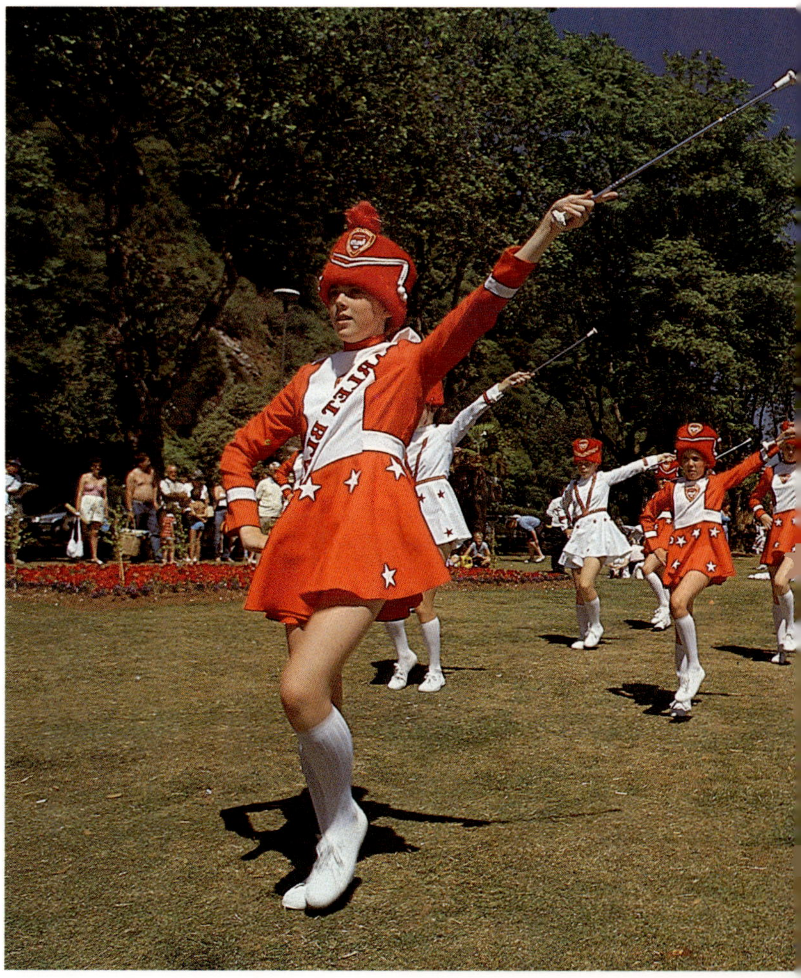

Drum majorettes are not easy to photograph; getting an angle which shows all the girls to advantage, without distracting backgrounds or an awkward horizon, requires thought. Here, the photographer has dropped his viewpoint to well below the girls' eye-line, which makes them look taller and allows a background mostly of trees. Shot from a normal adult eye-level, the picture would have been much less effective.

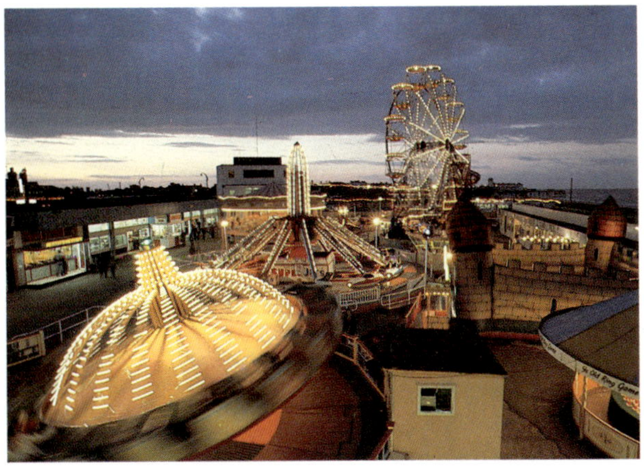

The very best time to photograph a fair is usually at dusk, when the lights are on but there is still some light in the sky. Longer exposure would result in much greater blur in the picture, as in the windmill arms on page 44.

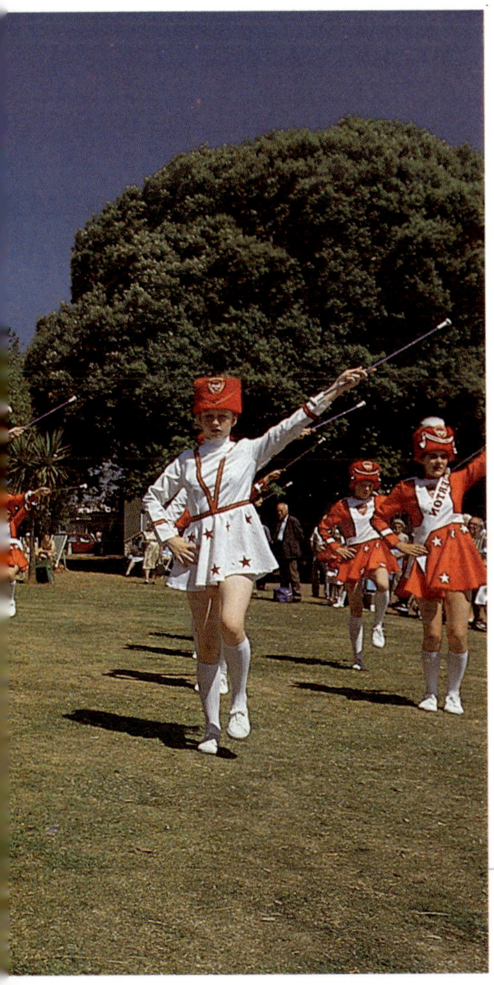

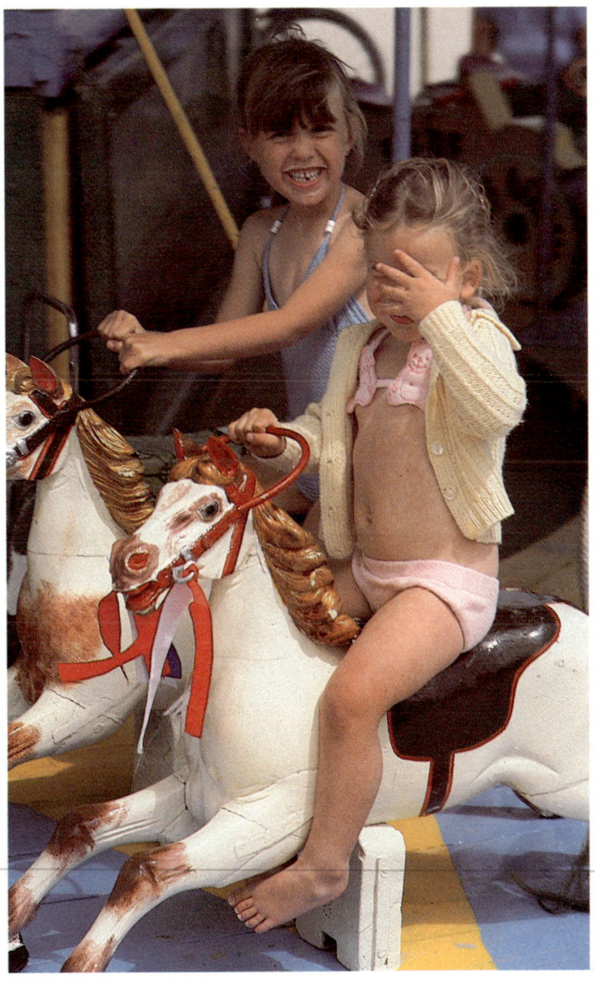

Children and fairground rides can make for appealing pictures, although pictures shot at night are sometimes more effective than daytime ones; there is something about the glare of a fairground's lights, and the smell of onions frying for hot-dogs, which is much more magical after dark.

High Days & Holy Days

The origin of the word 'holiday' is of course 'holy day': the only holidays which the majority of our mediaeval ancestors enjoyed were the numerous saints' days and religious festivals with which the calendar was punctuated. In our secular age, we have separated religion and recreation rather more, but there are still a surprising number of religious festivals, which can be visually attractive and extremely interesting whether you are religious or not. Easter and Christmas vigils are an obvious example, and can furnish some very striking pictures - but use a fast film and a quiet camera, as both flash and the slam-bang of a reflex mirror could destroy the mood of the occasion. Carol services are another obvious subject, and there are still surprisingly many local festivals like the beating of bounds, blessing of boats, and so forth. Some are on the way out, and they are worth recording while they still survive.

Our increasingly multi-cultural and multi-religious society also provides the opportunity to photograph a variety of religious festivals that is probably unparalleled in any other country. Of course, an unfamiliar religion may have its own pitfalls and taboos, but as long as you are respectful, most people will welcome the opportunity to explain to you something about their most cherished beliefs. Although British Hindu festivals cannot boast the splendour of the originals in India, there are still celebrations to be seen. The same is true of Islam, though Moslems are not much given to pomp and circumstance, and a truly orthodox Moslem will refuse to have his picture taken: the making of images is forbidden by the Koran.

If you live in the right places, though, you can witness everything from Druidic festivals to *Losar* (the Tibetan New Year). In the far North there is the Viking festival of Up-Helly-Aa, and in more and more towns there is a strong Chinese community who celebrate *their* New Year with the tradition 'Dragon Dance'; London's Chinatown, in Soho, is the best known.

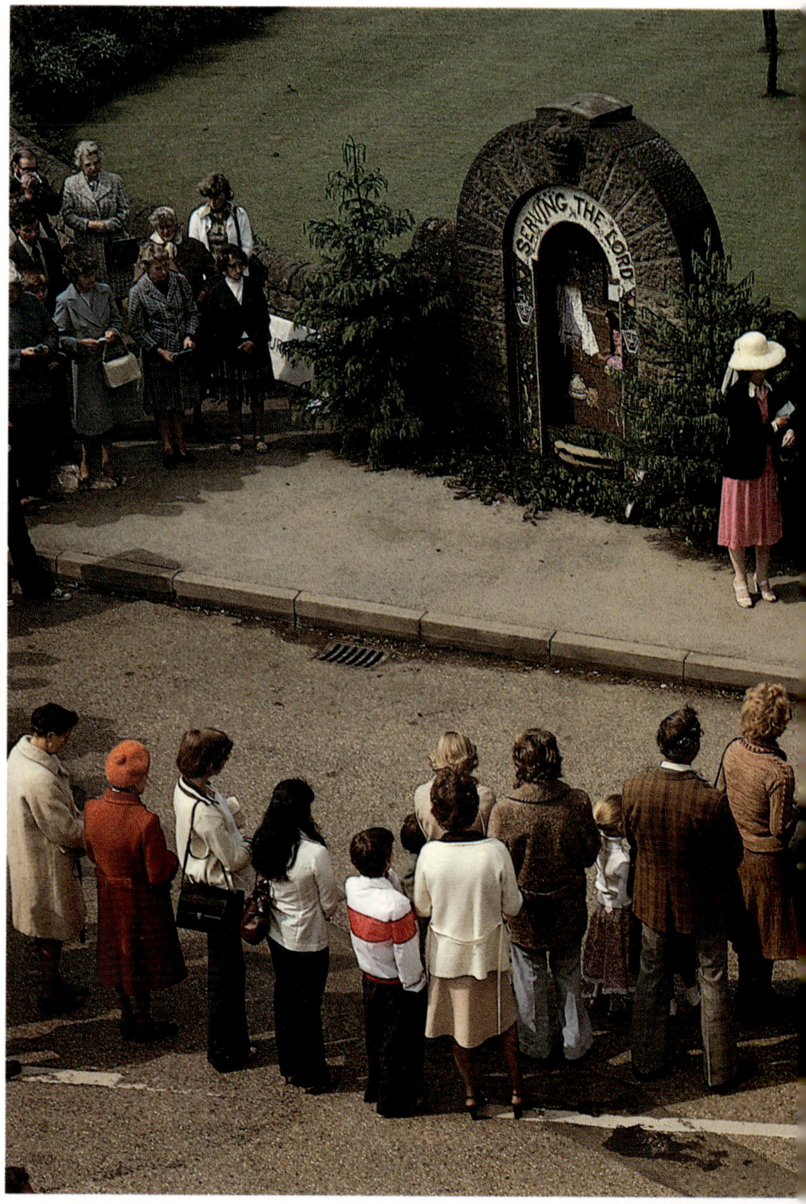

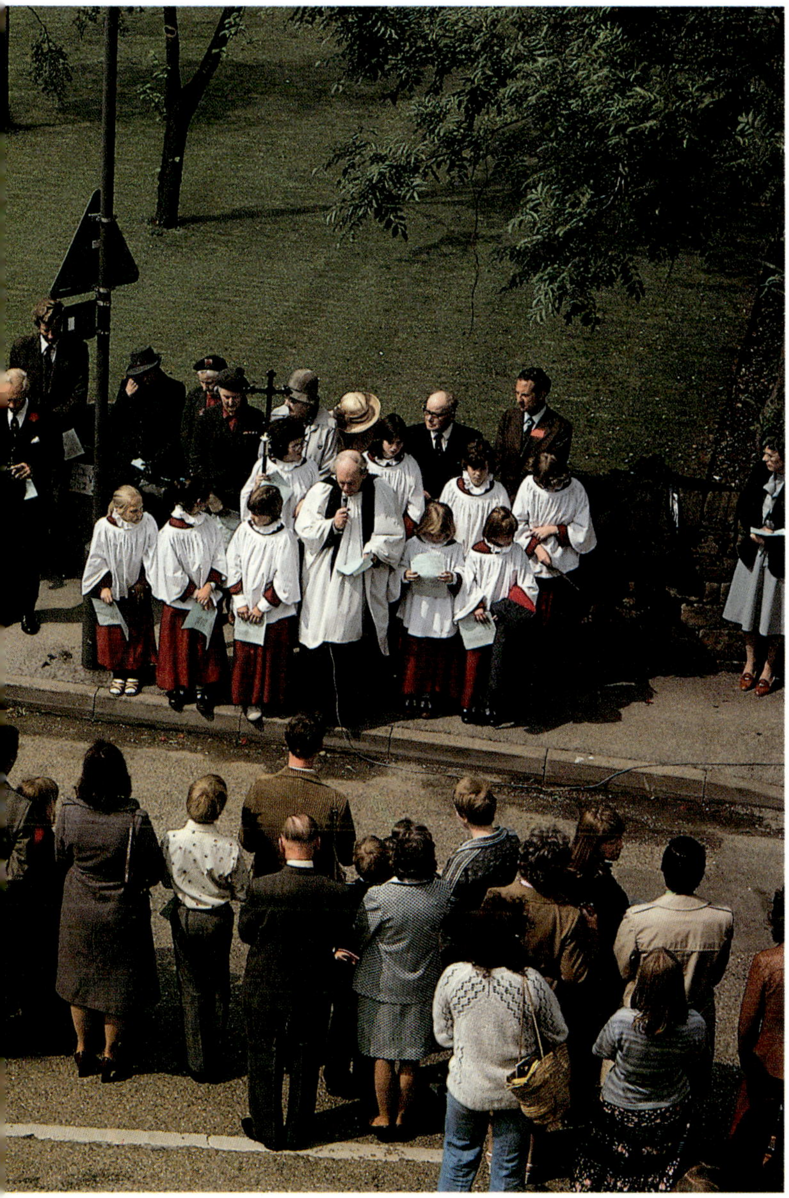

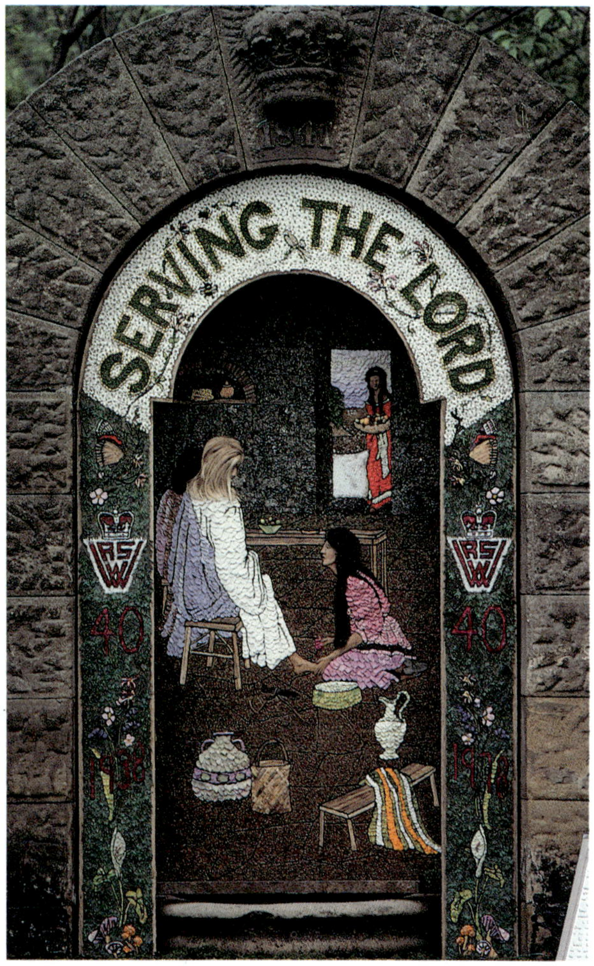

As well as the obvious feasts and festivals such as Easter vigils and Christmas midnight masses, there are all kinds of other religious festivals which survive in different areas. These pictures of Well Dressing in Rowsley shów a festival which is probably pre-Christian in origin, but which has been taken over by the church.

CHAPTER NINE

Equipment & Materials

The choice of equipment is between simplicity and versatility - though you can have both, at a price.

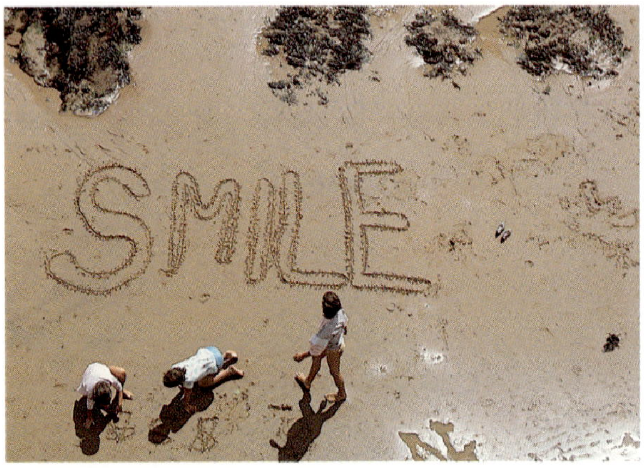

The most important thing for any photographer to cultivate is an eye for a picture; ultimately, equipment must be secondary to vision. A picture like this one, taken one evening in Sidmouth, could have been taken with any camera.

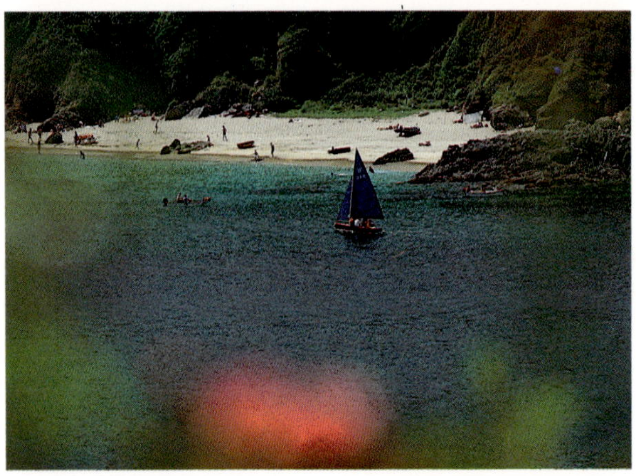

Although compacts are arguably best for photographing people, the reflex (see page 118) is generally agreed to be better for landscapes, as you can see what is in focus and what is not just by looking through the viewfinder. Here, out-of-focus flowers in the foreground add contrasting colour to deep blue sea.

Although this book is concerned mainly with how to make the best of the equipment you already own, there is no doubt that your choice of equipment will have a strong influence on your photography. Put crudely, the more you spend on a camera, the more versatile it will be.

But as we have already seen, versatility is not everything. Increasing versatility usually brings increasing complication, and many people are not interested in this: they want their photography to be as simple as possible.

This chapter, therefore, looks at the advantages and disadvantages of the different kinds of cameras. Inevitably, as professionals, the contributors to this book are biased: we use expensive SLR cameras (see page 118) with interchangeable lenses and all kinds of accessories. But most of us started out with simple cameras, often a lot more limited than the cheapest cameras available today, and if we had nothing else, we would go back to them. Photography is like a bug; if you catch it, you can really catch it seriously. For all of us, any camera is better than no camera.

It is also important to recognise that you don't *have* to catch the bug at all. If you want to keep your photographic life simple, do not be afraid to do so; don't be pressurised by the advertisements, or by equipment snobs who always have the latest super-expensive electronic wonder. The rest of this chapter - with the exception of the very end, which looks at how you can use all these pictures we have been urging you to take - is concerned with how to choose equipment (and film) and with how to get the best from your choice.

As you read the following sections, keep asking yourself the following five questions. See how well the different camera types meet your requirements, and choose accordingly.

- Am I satisfied with the camera I have got?
- Would I take any more pictures if I did change my camera?
- What do I want the pictures for?
- Am I prepared to take the extra trouble that a more expensive and more versatile camera would require?
- How much am I prepared to spend, and how much am I prepared to carry?

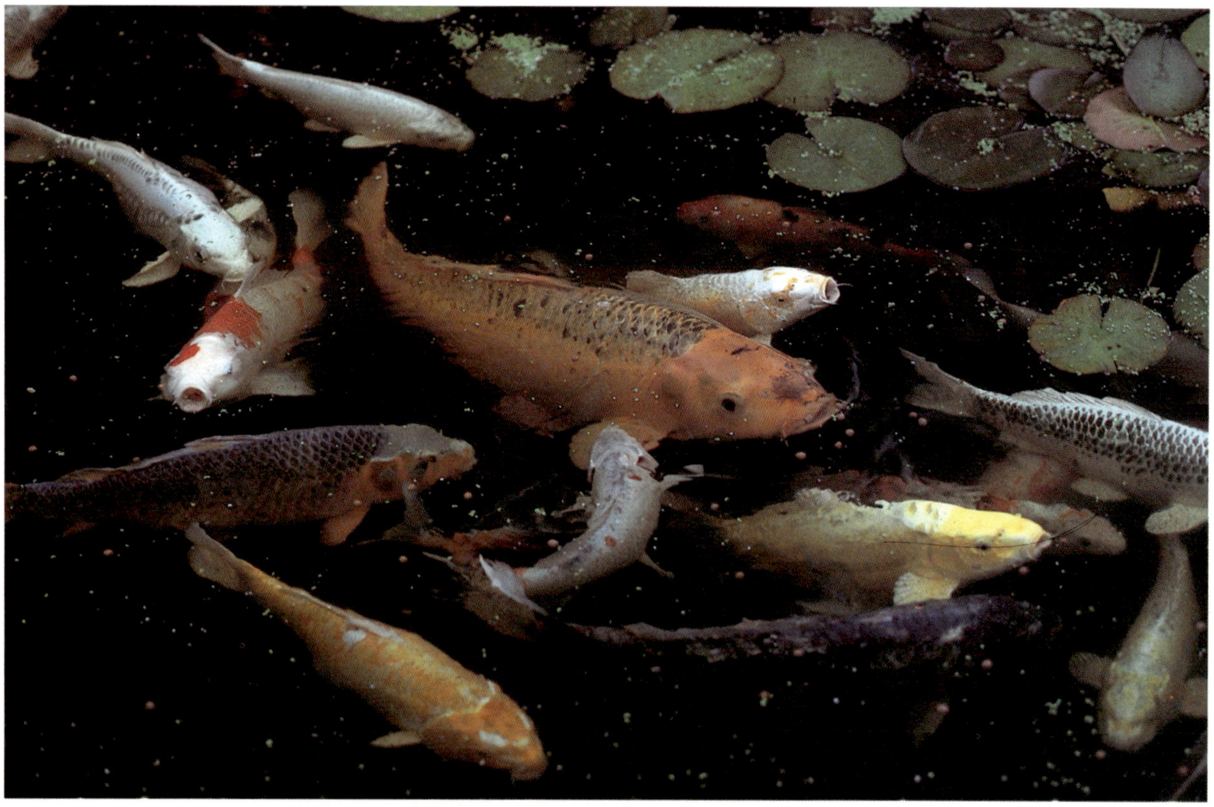

Even if you have an eye for a picture, your camera needs to be able to translate your vision into a photograph. For this sort of picture, a simple camera will do, but 35mm will give better quality than 110 or disc, and a 35mm SLR allows the use of a polarising filter in order to reduce surface reflections and increase colour saturation. You can also enlarge more from a 35mm negative; this would make a very fine 10 × 8″ (or larger) print.

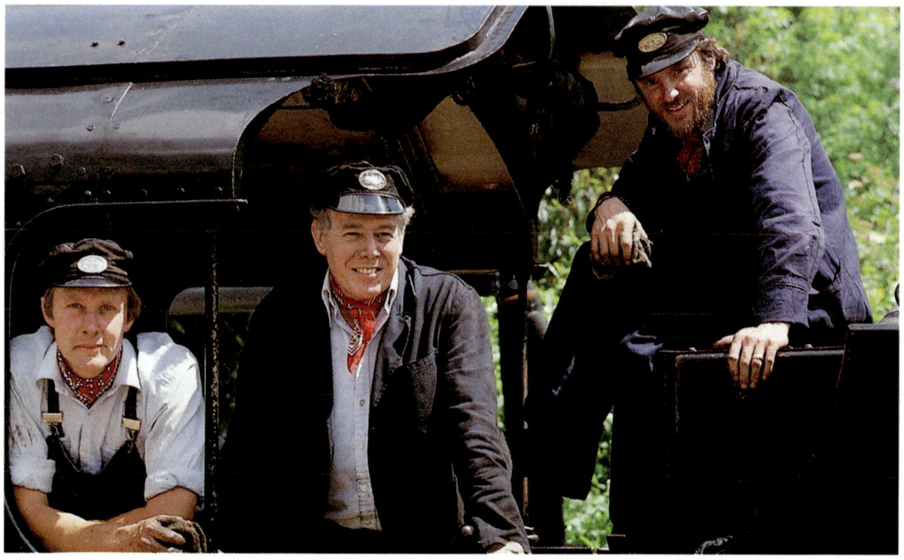

Even with posed shots like this one, you have to shoot quickly or your subjects rapidly become stiff and wooden-looking. The small, light, fast-handling auto-exposure compact camera is ideal for 'people' shots.

Disc & 110 Cameras

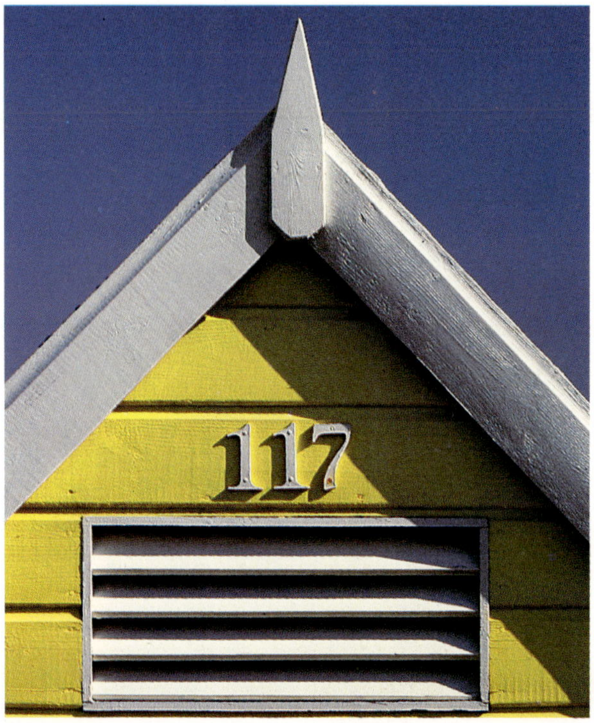

A picture such as this could be taken with almost any camera. The bold, graphic shapes are what make the picture work, and they would be as clear with a disc camera as with a much more expensive piece of equipment.

The advantages of disc and 110 cameras are not hard to see: they are cheap to buy, and they are easy to use. In fact, they are the perfect cameras for people who don't want to go to too much trouble over photography.

They do have one big drawback, though. Both disc and 110 cameras have tiny negatives, which simply cannot hold as much detail and sharpness as the bigger 35mm frame - or even as much as the old rollfilm box cameras, for that matter. Even at enprint size, the picture quality is distinctly 'mushy' and grainy when compared with a print from a bigger camera, and if you have ever tried to have a disk or 110 picture 'blown up' to 10 × 8" (20 × 25cm) you will know just how little detail you can expect.

This does not mean that these little cameras are useless, but it does mean that you have to be very careful what sort of subjects you photograph with them. Any picture which depends for its effect upon detail (such as a lot of people in one picture) or on texture (such as an old castle wall, or lush spring foliage) is likely to be very disappointing, whereas those pictures which depend on big, graphic shapes and masses of bold colour can be surprisingly effective. To take a simple example, a picture of a bed of flowers is likely to look like a bowl of Technicolor porridge, but a close-up of a single flower (if your camera will do close-ups) can be very effective.

The other main drawback of these cameras is that they are made for people who want their photography to be as trouble-free as possible. Well, we all want that, but as we have seen from the rest of this book, you have to take *some* trouble if you want really good pictures. Most people who buy disc and 110 cameras are prepared to put up with a certain loss of quality in return for ease of use, which is perfectly reasonable, but whether you are going to put up with that quality loss is up to you.

There are some disc and 110 cameras with all sorts of advanced specifications, but by the time you buy one of these you are spending the same amount of money as would buy you a 35mm compact, which is only very slightly more difficult to use, but will give you vastly better quality. About the only use for disc and 110 cameras is for the sort of pictures where the memory is more important than the picture; if you want pictures that you can be proud of *as pictures*, you will do better with 35mm.

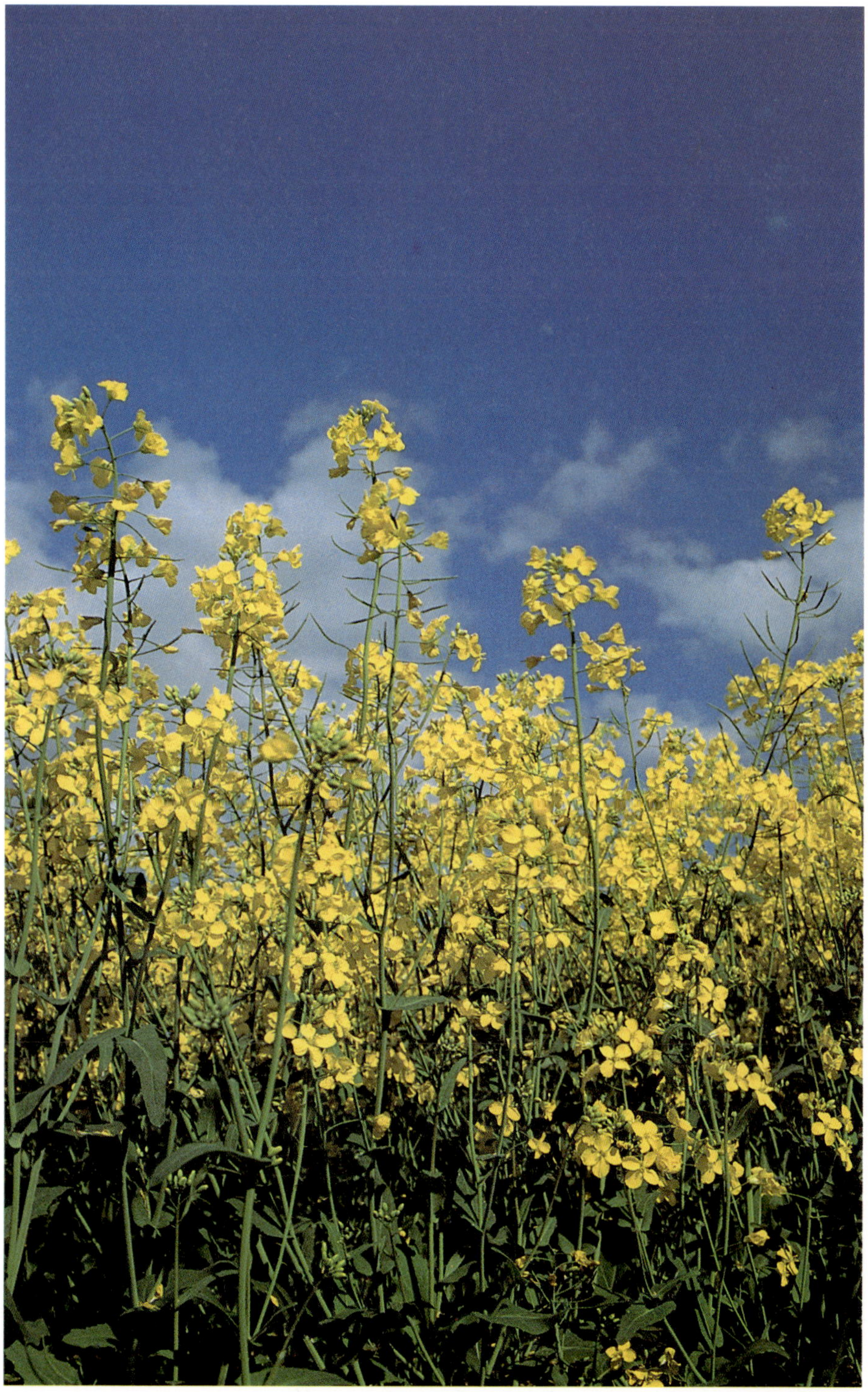

For a picture like this, where fine detail and the texture of the flowers and leaves is important, a disc or 110 camera would not really be suitable.

Instant Picture Systems

Polaroid introduced instant pictures to the world in 1948. Since then there have been tremendous strides in instant picture technology. In addition to their amateur products, Polaroid make all kinds of specialist films for technical and scientific purposes. In fact they make over 15 kinds of polaroid film but for our purposes the main types of film are the SX70 film, which requires no peeling apart, and the 'peel-apart' material.

Polaroid cameras are extremely easy to use and their great advantage is their immediacy; you can always shoot a picture again there and then and you can take extra pictures to give to friends as presents and souvenirs.

Another advantage of Polaroid cameras is that you don't have to finish a whole film, which can be as much as 36 exposures, nor do you have to wait to have the pictures processed.

Polaroid films are available everywhere and are easy to load into the camera. To make sure you get the right sort of film, it is a good idea for you to take your camera along to the shop with you.

Although there are no negatives from Polaroid colour film, Polaroid offers a copying and enlarging service. This

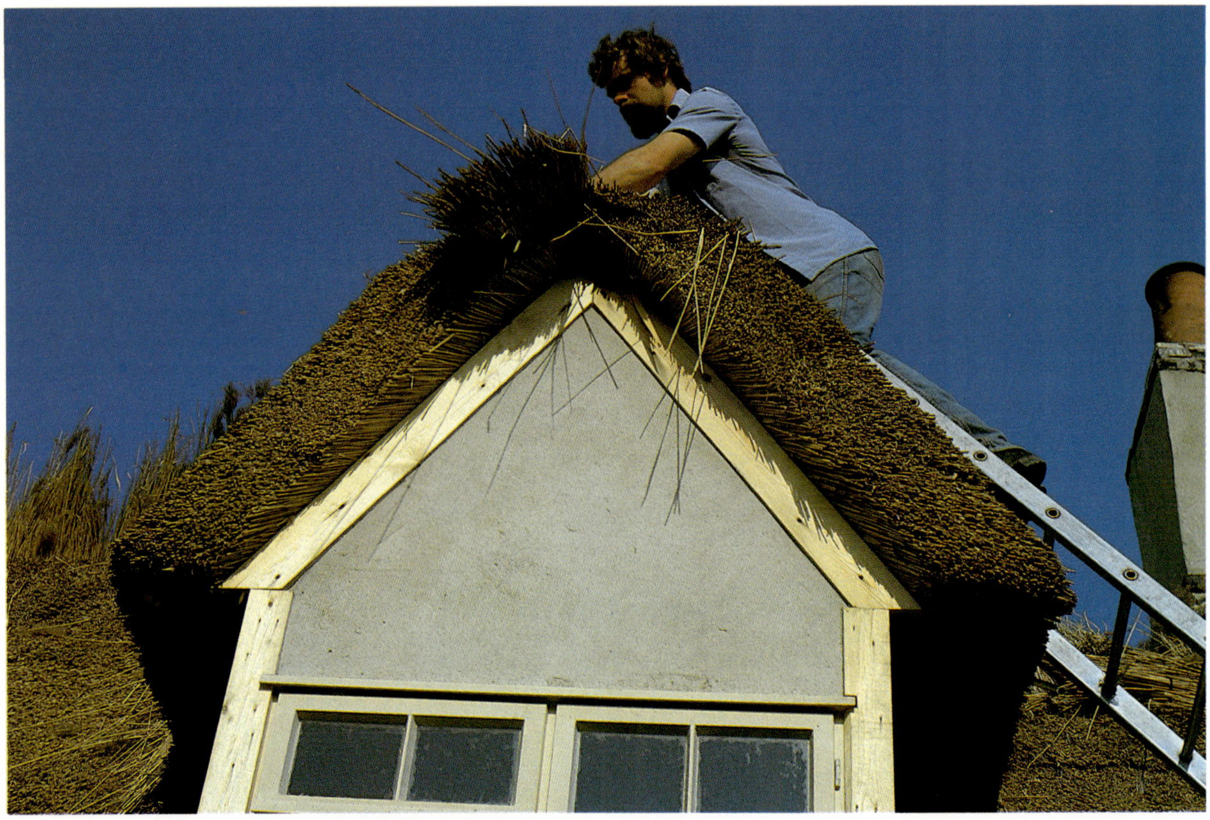

As with the Punch and Judy picture (far right), this picture of thatchers at work could be quickly and easily captured with an instant-picture camera. A great advantage of the self-developing print is that you can give a copy to the subjects, at the time. A slightly sneaky trick, of course, is that you keep the one which is better exposed or composed, and give them another copy!

removes the objection that some people had to Polaroid materials, which was that it was impossible to get copies or enlargements.

Another objection to Polaroid used to be that the quality was not as good as with conventional pictures. This is not true any more, if it ever was; in fact professionals who use Polaroid film to preview their pictures sometimes find that the Polaroid shot is the best one from the entire session. The quality has been known to be so good that these pictures have sometimes been used in the advertisements themselves!

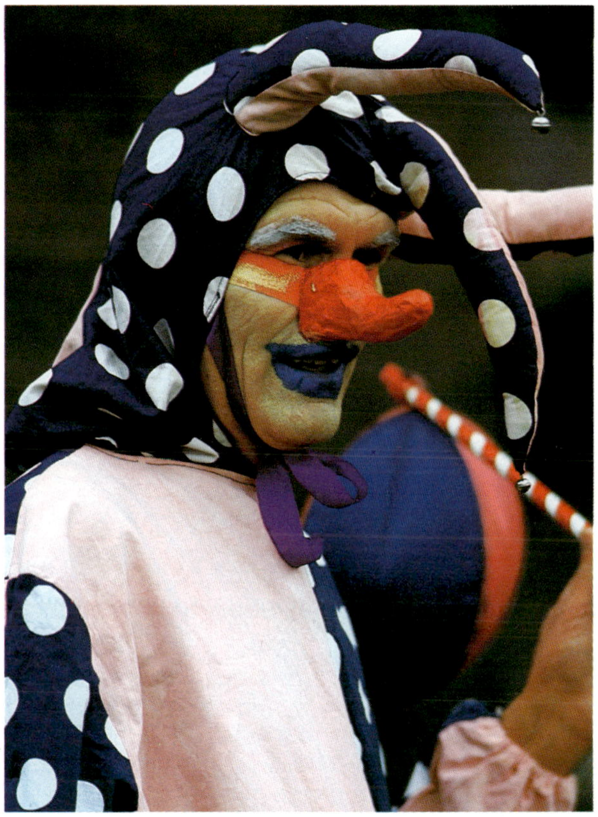

Possibly the most popular and best suited job that Polaroid cameras do, is recording parties or gatherings. Whereas other cameras might capture the spirit of a birthday party, a Polaroid can become part of that spirit, often helping to create fun and enjoyment on such occasions.

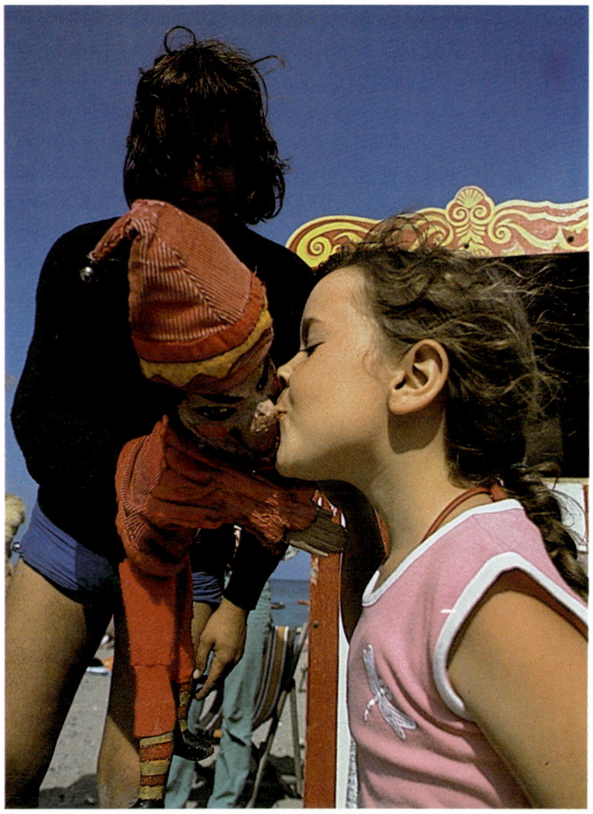

Punch and Judy shows are the sort of subject for which instant-picture cameras are ideal - those occasions when you want a rapid, unpretentious snapshot. If the exposure is not quite right, you can always repeat the shot when the picture has had time to develop.

35mm Compacts

With the 35mm compact camera, you begin to move into the realms of real versatility. They are not as complicated as they seem, and the more expensive models are very easy indeed to use. At the top of the range, there are auto-exposure, auto-focusing cameras which automatically read the film speed from the cartridge that is loaded into them: these are really no more difficult to use than disc or 110 cameras, but the results that you can get are very much better. If you do not want to spend so much, you can get cameras which still set the exposure automatically, but where you have to set the distance yourself, either by scale or with the help of a built-in rangefinder. When you load the camera, you will also have to set the *film speed* (see page 124), but if you always use the same film speed, you will not need to change this setting after the first time.

Setting the distance is not difficult, even by guesswork: small mistakes don't matter. The important thing is to remember to do it at all! If you have never used a rangefinder camera, go into a shop and try one out. It takes a few seconds to get the hang of it, and after that, focusing is very easy indeed. Some people prefer to set the focus themselves, because most autofocus cameras will only focus on the very middle of the picture. If you have (for example) two people standing side by side, this can mean that the camera focuses on the background behind them, and not on them at all! Besides, if you have already set the focus, the camera will take the picture within about 1/50 second of your pressing the shutter release: an autofocus can take up to 1/10 second. Think how fast a child's expression can change in that time!

With the very simplest cameras, you will need to set both the *lens aperture* and the *shutter speed* yourself, but even this is easy if you read the leaflet that comes packed with the film. The shutter speeds (as their name suggests) govern *how long* the shutter is open, and the lens apertures govern *how wide* the lens opens. Shutter speeds are easy, because 1/30 second is obviously longer than 1/60, and 1/60 is longer than 1/125, but apertures are a little tricky in that the *lower* the aperture number, the *wider* the lens opening and the more light it lets through. Aperture numbers follow an odd progression (2.8, 4, 5.6, 8, 11, 16, sometimes with 'in between' numbers), but if you just follow the film leaflet's instructions and set (for example) 1/125 at f/8 for a bright, cloudy day, you do not need to worry about exactly what they mean.

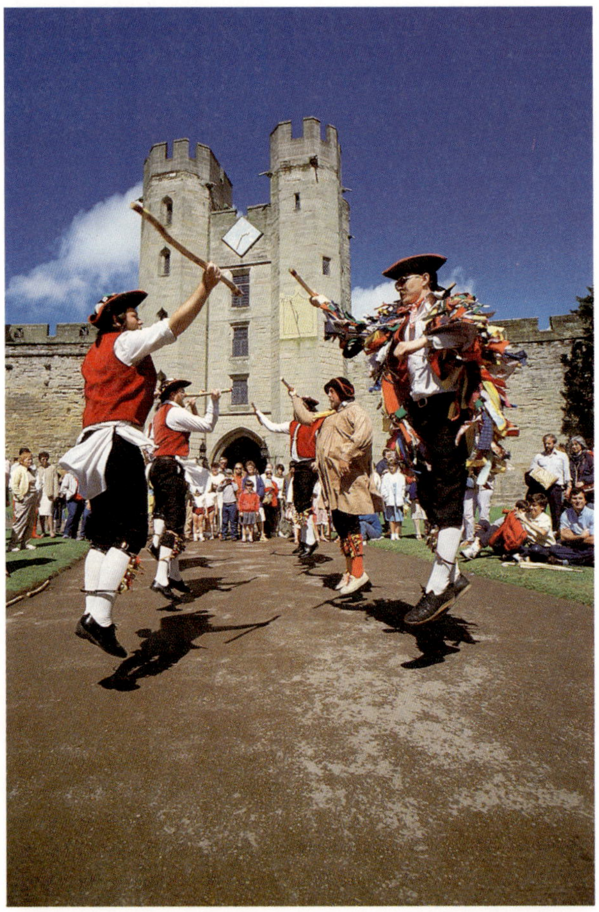

On a bright day, even an automatic camera should set a fast enough shutter speed to 'freeze' these morris-dancers in mid-air; but if you can control your camera, you would choose a fast, action-freezing shutter speed of 1/500 second. Crouching down for a low viewpoint accentuates the height of the jump.

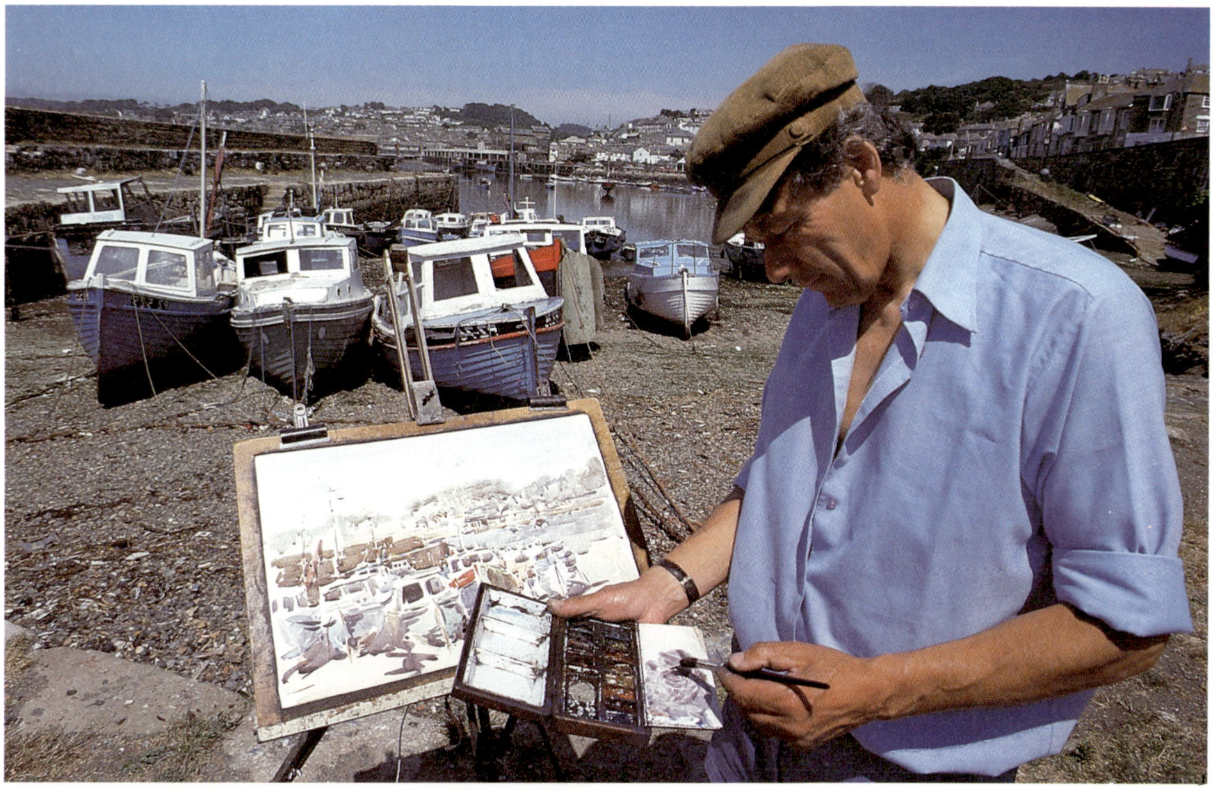

This is a classic example of the kind of picture which could be taken every bit as easily with a modestly-priced compact as with an expensive SLR (see overleaf). The only difficulty might arise if you were using an autofocus camera, which might focus on the boats instead of the easel; you need to keep your subject for focus in the middle of the picture with these cameras.

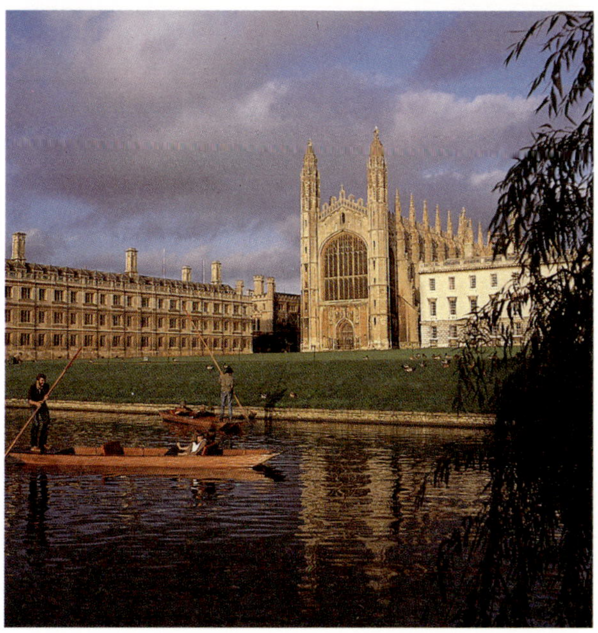

We have all been in situations where we have said to ourselves 'if only I'd brought my camera'. For those moments when no amount of waiting would have guaranteed the same mood, the compact 35mm is ideal since it can be carried in your pocket or bag and constantly be accessible.

35mm SLRs
Single-Lens Reflexes

For most amateurs, and many professionals, the 35mm single-lens reflex (SLR) is the ultimate camera. It is available with both automatic exposure and automatic focusing, though the latter is hardly necessary because you actually view the subject *through the lens of the camera itself,* and you can see whether it is in focus or not. This means that framing is never a problem, even in the close-up range, and that you can fit different kinds of lenses for different purposes (see overleaf).

For a first SLR, automatic exposure is invaluable, though it is worth spending the extra and getting one which also allows you to take control and set the exposures manually: this may not seem too important at first, but as you gain experience, you may find yourself wishing that you did have more control. Alternatively, if money is tight, consider buying a second-hand non-automatic camera with a *match-needle* exposure meter. This is exactly what its name implies: by matching two needles in the viewfinder, you set the exposure every bit as accurately as an auto-exposure camera.

Although there is undoubtedly a good deal of snobbery about cameras, there is no doubt that some are much better than others, and *Canon* and *Nikon* are the leaders in the professional market. If you buy an 'entry-level' camera from either of these manufacturers, you will be gaining access to the two biggest systems in the world, a point which can be very important if you get more seriously involved in photography later. Other well-known cameras include *Contax, Leica, Rolleiflex, Olympus, Pentax, Konica, Minolta,* and *Yashica,* though the first three are frighteningly expensive.

The enormous advantage of the SLR is not so much its image quality (which is not necessarily any greater than that of a first-class compact), but its versatility. Even with the standard lens you can take pictures by ordinary room-light, without flash: a typical f/1.8 SLR lens needs less than half the light of an f/2.8, or about a quarter of the light of an f/3.5. The range of shutter speeds is much greater, too: an eight-second exposure (perfectly possible with most automatics) allows 256 times as much light to reach the film as the typical 1/30 second of a compact camera! Of course, you will need to support the camera rigidly for exposures of more than 1/30 second, or *camera shake* may blur your pictures, but with a tripod or even a table or wall to support the camera, you can achieve some wonderful effects.

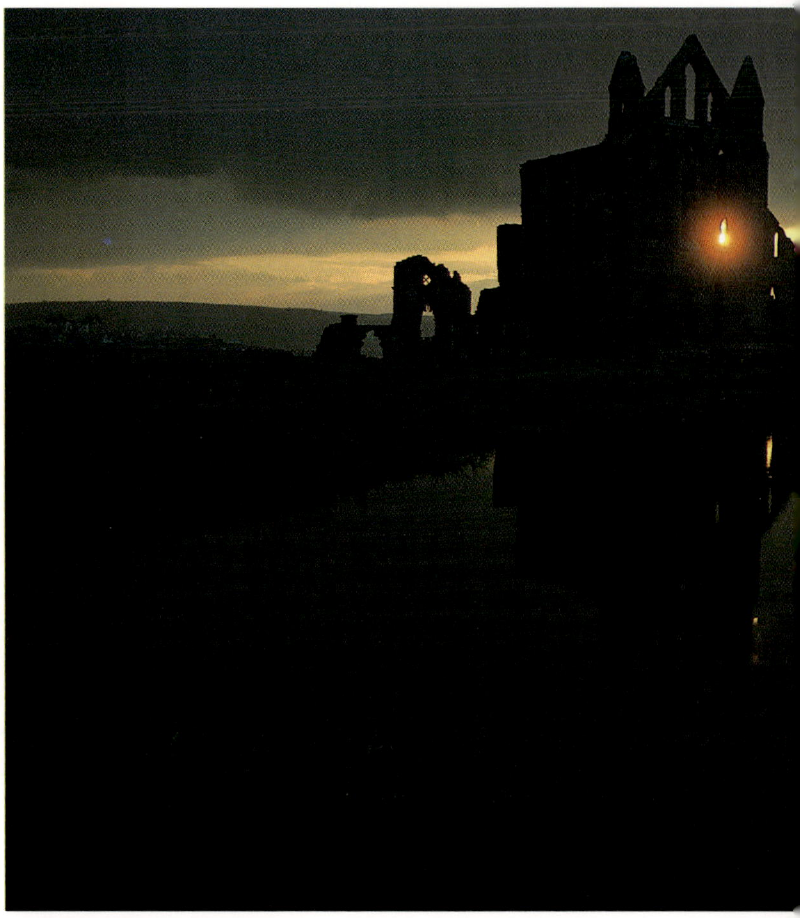

If you want to line up two components in a picture - the sun and the window, in this example - the SLR makes it very much easier. At this distance, a viewfinder camera would be accurate enough, but as you get closer and closer, there is more and more difference between what the viewfinder sees and what the camera lens sees.

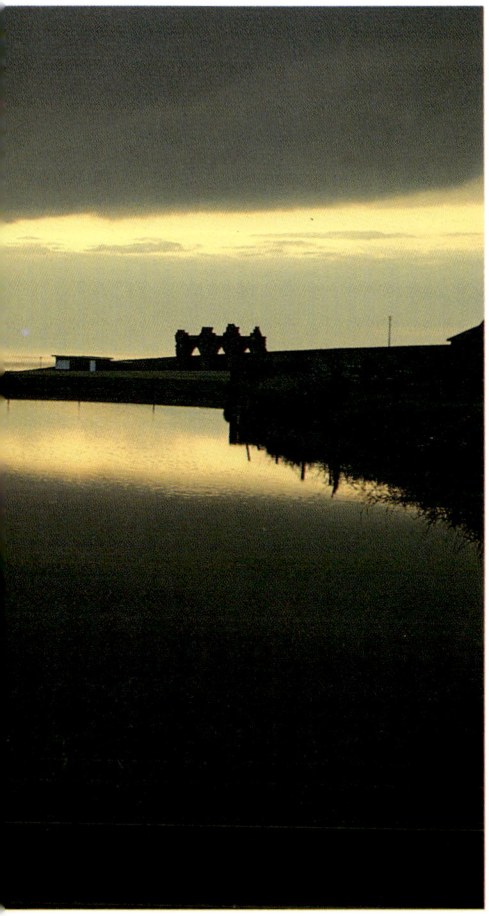

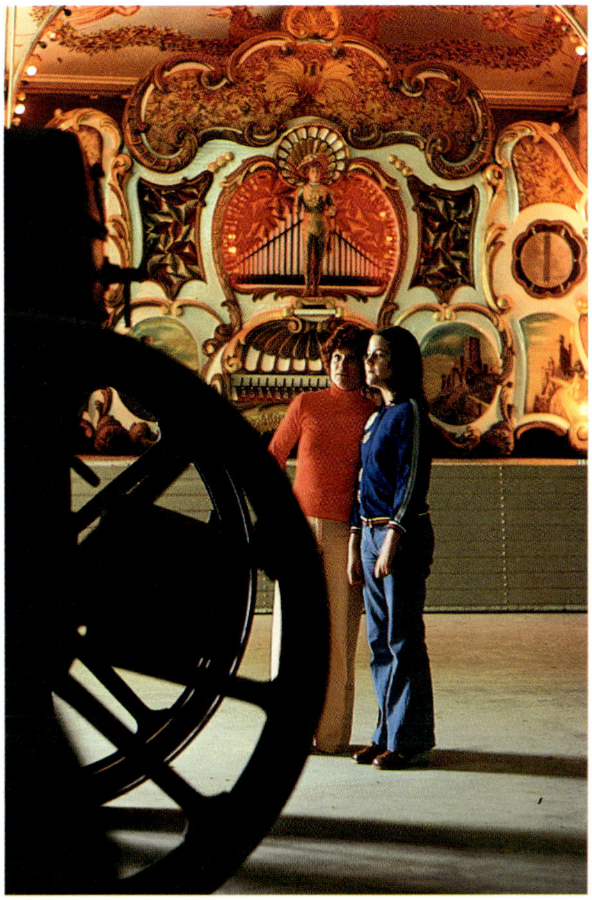

A major advantage of the SLR is that you can see what is in focus and what is not. In the clown picture (below), the background has been allowed to 'go soft', out of focus, by using the lens 'wide open'. In the museum picture, on the other hand, the lens has been stopped down (ie, the aperture has been reduced) to keep both the foreground and the background reasonably sharp.

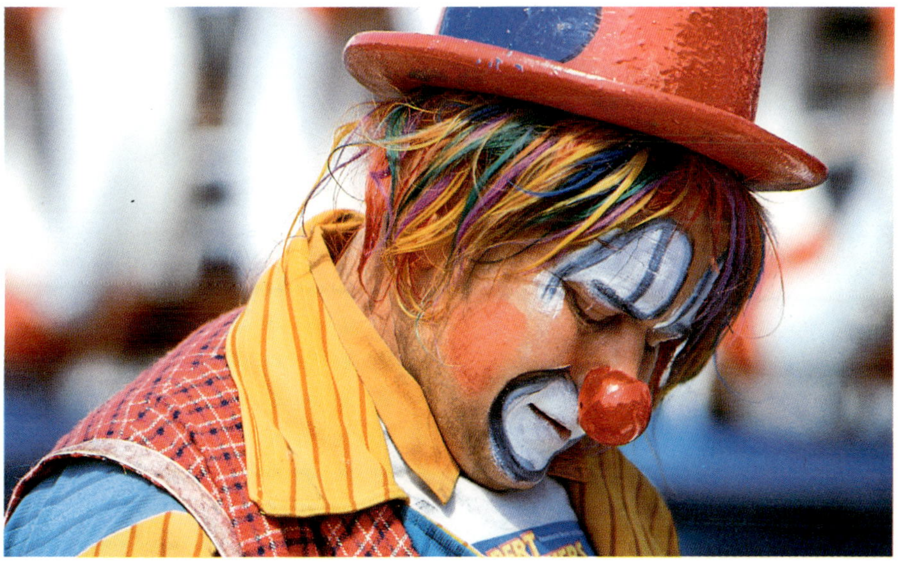

Additional Lenses

One of the great attractions of the SLR is of course its ability to accept different lenses. The important things about a lens are its speed, which we have already mentioned, and its *focal length.* As a rule, the standard lens supplied with an SLR has a focal length of around 50mm; anything longer than this will act as a magnifier, and bring the action closer, and anything shorter will act as a 'wide-angle' and get more in. There are three kinds of *interchangeable lens* to think about.

The one which everyone thinks of first is the *zoom,* which is certainly fascinating and versatile, and which allows you to 'zoom in' or 'pull back' on your subject in order to get *precisely* the right framing. On the other hand, zooms are always bigger and heavier than 'prime' standard lenses; they are *slower,* so that you cannot take pictures as easily in poor light (the maximum aperture of a zoom lens is usually less than that of a compact camera's lens); and only the better (and more expensive) zooms can deliver image quality which is as good as any 'prime' or non-zoom lens, though if you only shoot colour negatives, this unlikely be too noticeable. Tele-zooms, such as a 70-210mm, will usually deliver better quality than wide-angle or wide-to-tele zooms.

The second kind is the *telephoto.* There is actually a technical difference between 'telephoto' and 'long focus' lenses, but it need not concern us here. Telephotos act like telescopes, bringing everything closer. Some people find that an 85mm, 90mm, or 105mm 'short tele' is their ideal lens; others prefer something like a 200mm, which really brings things closer. 'Prime' telephoto lenses are cheaper, (usually) faster, and often lighter than zooms, so they are well worth considering if you are interested in pulling things closer.

Thirdly, *wide-angles* are (usually) the most neglected by amateurs and (usually) the most popular with the professionals, as they allow you to show more of a scene when your viewpoint is restricted and offer a far greater depth of field. A 35mm lens is a very modest wide-angle, indeed many compact cameras have a 35mm lens as 'standard', and some professionals habitually use them on SLRs instead of a 50mm. While 28mm is a useful focal length, for really dramatic effects, a 24mm, 21mm or an even wider lens can be used, but perspective can look strangely exaggerated.

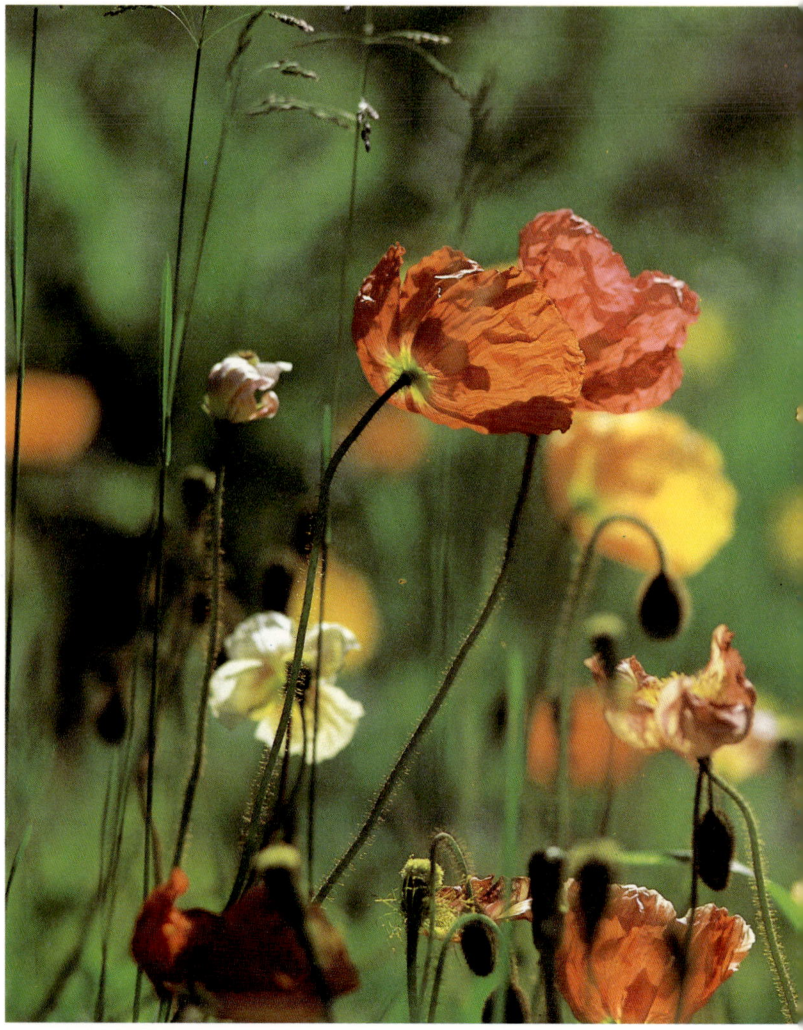

The 'close-up' or 'macro' lens is designed to enable focusing at very close range, something which an ordinary lens without special attachments is incapable of doing. In general the macro lens comes in two focal lengths, 50mm or 100mm and besides close focusing, can be used normally as an ordinary lens. A number of zoom lenses on the market have an optional macro facility, which combines the benefits of a telephoto with that of close-up photography.

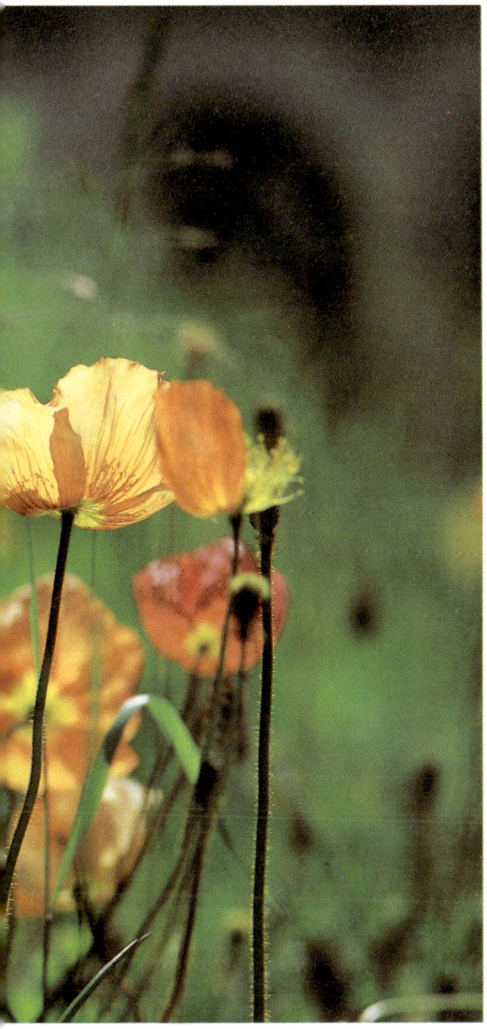

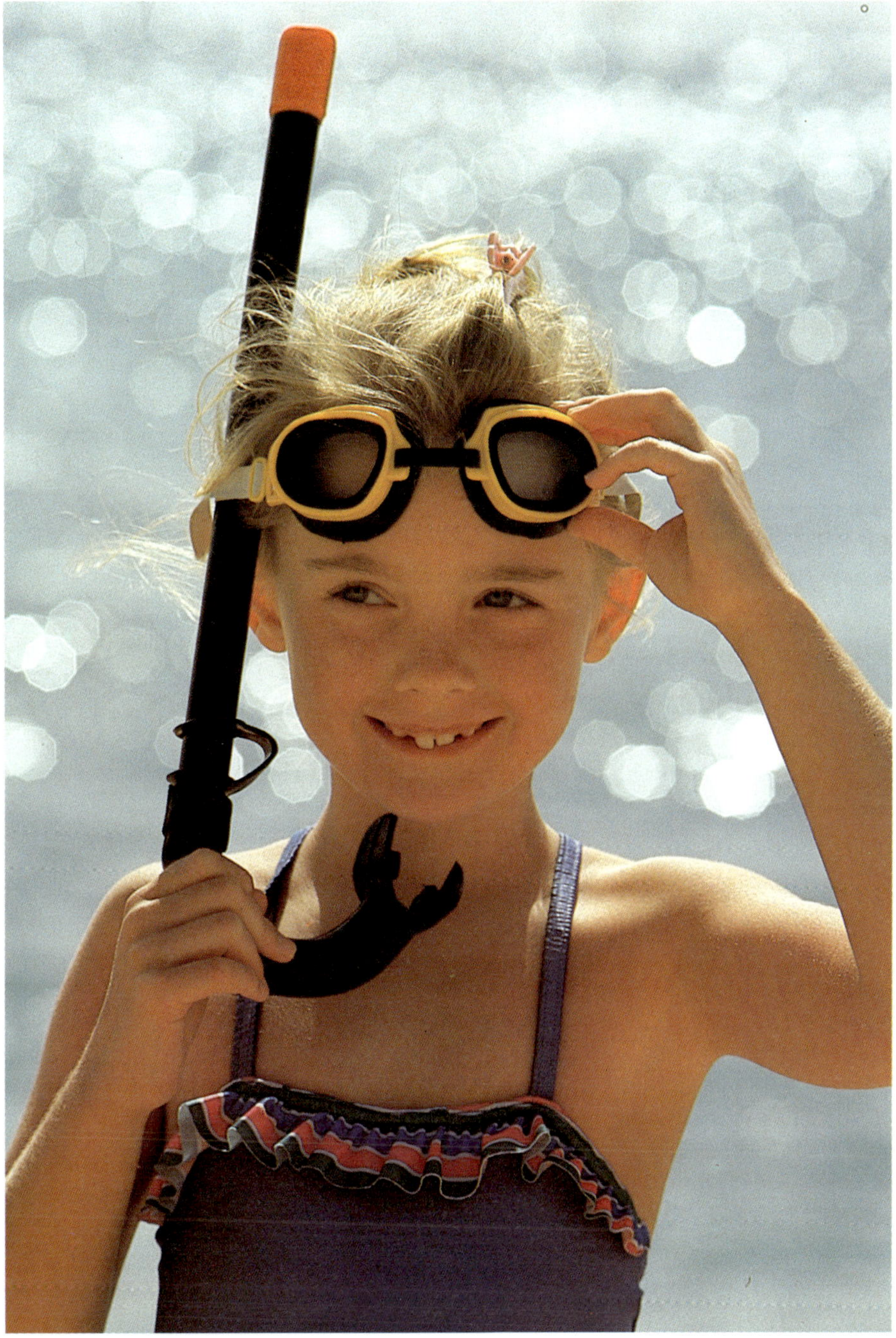

The 'telephoto' or 'long' lens can be invaluable in situations where you can not, dare not or are prevented from, moving in close to your subject. Sporting occasions, wildlife photography or any of the numerous events which are bedecked with barriers, all present the photographer with instances which call for a long lens. However, such a lens is not by any means limited to the metaphorical jumping of obstacles. In portraiture, lenses ranging from 90mm upwards to 200mm are ideal. Focusing on the subject will throw the background out of focus, as in the above picture, which is usually preferable to a clutter of infringing shapes behind the sitter.

Accessories

The accessory which most amateurs think of first is a motor drive, but it is very doubtful whether these have any advantages over a well-tuned thumb, at least for most amateur work. They are expensive, and they do tend to eat up film, so they are probably things to get only when you are absolutely *sure* that you need one - which is not a bad rule-of-thumb to apply to buying any new equipment.

A far more important accessory, and one which is often supplied with the camera, is the humble lens-shade or lens-hood. Not only does this improve the colour and sharpness of pictures by cutting out extraneous light: it also protects the lens from rain, from sticky little fingers, and even from knocks, as the shade both absorbs the worst of the blow and distribûtes the shock evenly around the lens mount, instead of making a 'ding' in the filter mount. Rubber lens-shades make particularly good shock absorbers.

Many people like to use a plain filter ('UV' or 'skylight') to protect their lens; others prefer to put the lens cap on whenever they are not actually taking a picture. Either approach is defensible - the filter may take the ultimate edge off the definition, but it does leave the camera ready for action, which the cap does not - but leaving the lens unprotected is very unwise indeed, as dust and fingerprints will ruin the quality of your lens, and make your pictures flat and flary. If you have to clean a lens - and it should be done as rarely as possible - you should blow any loose dust off with a blower brush, and then clean the lens itself with a piece of lens tissue. Both lens tissue and blower brushes are available at camera stores.

Other filters, especially 'effects' filters, should be used with care: you can get some wonderful effects with Cokin filters (and their imitators), but you can also turn an ordinary boring picture into a boring picture with funny effects tacked on. Arguably, a really good photographer would never need these filters at all, but not many are that good!

The only other accessory which most people ever buy is a flash gun, and opinions are divided on these, with some professionals swearing by them, and others at them. On the credit side, they are useful when there is no other way of getting a picture: on the debit side, the effect is usually harsh and unflattering, with ugly hard shadows around the subject. Besides, modern fast films mean that you can get much more natural-looking pictures without flash, at the expense of some increase in *grain* (see overleaf).

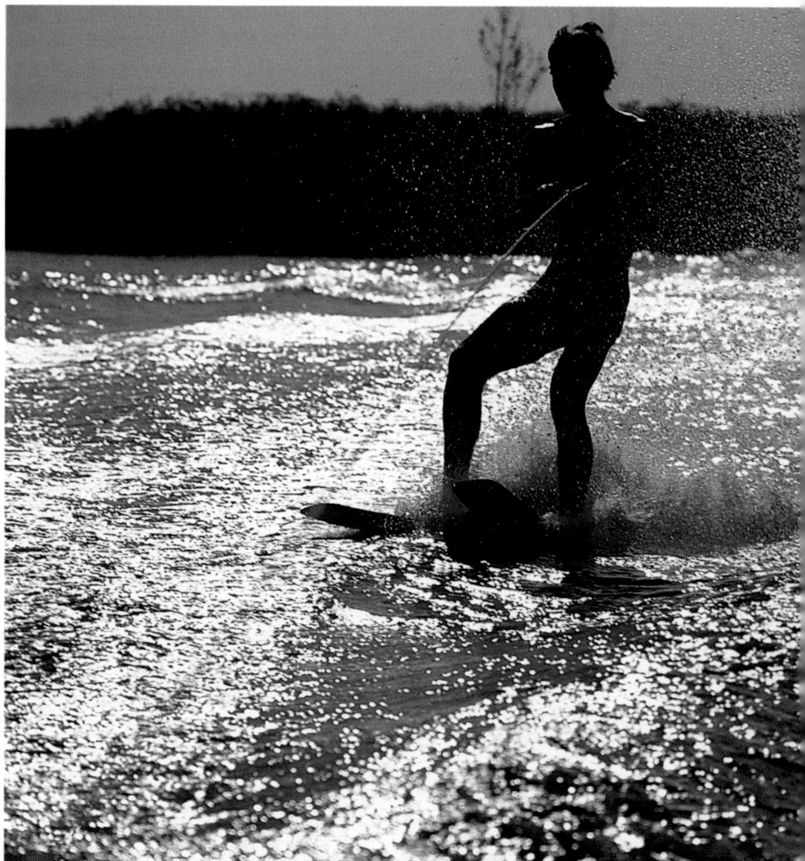

It is always worth looking through accessory manufacturers' catalogues, because although a lot of the accessories offered are of dubious usefulness, there are others which may suit your particular needs. For example, Ewa Marine make a sort of camera 'rain cape' which can protect your camera from flying spray in conditions like this.

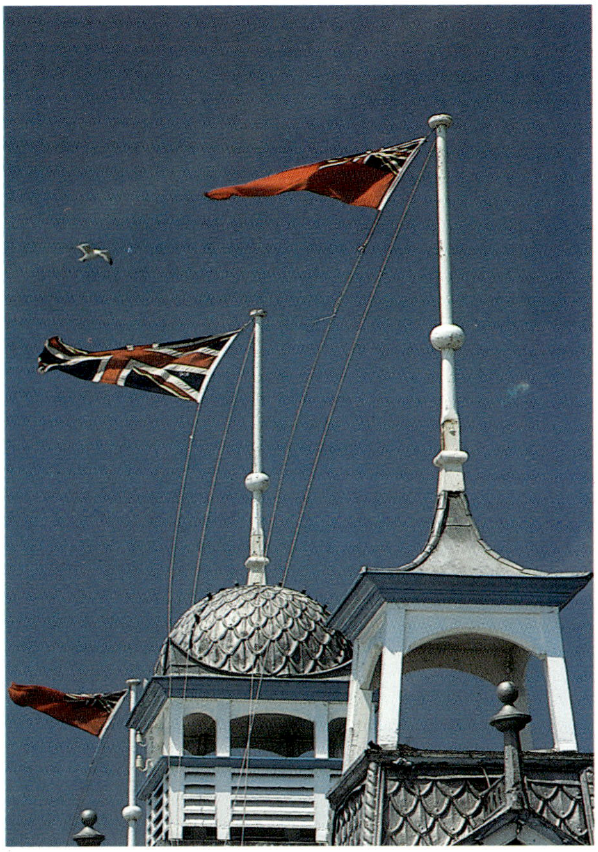

Once again, two accessories were used: a polarising filter, to darken the sky, and a lens hood or lens shade to cut down flare which could degrade colours and 'flatten' the image. You need an SLR to use a polariser conveniently, but you should use a lens shade on any camera that can be fitted with one.

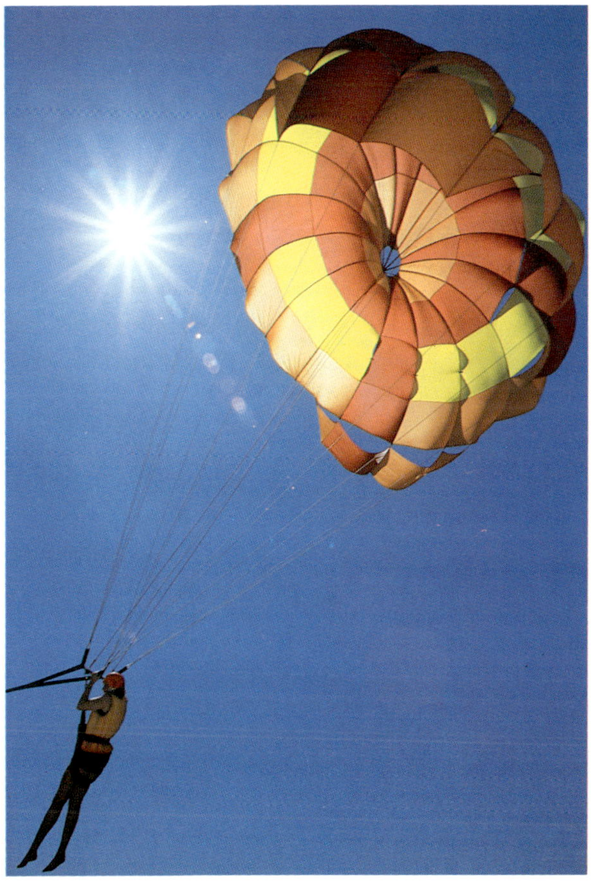

If a telephoto lens is too expensive, a useful addition to your equipment might be a 'tele converter' to enable shots such as this one to be taken. Events such as parascending or indeed any fast-moving sport can benefit from the use of a motor-drive/auto-winder, which allows the photographer to concentrate more on the subject than the equipment. On occasions such as these, winding on manually can upset the composition at a time when there will be no second chances.

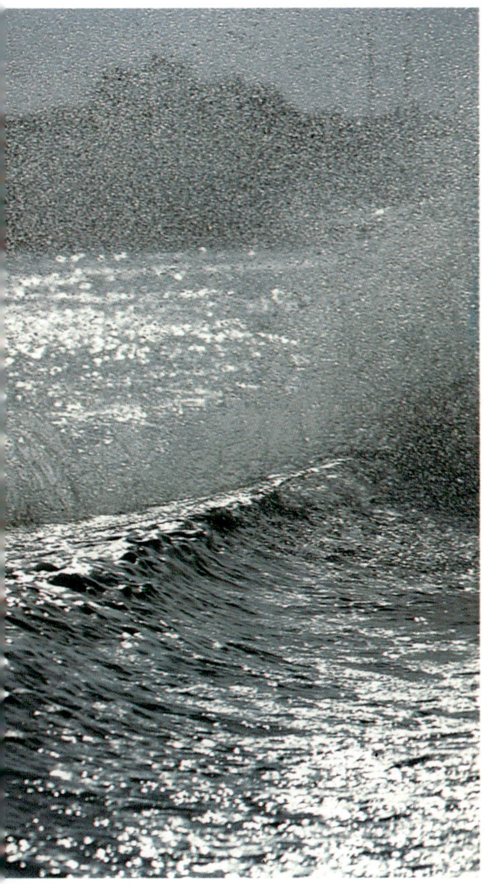

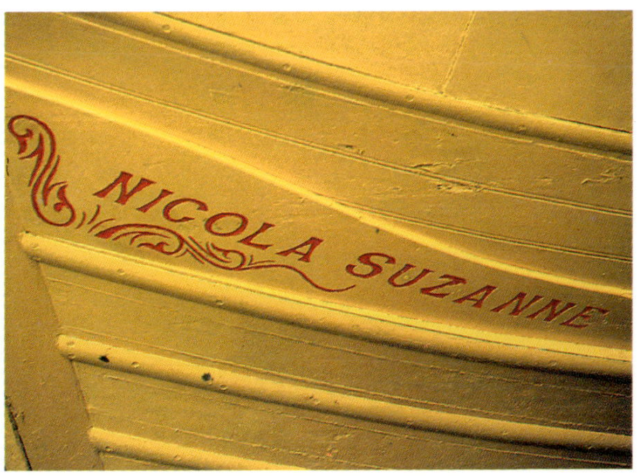

A flash gun is a useful piece of equipment, not only to illuminate subjects taken in the dark, or in dim light, but also to soften shadows in sharp, raking light.

Film & Processing

Colour print film is overwhelmingly the most popular medium for amateur photography of all sorts. With this sort of film, it does not matter much which brand of colour film you choose, provided it is reasonably fresh; all film boxes carry an expiry date, and unless the film has been stored next to a radiator or in a shop window (which can be a lot hotter), in-dated film is likely to be all right. If it has been stored in a reasonably cool place, film which is a year or more past the expiry date can still be used with confidence.

What is much more important is the *speed* of the film, and *where you have it processed.*

Speed is a measure of how much light a film needs in order to record an image. A 'fast' film needs less light than a 'slow' one. The standard measure of speed is the ISO (International Standards Organisation) rating, which is effectively identical to the old ASA (American Standards Association) rating; the two terms are used interchangeably by most people, and many cameras still have their speed setting dials marked in ASA.

The usual ISO speed scale is arithmetical, so that an ISO 400 film is four times as fast as ISO 100. It might seem that the faster the film, the better, but the drawback of the faster films is that they are also *grainier;* that is, if they are enlarged, the actual structure of the dye image on the film starts to become visible rather sooner than with slower films. You can usually begin to see the dye structure of an ISO 100 film at about 5× enlargement (5 × 7-½", 12 × 18cm for 35mm), and it is quite obvious at 8x (the standard 'ten-eight' enlargement), but with an ISO 400 film it is easily visible at 4×, and even an enprint (about 2-3×) from ISO 1000 film shows distinct grain. Grain is not necessarily a disadvantage, and indeed it can even be used creatively, but if you want the sharpest possible pictures, you should use ISO 100 film.

It is also a useful trick always to *overexpose* colour negative film: most professionals will set the film-speed (ISO/ASA dial) a notch or two lower than the nominal speed - 80 or even 64 for ISO 100, 320 or 250 for ISO 400. The slight loss in speed is offset by a gain in quality, especially in poor light, where you will not get the sickly greenish shadows which you sometimes do if you expose the film at its recommended speed.

As for *where* you get your processing done, the best advice is to find somewhere you can trust, and stick with them. Although an increasing number of shops do their

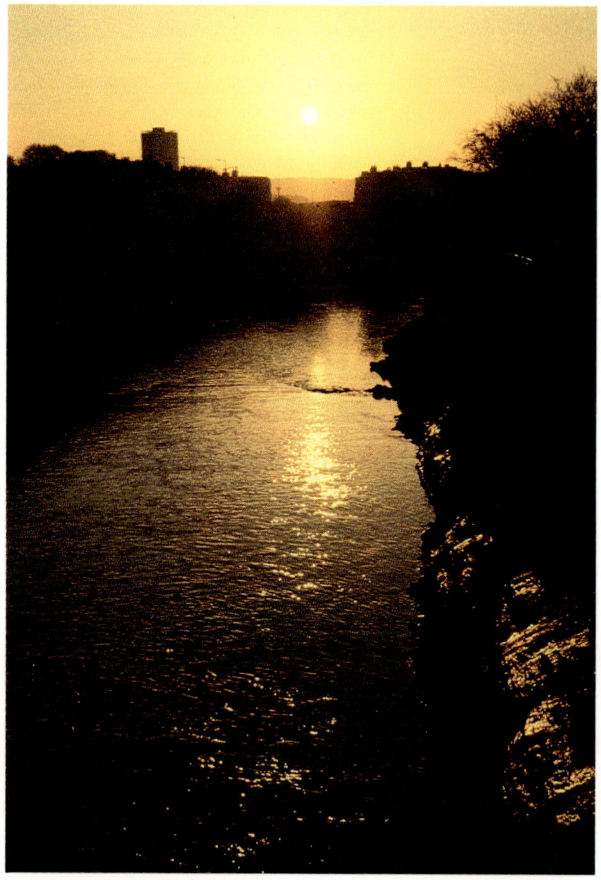

You do not need 'trick' filters at sunset; shooting straight into the sun, and underexposing the film (by resetting the film speed dial on the camera 2-4x higher than the actual film speed) can produce this kind of effect.

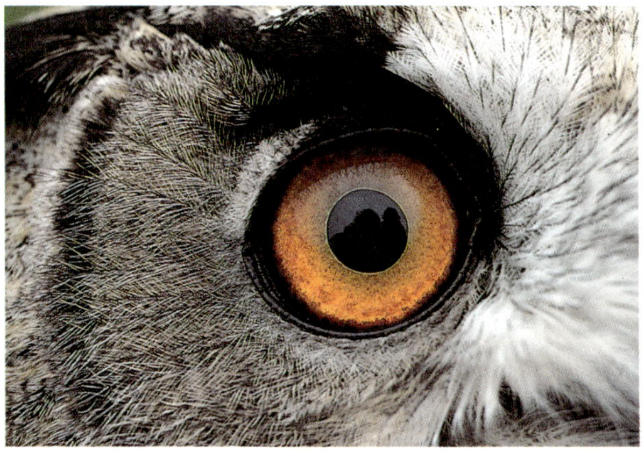

Kodachrome 25 is renowned as the sharpest colour film on the market; only Fuji's ISO 50 film and then Kodachrome 64 even come close. There is no way that you can get this sort of sharpness with colour print films, but Kodachrome tests the best lenses to the limit.

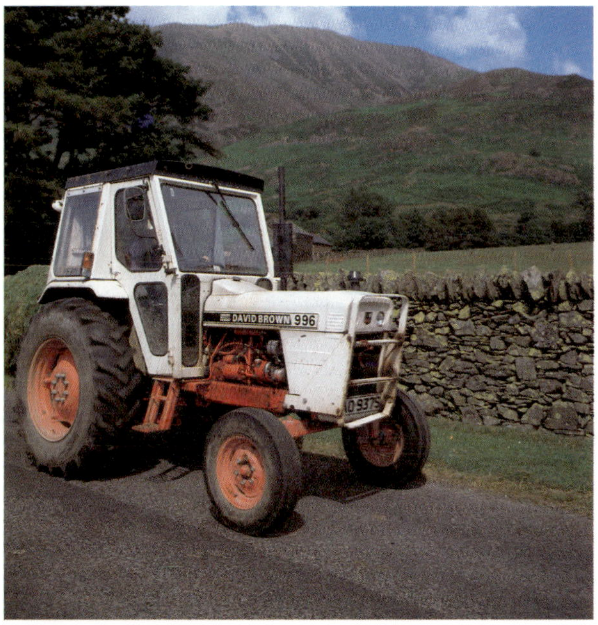

Manufacturers' films vary greatly in their colour rendition, often particularly noticeable with reds and blues. You will have to stick with a film for some time to learn how it responds to specific lighting conditions.

own processing, most send their films to a nearby processing lab, and some of these are better than others. It is usually better to deal with a camera shop rather than a chemist's, because they will be able to tell you when the faults are yours and when they are the lab's; they can explain where you went wrong, if it was your fault, or back you if the lab is at fault. On the other hand, it is not usually worth going to a processing lab which caters for professionals, except for big, high-quality reprints, as the prices will be two or three times as much, and the results are not much better than from a good amateur lab. The two most useful pieces of advice are first, not to keep chopping and changing, because you will never build up a working relationship with the lab or shop, and second, not to be tempted by price alone - though that is not the same as saying that the most expensive are always the best!

If you decide to use colour slides instead of colour print film, the advice is completely different. First, the brand of film matters considerably: slow films are sharper, and colour balances each have their own 'personality'. Second, you should *underexpose* slide films very slightly to get the best results, rating ISO 25 at 32, 50 at 64, and 64 at 80 - this is one click of the film speed dial on most cameras. Faster slide films than ISO 64 are only worth considering if you really need them, unless you want to use the bigger grain of the fast films creatively. Thirdly, professional labs *do* give better results, with fewer scratches, though you will usually have to mount the film yourself. Finally, professional labs offer a two-*hour* turnaround, which is pretty quick by any standards, and cost very little more than amateur labs. Kodachrome is a special case, as only Kodak can process it outside the United States.

You can also get prints from slides; those from amateur labs are good, but those from professional labs can be superb. Of course, you need only have the slides you want printed, instead of the whole film.

Finally, black and white does have a charm of its own, but it is very difficult to get good trade processing. You can either do it yourself (which is outside the scope of this book) or you can try one of the small specialist printers who advertise in photographic magazines. Be warned, though, that black and white is likely to cost *more* than colour, nowadays!

Using Pictures

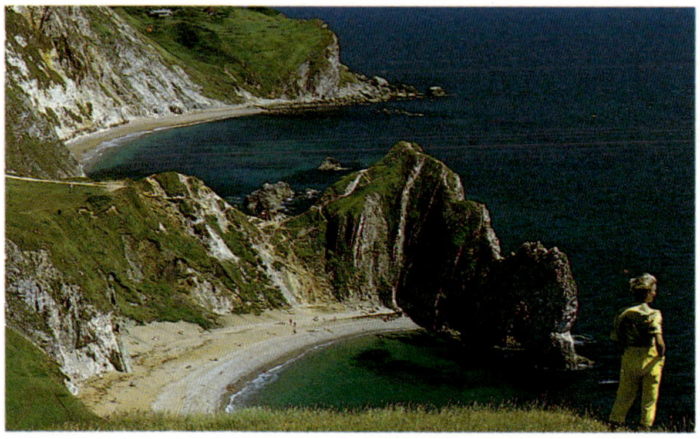

This is a superb photograph which could well stand enlargement for hanging on the wall, as well as being a good picture for the family album. The range of colours and the use of shape is intriguing, and the whole feeling of the photograph is one of happiness, summer, and fresh air.

We have now come full circle. At the beginning, we said that this was a book about memories. Now, we look at how to use photographs to hold on to those memories.

The most obvious way is the album. The days of the Family Album, to which a few pictures were added every year, are gone: photography is so cheap now that most people could fill an album in a year or less. A set of albums can, however, give great pleasure.

The important thing is editing. When you get your prints back, be ruthless. Throw out all the ones that are sub-standard; give away the duplicates and near-duplicates. Then, arrange the cream of your pictures in order, and (if you feel the need) add captions. The result will be a book that grows more valuable with the passing years.

Another way to use prints is to hang them on the wall. Many sizes of enlargement are available from both prints and slides, and while the minimum size that is usually worth hanging is usually 5 × 7″ or so, you may want to consider anything up to poster-sized (20 × 30″) prints of certain subjects - especially landscapes.

If you decide to use slides, then you need to be even more ruthless than with prints when it comes to sorting and structuring, and if you are going to show them to other people, prepare your slide show carefully and keep it short. Put the slides in order, and do what the professionals do: in the bottom right-hand corner of the mount, as the slide 'reads' correctly when you are holding it, place a numbered thumb-spot. That way, you can keep the slides in order and you can see at a glance which way round they should be placed in the projector. A well-presented, well-structured slide show can be a pleasure: the other kind, as we all know from seeing our friends' shows, can be purgatory. If you want to show more than (say) 50 slides, make two separate shows; you can decide whether to show the second set after seeing your audience's reaction to the first!

Last of all, you may want to enter competitions. These are always something of a lottery, because they depend so much on the judges' individual preferences and prejudices; this is why so few professionals bother to enter. But you can increase your chances dramatically by following a few simple guidelines.

First, *read the rules.* You would be amazed at the number of people who send in landscapes when the subject of the competition is people, and vice versa. Send in prints if they ask for prints, slides if they ask for slides.

Second, make sure the technical quality is good. Fuzziness and poor colour will almost certainly lead to your pictures being rejected on the first round of selection, because many other photographers will be of a near-professional standard.

Third, do not send pictures that you treasure unless you are sure you will get them back. By the same token, never send pictures to any competition where it says anything like 'all entries become the property of the organisers': that is a rip-off.

Fourth, make it easy for the organisers to send your pictures back. Write your name on prints or slide mounts (with a soft pencil to avoid damage to prints) and enclose return postage.

Lastly, when selecting pictures for a competition, go for IMPACT! A picture with a clear, simple subject and composition which fairly jumps up and hits you between the eyes stands a better chance than a subtle picture which requires close study to communicate its best.

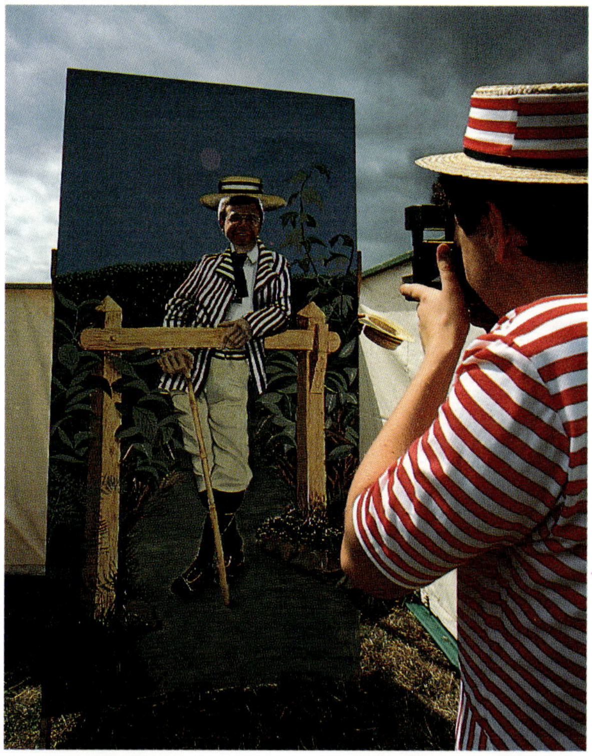

A picture like this one might do well in a competition: the brightly-striped outfit worn by the beach photographer would immediately attract the judges' eyes, and they might then go on to spot the humour of the photograph.

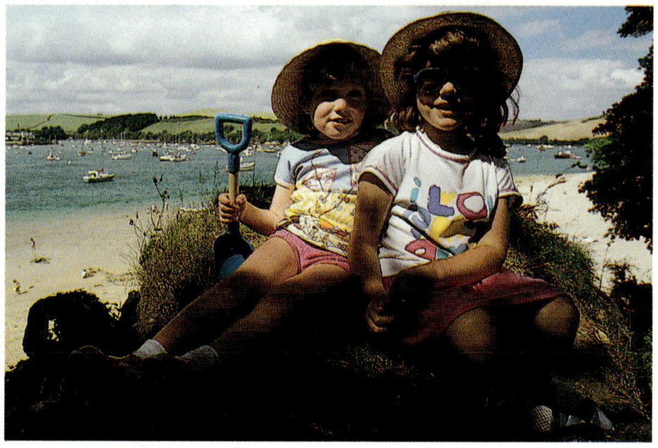

Always be careful in choosing the people to whom you show your pictures. Obviously, members of the family and close friends will like this, but many others will see it as 'just another picture of the kids'. A really sophisticated photographer, on the other hand, might be very impressed: it captures the spirit of the seaside.

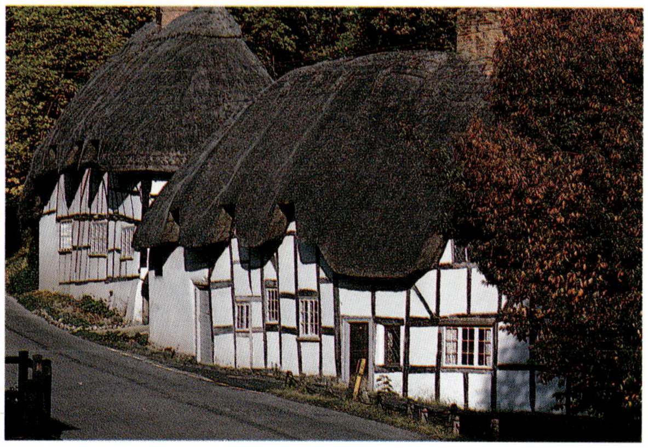

This obviously goes beyond being a snapshot, but it is not a sophisticated picture: it is a bit too 'chocolate-boxy' for that. It is very attractive, but it might become cloying if you hung it on the wall and had to look at it for long.

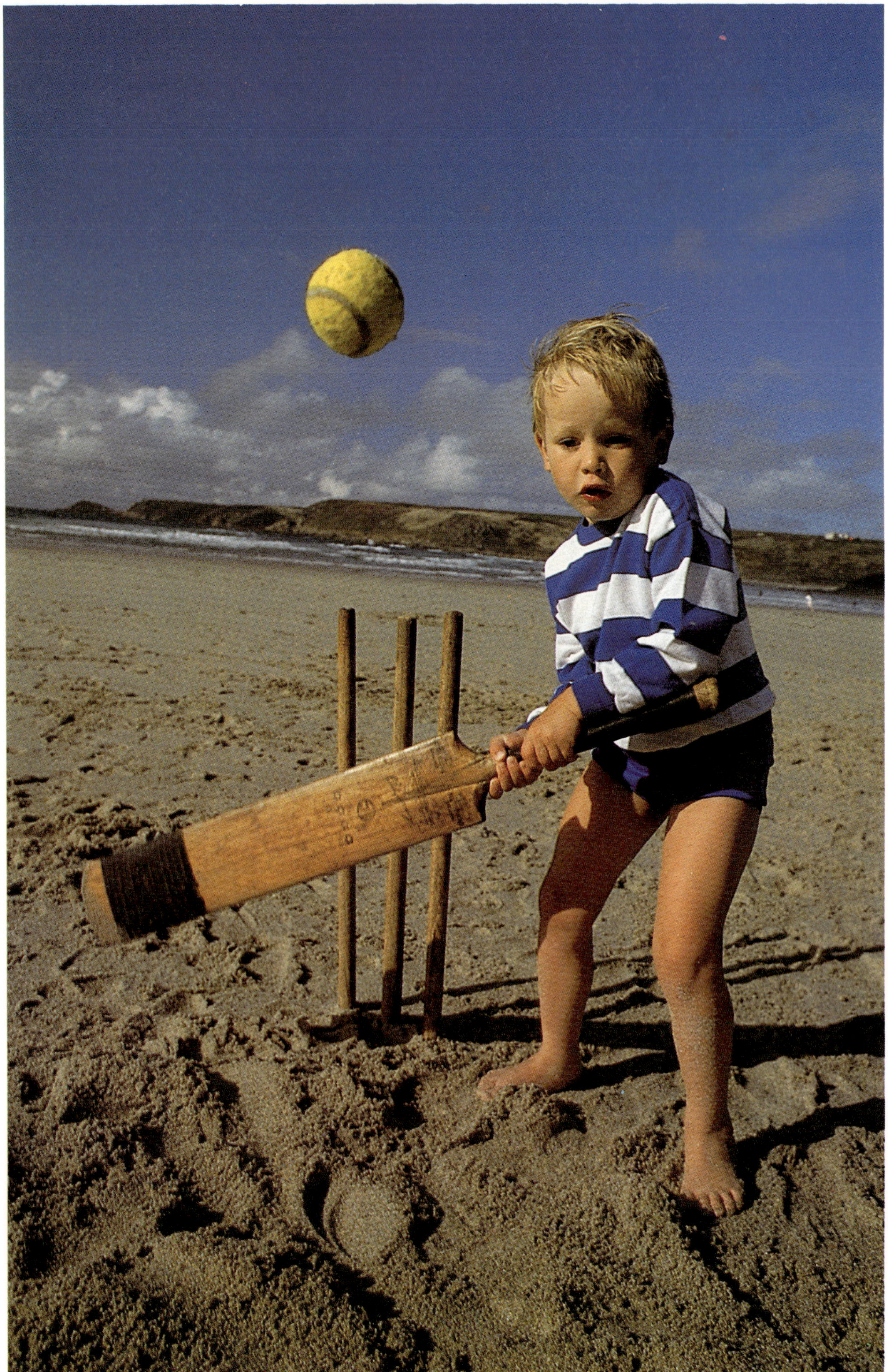